Paula's prepar... ... inches of water in the tub, just ... ... ture. Gentle shampoo for the bright red nail. Special soap for the alabaster skin. A soft little washcloth. A plastic duck.

"I put her in the bathtub. And then I walked out. I didn't *decide* to walk out. I didn't decide anything. I just walked out."

She prowled the house, from one corner to another. Down the hallway to the nursery, half expecting to see the baby there. Back the other way, past the closed bathroom door. "I was cryin'. I was always cryin'. I said to myself, am I really doing this? And first I said, no, I'm not. And then I said, well, maybe I am."

To the dining room, around the table. To the kitchen, looking for something, unable to remember what it was. Back to the nursery, circling, hurrying. "I felt like I was rushing, but I also felt like I was moving real slow." And when all the bungalow's corners had been explored, when there was nowhere else to wander, when her expectation overcame her dread, she paused before the door of the bathroom and turned the knob. The door swung open slowly, silently.

Loralei lay mute and motionless. The once-warm water spread like a sheet of glass over her, and her pale skin had turned faintly blue. . . .

DYING DREAMS

THE SECRETS OF PAULA SIMS

Audrey Becker

POCKET BOOKS

New York   London   Toronto   Sydney   Tokyo   Singapore

"Lorelei," lyrics and music by Dennis De Young and James Young, copyright © 1975 Almo Music Corp. and Stygian Songs (ASCAP). International Copyright Secured. All Rights Reserved.

An *Original* Publication of POCKET BOOKS

POCKET BOOKS, a division of Simon & Schuster Inc. 1230 Avenue of the Americas, New York, NY 10020

ISBN: 0-671-73232-3

First Pocket Books printing May 1993

10 9 8 7 6 5 4 3 2 1

POCKET and colophon are registered trademarks of Simon & Schuster Inc.

Cover photo by *The Peoria Journal Star*

Printed in the U.S.A.

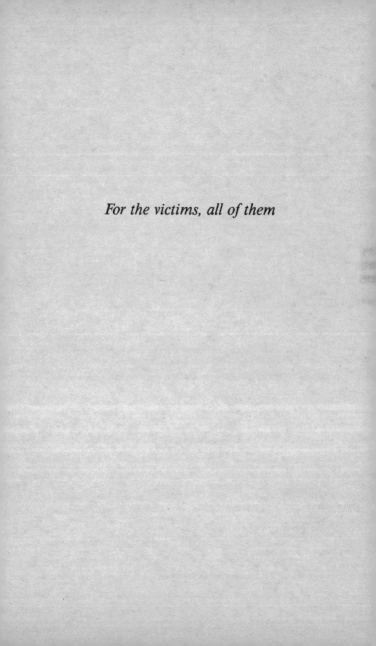

For the victims, all of them

Acknowledgments

Many people whose lives were touched by the events covered in this book shared their knowledge or their memories with me in interviews between January, 1990, and July, 1992. Some of the interviews were brief; some stretched over several days; some went on for months.

I am particularly grateful to those people who were part of the story. For many of them, telling it was painful. I admire Paula's courage in deciding, finally, to speak, and I thank her for choosing me to listen. My deepest appreciation goes to Rhonda Henson Scott, June Bland Gibson, Debbie Fuller Wolf, Mike Wolf, Danny Hall, Marla Lowe Rogers, John and Uldene Jackson, Mike Buck, Julie Fry, Stephanie Werner Cook, Jennifer Sheppard Yates, Kay Hanks Stassi, Pamela Johnson, Ernest Springer, Charles Saunders, Paula Welch, and Dr. Mary Case. I am indebted also to the people who appear in this book as Stella and Marvin Hyatt, Gayle Allard, and Terri Sims; they requested that their real names be changed.

There were others who offered their information with the understanding that they could remain anonymous. I thank them also.

Some lawmen were generous with their specific recollections of the investigation. I wish to acknowledge the contributions of DCI Agent Jim Bivens, Jersey County Sheriff

ACKNOWLEDGMENTS

Frank Yocom, Illinois State Police Officer Mike Donovan, former Alton Officer Bob Eichen, and former Brighton Officer Chris White.

Many members of the press offered data, reactions, or advice. I am grateful to Roger Kramer and Bea Venezia of the *Telegraph*, to Lorraine Orlandi of the *St. Louis Sun*, to Rich Wooley of KMOV-TV, to Charles Klotzer of the *St. Louis Journalism Review*, to Debbie Clay of the *Home Press*, to Jayne Matthews of the *News Democrat*, and to artist Gary Jameson.

John Badman of the *Telegraph* did fine pictorial work over a long period of time, and I thank him for sharing his efforts. My appreciation goes also to photographer Eric Behrens of the *Journal Star*, who managed to get excellent pictures despite the confusions and restrictions of the trial.

I am deeply indebted to Dr. Diane Sanford and other mental health professionals who felt strongly about the issues and were willing to speak their concern.

There were courthouse personnel who made my job easier. My gratitude to Dina Burch, James May, Dorothy Warren, and William Portell at Edwardsville and to Linda Smiddy at Peoria.

I must acknowledge my debt to my agent, Joyce Flaherty, for pushing, pulling, cajoling, scolding, and everything she did beyond agenting, and to my editor, Judith Regan, for her continued interest, incredible patience, and long-distance perception.

I am indebted to Dale Myers and Shirley Giebel for their encouragement and suggestions, and to Pat Capon for cutting the trees to get to the forest.

And I thank my son Barrett for his understanding when Mom was late and dinner was Swanson's.

A.B.

Oh! that a dream so sweet, so long enjoy'd,
Should be so sadly, cruelly destroy'd!

Thomas Moore
Lalla Rookh, 1817

Connection

I HAD LIVED IN ST. LOUIS JUST A FEW MONTHS WHEN ROB SIMS, IN a town forty miles from me, flagged down the police to say that one of his baby daughters had been "kidnapped again." I soon became as caught up in the case as everyone else; it played out in front of us, filling our television screens hour after hour during the spring days of 1989.

As a newcomer to the area, I hadn't heard about the first "kidnapping," the one that had occurred three years earlier, but its gruesome details were repeated in story after story. Who could do such a thing? Who could do it twice?

When law officers and news cameras pointed at the parents—tall, young, taciturn Paula Sims and her bearded, deep-voiced, overall-clad husband, Rob—I was not surprised. Having worked as a television reporter and news anchor, I knew that there was a plethora of odd and dangerous people in the world and that some of them couldn't be trusted with their own children.

In the weeks that followed, however, the singularity of this case became apparent. Police, usually terse and evasive, held news conferences to recount their progress. Residents camped outside the home of the suspects, hoping to be present when an arrest was made. A defense attorney stood at a pay phone in the glare of television lights, trying to convince a judge to give him access to his client. This was unlike any investigation I had known; I was sure the case was one I wanted to explore.

I showed up at pretrial hearings and watched Paula, mute and blank-eyed as she sat beside her husband. I attended the four-week trial and saw her stony stare, day after day. I came away knowing something about the "case," but almost nothing about the defendant, the silent young mother whose babies had perished.

In the wake of the verdict I cautiously approached her friends; I was surprised by their willingness to talk. They were as mystified by the tragedy as everyone else. The Paula Sims they knew could never have hurt a child, they told me. Never. "She was just like us," one said.

I contacted Paula in prison, as did many other journalists. She did not respond.

I pursued the enigmatic husband and father, Rob Sims, who never said he wouldn't talk but never said he would, either. I filled in his silence by tracking down other women in his life, women who had worked with him, or lived with him, or married him.

The clues trickled in, one interview leading to another. Lawmen offered recollections. Psychologists offered opinions.

From time to time throughout the first year of my explorations I sent entreaties to Paula. One of her friends told her of my efforts and urged her to consider talking, but she remained resolutely silent. She had made her decision, I concluded; I had no choice but to accept it. I ceased to write; continuing to do so seemed almost harassment.

I set about assembling the clues, tracing the history of the Simses, not from their own words but from the words of those who knew them, probing the elusive nature of their relationship, looking for the pathological elements that had led to tragedy. By January of 1992, six months after I gave up hope of word from Paula, I was typing a manuscript.

2

DYING DREAMS

One wintry day I saw a greeting card that seemed right for her. I don't know why the card caught my eye; I no longer remember what it said, or how I signed it. I'm not even sure why I sent it. I suppose it was because she had occupied my thoughts for two years, and as I finished work on her story I wanted to offer something, some message of connection. Perhaps I was thinking of it as a farewell.

A week later my phone rang. "This is the AT&T operator with a collect call," a voice said. "Caller, will you state your name, please?"

The response was quiet but sure: "This is Paula."

In the months that followed Paula and I sometimes discussed that call and the leap of faith she took in making it. At first she seemed not to know why she had broken her silence. "I thought you probably had most of it figured out," she said. "Maybe I just wanted to be sure you got it right."

But as she shared her story, telling it in increments small enough for her own acceptance, verifying the recollections of others, filling in the blanks, her reason for speaking out became clear. She simply could not bear to continue the lie. Time and reflection had added weight to her awful burden. For her soul, her sanity, and her dead babies, she had to tell the truth.

I

Loralei

1

THE SUN WARMED *STELLA HYATT'S SHOULDERS AS SHE WAVED *Marvin off to work and started the mower. She felt a bit of morning breeze fan her cheek, but she knew the temperature would climb, for the weather on June 17, 1986, was typical for southwestern Illinois, building to a sweltering stickiness during the day, cooling to the point of chill at night.

By midmorning the air hung hot and heavy. A trickle of perspiration snaked its way down Stella's spine. The lawn spread out before her, five acres waiting to be leveled into a uniform green carpet. The task seemed endless, almost too much for a woman her age.

Heat and hunger drove her inside at noon, but she was back by 3 P.M., walking the mower over the gently rolling ground. She paused when she caught sight of her young neighbor, Paula Sims. The Simses' next-door house was set back a football field's length from the road, and Stella raised a hand in long-distance greeting as Paula, still showing the

_____
*Names marked with asterisks are pseudonyms.

7

abdominal puffiness of recent pregnancy, began a slow approach to the mailbox.

A week had slipped by since Stella's visit with Paula and the new baby, and she was eager to hear how things were going. "How's our little girl?" she called, stopping the mower and stepping to the road as she pushed the curly gray hair from her damp forehead.

"Just fine. She's gettin' a little potbelly on her," Paula replied.

Stella smiled at the image. Loralei with a little potbelly! She was such a beautiful infant, creamy skin and golden-red hair, the kind of baby that would make any grandmother beam with pride. Stella had grandchildren of her own, but she felt a special connection to the new baby girl. She had grown close to Paula during the pregnancy, talking through the long winter afternoons, sharing memories of her own children, answering questions about babies, about what to expect and what to avoid.

A week earlier, when Paula had placed the infant in her arms, Stella's face glowed. She would have been content to sit for hours cuddling the tiny bundle, maybe even rocking her to sleep. And Paula looked so happy! "This is what life is all about, isn't it?" she said.

"Yes," Stella agreed. "Oh, yes!"

It was a moment to savor, a moment that made her smile as she recalled it. But then Rob Sims came halfway down the stairs to the basement family room, and the moment was gone. Paula reclaimed the baby and placed her in the bassinet.

The abruptness of the action startled Stella. No word passed between the Simses, but there was a change in the air, an edge that made things uncomfortable. Maybe that was the reason she had stayed away for a week. She knew, from watching the comings and goings of the silver Jeep, that Rob was working the night shift; during the day he was home sleeping. Soon the shifts would rotate, and Paula would be alone during the afternoons. This was the time to visit, the time the two women usually visited, when they could be easy and natural with each other.

"I can't wait to see Loralei again." Stella made the question a casual one: "When does Rob's shift change?"

"Day shift starts Thursday," Paula answered.

"Thursday," Stella repeated, looking forward to kissing and stroking the little red-haired girl. "That's when I'll be over. Thursday." She nodded good-bye and turned her attention back to the mower, having no reason to suspect that she would never again see tiny Loralei Marie Sims.

Stella was out once more, taking advantage of the evening coolness to pull weeds from her flower bed, when Rob Sims drove by at 8:30 P.M. He was leaving earlier than usual, she noted as she waved.

The cool darkness was welcome. Stella was more than ready for bed after she and Marvin heard the weather forecast on the 10 P.M. news. Even hotter tomorrow. She was glad she had finished the lawn. She turned off the TV and started toward the bedroom, conscious of the ache in her muscles. Marvin detoured to the kitchen for a drink of water and gazed absently through the open window above the sink, savoring the smell of new-cut grass and the pleasant stillness of the night. "Do you remember if I locked that basement door?" Stella called.

"I'll check it," Marvin offered.

Stella waited in the living room for his return, yawning and rubbing her tired back. She jerked involuntarily, a spasm of surprise, as a fleeting figure crossed the picture window. Before she could do more than draw a sharp breath, pounding erupted at the front door.

The noise bounced off the walls in the basement. "What the—!" Marvin muttered. His first thought was that it was kids, some silly prank, some run-to-the-door-and-knock dare thought up by juveniles with too much summer time on their hands.

Stella squinted through the door's peephole. "Who are you?" she called. "What do you want?"

"It's Paula!" came the frantic reply. "Let me in!" Muffled words broke through as Stella fumbled with the lock. "My baby! Please!" Paula Sims charged through the opened door. "Help me!" she sobbed. "He stole my baby!"

"What?" asked Stella. "Who?"

"A man with a gun," Paula gasped. "Call the police!"

Stella stood frozen, trying to absorb the unlikely message. She turned to Marvin, who hurried up the stairs. "Oh, my God," she said as she reached out to her weeping neighbor, "someone took Paula's baby! Someone took Loralei!"

Words tumbled hysterically from Paula: "Masked man . . . gun . . . gloves . . . bassinet!"

Marvin's move to the phone was automatic. The sheriff's dispatcher was as astonished as the Hyatts. A stolen baby? In Jersey County? In the peaceful green fields of Illinois? *A stolen baby?*

Marvin relayed the details as Paula sobbed them out: "Downstairs in the family room . . . lay down on the floor . . . baby gone from the bassinet."

Stella tried to piece the information together, but Paula was almost incoherent. "My baby," she repeated, "he took my baby!" She paced, her thongs flapping against her heels as she clutched the bottom of her T-shirt and turned it into knots. She covered her face with her hands, collapsing on the couch. Then she was up again, looking out the living room window, grabbing Stella for support.

The surprised sheriff's dispatcher volunteered to notify the Brighton police. The area in which the Simses and Hyatts lived was outside the village limits of Brighton by a half mile, but the police would certainly arrive before sheriff's deputies, whose headquarters was eight miles away in Jerseyville.

"I want to call Rob!" Paula cried. "I've got to call Rob!" She was headed for the door.

"Soon as I finish with the sheriff," Marvin assured her. "Wait a minute, Paula. Don't go back there!"

Stella forced her to sit down. "My baby's gone," Paula wept. She was beyond consolation. "I've gotta call Rob!"

"You mustn't go out there," Stella echoed the warning.

"What's his number?" Paula asked. "I can't remember Rob's number." She was on her way to the door.

"Don't leave," Stella begged.

"Paula," Marvin cautioned sternly from the phone, "you don't know what you'll find."

But Paula was gone, her thongs flapping away into the darkness.

Marvin hung up the telephone. He and Stella stared at each other in the sudden silence of the house. "We're in our pajamas," he said. "We better get dressed."

Stella's heart pounded as she hurried along the three hundred feet of the Simses' driveway, now running, now walking. Her crunching footsteps punctuated the rustling of leaves and chirping of insects, but there was no comfort in the familiar sounds. As she passed through the pale spill from the dusk-to-dawn pole lamp every dark shape in the landscape seemed ominous: the large tree on the right where the narrow road curved and dipped, her own carefully tended fruit trees on the left. She wished Marvin were with her, but he waited at the end of the driveway for the arrival of police officers and sheriff's deputies. They might have trouble finding the location otherwise; the Sims house was set so far back from the road they could miss it entirely.

Stella peered at the moonlit home before her. It looked usual, ordinary, nestled in its backdrop of woods, a placid pond on one side. She moved carefully across the redwood-stained deck on the corner of the house, for there was a step midway that, even in daylight, was hard to discern. Shadow, Paula's collie, heard her approach and responded noisily. "Shh, quiet, Shadow," said Stella as she felt her way past the cushioned bench and chair to the front door. The name Sims was burned into a wood plaque beside the entrance. To the right of the screen a white rectangle's black letters warned "Do Not Disturb." Almost directly opposite, a jagged vertical slit suggested that someone had not heeded the admonition, but Stella did not see it, for the porch light was dark as she waited at the door. She stood still, listening as Paula, her voice high and sharp, tried to make Rob understand that their baby daughter was gone, snatched from her bassinet by—by whom? Stella peered into the dim house. Its order gave no hint of intrusion. It looked exactly as it had when she'd visited. Neat. Clean. Everything in its place.

"Come home," Paula begged Rob. "Come right home." She stifled a sob as she replaced the phone and motioned Stella inside. A loud squeak accompanied the opening of the door, and the collie bounded out to the deck, barking. Paula had told Stella that she was never afraid, not even during Rob's midnight shifts, because she had Shadow. "Come here, girl," coaxed Stella. "Shadow, come here."

The dog wouldn't respond to her beckoning, dashing instead to the darkness on the deck and beyond. Was she chasing something, someone? Stella didn't know what to do. It seemed odd to worry about a dog when a baby was missing. "I can't get Shadow," she reported.

Paula stepped out on the deck. "Get inside," she ordered the dog. "I've already lost my baby. I can't lose you, too."

At 10:15 P.M. Robert Sims brought his silver Jeep to a stop in the parking lot of Jefferson Smurfit, the paper processing company where he had worked for six years. He met a coworker, Roger Mauser, and the two men entered the plant, making small talk along the way.

Sims went to his locker to exchange his street clothes for the shirt and overalls he wore on his shift. Carrying his lunch box, he walked to a bulletin board and scanned it for company or union notices. He stepped into an office to check the coal-unloading sheet, noting how much had been unloaded already and calculating how much had to be accomplished on his shift. It was there that another employee, Tod Bartholomew, found him. "Get to the steam and power office!" Bartholomew ordered. "You got a phone call!"

Rob hurried to the room where Paul Minor and Richard Combs, bosses of the incoming and outgoing work shifts, hovered by the phone. Combs had been talking to Paula, trying to calm her, trying to make sense of what she said while men searched the plant for Rob. "You'll be goin' home as soon as you talk to your wife," Combs advised as he handed over the receiver.

"Paula?" Rob's expression changed as he listened. "You're kidding," he protested. But the worried faces of the shift bosses and Paula's hysterical tone belied any kidding. He listened again, shaking his head. "I'm comin', Paula," he promised. "God damn!" he stammered as he handed the receiver back to Combs. "You're not gonna believe this. Someone just took my baby!"

Stella followed Paula down the stairs that led to the basement family room. To the right of the bottom step was the bassinet, its wicker covered by a blue blanket that reached the floor. A pink-flowered mattress pad softened the bottom; folded towels offered extra protection at the ends. But there was no baby, only a white receiving blanket, its corner turned back neatly, delicate pink and blue figures decorating the gentle fold.

Paula stood helplessly in the center of the room, her words escaping between little sobs as she indicated the easy chair in which she had been sitting while she watched the Channel 2 news. The stairway cut across a wall directly behind the television set, but the dark, masked figure had crept almost to the bottom step, Paula pointed out, before she had noticed his presence. "Lay down on the floor," he had ordered, "and don't move for ten minutes, or I'll kill you."

She had done as she was told, she said, stretching out on the mottled embossed carpet, her head toward the sliding glass doors that opened to the backyard. The bassinet was behind her, hidden from her view by the couch, but she had heard no sound from it, no noise at all but the intruder's footsteps as he mounted the stairs.

She had stayed on the floor at least five minutes, she told Stella, until she had heard the loud squeak that always accompanied the opening of the upstairs screen door. When that was followed by the click that signaled the door's closing she had scrambled up. Only when she hurried around the couch had she realized the bassinet was empty.

The television's late-night images still flickered across space. Stella looked around the wood-paneled room, so unremarkable, so neatly kept. Blankets protected the furniture from wear and dog hair; a polished brass teapot adorned the freestanding fireplace; a Foosball table waited in a corner. How could such a thing have happened here, here where everything looked so normal? Stella turned off the TV.

Paula huddled in the easy chair, her arms hugging her legs, her figure rocking back and forth. A table with baby supplies stood beside her. Stella had checked them before the baby's birth. Disposable diapers, powder, alcohol, cotton balls, tissues. "Do I need anything else?" Paula had asked. Stella had been unable to think of anything more. It was all there beside the chair. The cozy family room contained everything a young mother could want. Everything except a baby.

Paula's words tumbled on as she relived the nightmare for her neighbor, telling how she had run up the stairs, shoved her feet into her thongs, and dashed out through the squeaking screen door, across the deck, onto the lawn. There she had seen something, a shadowy figure along the driveway. Maybe she had heard footsteps in the gravel; she wasn't sure, but she had followed, running, panting, desperate, all the way to the road. And then nothing. No figure, no car, no footsteps, no baby cry. Only the lights of the Hyatts' house, so she had come to beg for help.

Suddenly Paula was up, drawn to the bassinet as though she didn't believe its emptiness. "My baby," she wept. "My baby's gone." She mounted the stairs with unexpected purpose and prowled the upper floor, circling the dining room, opening the bedrooms.

"What are you doing?" Stella asked, following.

"Looking for Loralei," Paula answered, a breathless whine in her voice. "Maybe he hid her. Maybe she's here somewhere."

"No, I don't think so," Stella said gently. "The police will be here any minute, Paula. Why don't you turn on some lights so they can see where they're going?" Paula flicked the switches that brought light to the dining room and the deck. "How did anyone get in?" Stella wondered. "Did you have the door locked?"

"Just the screen door. That was locked."

Stella looked toward the entry, now splashed with light from the bulb outside. "Look!" she exclaimed. "Your screen is cut!"

"I thought I was safe here," Paula protested as she examined the slash. She slumped despondently into a chair at the dining room table and laid her head on her arms. "Rob loved the baby so much," she moaned. "He left early just to get some things for her. He loved her so much. We had so many plans."

Dave Heistand had been home just long enough to kick off his shoes and change into his pajamas when he and Linda were startled by squealing tires and a honking horn. Rob Sims flung open the front door and fell into their living room. His face was ashen; his hands trembled; he seemed scarcely able to breathe. "You've got to help me," he gasped. "I can't drive any further. They stole my baby!"

The Heistands didn't understand. They had heard Loralei fussing in the background just the night before, when the Simses phoned to wish Dave a belated happy birthday. Only a few days before that they had seen her, a beautiful red-haired baby. Loralei—stolen?

Within minutes Dave was dressed, ready to drive, ready to do anything he could.

"What have I done to deserve this?" Rob Sims lamented as the two men sped through the night.

2

THE SHERIFF'S CAR RACED THROUGH THE TWO-LANE DARKNESS, red lights flashing in constant rhythm over fields and trees. Kidnappings were not unknown in Jersey County, but usually they were easily explained: antagonism between ex-spouses, a disgruntled father or mother. From the little sheriff Frank Yocom knew about the Sims case, this was something entirely different.

Yocom had never met the people who lived in the brick house, but he knew the setting. He knew all four hundred square miles of Jersey County. Its turns and twists, its hills and valleys were committed to his memory, as were many of its twenty thousand residents.

Yocom had recently won his fourth election, but he was recognized as much for his distinctive presence as for his electoral victories. His girth was remarkable, and he wore his belly almost as a badge of authority. "How does Frank manage to hold up his pants?" townspeople joked.

As he sped along a route that he had traveled many times Yocom again pictured the area, the house set back from

16

Cotter Road. So remote, so quiet, he thought; an odd place for a kidnapping.

Dave Heistand's car raised a cloud of dust as it crunched to a stop in the driveway. A paunchy, bearded man wearing bib overalls bolted from the passenger side. "Where's Paula?" he demanded. Marvin Hyatt pointed to the house, and the man leapt the steps, stumbling and cracking his shin on the rise in the deck.

"That's Rob Sims," Marvin explained to the lawmen gathered in the driveway.

Sims was back outside almost immediately, limping slightly. "What are you guys doin'?" he asked the sheriff's deputies. He looked at young Brighton police officer, Chris White. "Have you got any roadblocks up? Did you call the FBI?"

Deputy Hazelwood stepped forward. "What we need is information. Have you noticed any strange vehicles? Any cars that aren't normally around?"

Rob recalled a blue Ford Falcon that had been parked east of the driveway as he left for work. He had stopped to tell the driver not to fish in the pond. The warning didn't seem to sit well, so he had made a note of the car's license. He gave the number to Hazelwood.

And on the Sunday that Paula and Loralei had come home from the hospital, he went on, two men in a pickup truck got nasty when he wouldn't let them fish. They drove over the front lawn after he ordered them to leave. He didn't have a license number, but the pickup was an older model, a "shitty green" color.

Hazelwood nodded. "Anything else?"

Hang-up phone calls, several of them, Sims replied. Someone who listened but said nothing, just hung up. It seemed peculiar, since the phone number was unlisted.

Hazelwood made notes.

"And there was a nurse at the hospital." Rob spoke slowly. "She said Loralei was such a pretty little girl that she ought to steal her."

Hazelwood stopped writing and looked at the red-haired man.

"I'm sure she was just kidding," Rob added.

Hazelwood nodded.

"How come the sheriff's not here?" Rob asked. "Where's Yocom? Is he coming?"

"He's on the way," the deputy replied. "Why don't you go inside and wait with your wife until he gets here?"

Rob turned slowly and limped back to the house. "We never shoulda put the birth announcement in the paper," he muttered. "That was a mistake. We never shoulda put it in the paper."

Frank Yocom turned off the siren as he pulled into the long driveway. Two of his deputies' cars were there already, as well as a cruiser from the Brighton police. "So what have we got?" Yocom asked Hazelwood and Deputy Roger Long.

The deputies introduced Chris White of the Brighton Police Department and Don Stewart, a member of the village police board who had chosen this evening to exercise his "ride-along" privilege. Their squad car had been the first to arrive at the scene.

The baby was taken from a bassinet in the basement, Chris White explained, a bassinet that wasn't visible from any window. And it was obscured by the couch, so it couldn't have been seen through the basement's sliding glass doors. No casual prowler or Peeping Tom would have been able to tell that there was a baby in the house unless he had *heard* her. But the mother said the baby was quiet, asleep. The circumstances suggested to White that perhaps the child had been taken by someone who knew she was there, someone who had come specifically to get her.

At first he concentrated his efforts on calming the mother, on getting her to give him a better picture of the kidnapper. It might be someone familiar, he reasoned, someone who knew that she had a baby, maybe someone who had been in her home before. But she could give him only a sparse description: a tall man with a deep voice, black T-shirt, and black stocking mask.

When Deputy Hazelwood arrived he tried for more detail. Maybe the gun was the problem, he figured. Face to face with a gun, the mother might not have been able to see anything beyond the barrel. Her attention, her fear, could have concentrated on the weapon rather than on the man who held it. "Can you describe the gun?" he asked.

"It was just a gun," she said.

"Was it blue or silver?" he persisted.

She shook her head. "I don't know."

"Was it like this gun?" Hazelwood showed her his service revolver.

"It was just a gun." Sobs overcame her.

When the officers searched the house they found only the slit in the screen. No broken window, no open doors or drawers, no telltale token of a masked intruder. When they turned on their cars' headlights, aimed their spotlights, and grabbed their big rechargeable Kell lights, the darkness stayed unyielding. No footprints, no discarded mask, no gun, no baby.

The first cryptic message, teletyped across the state at ten minutes before midnight, reflected their frustration:

ILLINOIS STATE POLICE EMERGENCY RADIO NETWORK (ISPERN)
MESSAGE #361
CHILD ABDUCTION 67 1 W OF CITY LIMIT ROAD 2235
ONLY INFORMATION WE HAVE AT THIS TIME IS A MALE MASKED SUBJECT ENTERED A HOUSE WITH A GUN AND ABDUCTED A CHILD
NO VEHICLE DESCRIPTION OR FURTHER INFORMATION AT THIS TIME

"Nothing? No motor, no lights?" asked Sheriff Yocom.

"That's what she says," confirmed Hazelwood. "Nothing."

"That's damn strange," said Yocom. "Nothing."

The squeak of the front door startled the sheriff as the deputies led him into the house. Paula sat in the dining room, her head leaning against her husband, who stood by her chair. Her sobs were dry, short little gasps of breath. "Mrs. Sims," the sheriff said, "I'm Frank Yocom. Can you tell me what happened?"

She went over it again, leading the sheriff downstairs, just as she had led Stella, and then the Brighton police, and then the Jersey County deputies. She pointed to the easy chair, the stairway, the empty bassinet.

"Did you ask him what he wanted?" Yocom inquired. "Money? Drugs? Whatever."

"No." She shook her head. "I didn't ask him." Rob Sims put an arm on his wife's shoulder. She sobbed. "My baby's gone!"

"Did he say he wanted the baby? Did he say that's why he was here?" the sheriff pressed.

She brought her hands to her face and spoke in a tiny whine. "He just took her."

Yocom watched. He couldn't get a handle on her gasping sobs. He had heard the gut-wrenching, soul-tearing cries of bereaved mothers. He had seen shock so severe that the victim was unable to react to anything. He had never before observed this kind of reaction. The weeping woman was able to repeat some details of her experience coherently and, from what he could tell, consistently. At a certain point details ceased.

The sheriff had a dozen questions: Why didn't she see her baby in the kidnapper's arms when he climbed the open staircase? Why did she lie on the basement floor for five minutes even though she heard no noise from above? Why didn't she peek to see if her daughter was safe? And how could any intruder have been so quiet, his footsteps on the floor above making no sound at all as he presumably walked from room to room carrying the baby?

Yocom didn't ask the questions. He was afraid to push the young mother too much. Still, he knew there should be more. Something was missing. He studied the woman's face. The pressure of her hands left red marks on her cheeks. Her eyes were small, swollen from crying, but there were no tears, just heaving sobs. She appeared to be in her mid-twenties, as tall as her husband, maybe taller. Yocom guessed her weight to be about 150 pounds, with the thickening of her abdomen, the stretched stomach muscles of pregnancy, still apparent. Her arms were thin, her fingers long. Her light brown hair was messed, straggly. Curly tendrils lay in clumps on her neck and shoulders, sometimes clinging to her cheeks, pressed there by hands that she seemed unable to control. There was a delicacy to her facial features. Under different circumstances Yocom might have considered her pretty. She laid her head on her husband's shoulder. "My baby's gone," she repeated plaintively. Her husband patted her arm.

The sheriff knew there was no way to predict a victim's reaction to tragedy, but the young mother's responses seemed peculiar. Her cry was odd, hollow. Her eyes darted about except when her head was on her husband's shoulder. She declined a suggestion that her parents be notified, saying that her mother was "the nervous type." Yocom was grateful that Stella Hyatt was available to serve as a stabilizing influence, but still he worried. Was this a woman who might go into shock? He led the uniformed men to the yard and spoke quietly to one of them: "Let's get an ambulance out here. Just in case."

Rob Sims trailed the last man out the squeaking door, leaving the two women inside. The house was suddenly a vacuum of silence. Paula glanced at a clock and caught her breath. "I've got to warm Loralei's bottle," she said, as though scolding herself. She opened the kitchen refrigerator and stared at its light. "No," she said, "no, that won't do any good. Loralei's gone."

Stella took a deep, slow breath. She felt the walls closing in. "Come on, Paula," she said. "Let's go outside."

Sheriff Yocom knew that the situation required expertise and manpower beyond the capabilities of his county. He phoned an emergency number in Springfield, requesting help from the Illinois State Police and its Department of Criminal Investigation.

"What about an airplane? Or a helicopter?" Rob Sims was at his elbow, making persistent suggestions.

"What time did you leave home?" the sheriff inquired. He was looking for information about the couple's life-style, something that might offer a clue to the motive, if not the identity, of the kidnapper.

More than an hour early, Rob explained, in order to take care of some errands on the way to work: a stop at Toy Chest to exchange a crib mobile the baby had received as a gift, a mobile identical to one he and Paula had purchased themselves. A stop at Target to drop off three rolls of film, photos of Loralei. "Bought four baby-bottle nipples and looked for a flashlight I saw advertised. Flashlights were sold out, but I got a rain check. Looked for a Garden Weasel, but I couldn't find any. Went to Venture. No Garden Weasel there either. Bought a can of car wax. Receipt's probably in my Jeep. Bought me a set of spark plugs, too, but I don't know what happened to the receipt for those. Left Venture around ten. Got to work by ten-fifteen."

It was a specific accounting. Almost too specific, Yocom thought. "Do you have any notion who might do something like this?" the sheriff asked. "Any enemies?"

Rob shook his head. He talked again of men annoyed when they were denied permission to fish in the pond. Yocom struggled to make the mental leap from disgruntled fisherman to baby kidnapper. The blue Falcon's license number wouldn't be difficult to check, but a beat-up "shitty green" pickup could present some problems. The hospital nurse seemed an even longer shot. Surely her words were just an offhand compliment, but that, too, would have to be checked out. Tomorrow. Tonight he needed dogs. His own department had none. The Brighton police had none. The Illinois State Police had K-9 units, but they would have to come all the way from Collinsville, almost forty miles southeast. A call on his car radio gave Yocom the news that the dogs would have to travel even further than that; they were at a K-9 certification seminar in Springfield, fifty miles north.

Someone remembered that local newspapers had carried word of a K-9 recently acquired by the nearby Wood River Police Department. Yocom called for it. The dog, Tracker, and his handler, Ralph Timmons, covered the twenty-seven miles in only twenty-two minutes. It was their first assignment; they were eager to work. Not long after, the state police units dispatched from the seminar began to arrive, first Mike Donovan with Jud, then Jim Buysee with Bear.

Led by their handlers, the three dogs sniffed everyone at the scene, lawmen as well as civilians. The animals' sensitive noses would categorize those human odors and then ignore them, instead going after whatever "unknown" scent they encountered. The target area was the gravel drive, the hundred yards where Paula Sims had followed crunching footsteps. The dogs should pick up the trail of the suspect, lead their handlers the length of the driveway, and head east or west on Cotter Road, indicating the direction in which the kidnapper had made his escape.

The German shepherds zigzagged across the gravel, sniffing past the cars, past the dusk-to-dawn lamp pole, past the midway point where the lane bent and dipped. Donovan returned to the yard to share his concerns with Yocom. The dogs found no trail, no "hot scent" on the driveway. What was more, Cotter Road had just two lanes and narrow shoulders. Any car parked on it would block traffic in one direction or the other. No one intending a crime would conspicuously block half a road with his vehicle. It seemed more likely that the getaway car had been parked in the mouth of the driveway, the only wide spot. But the mother had said nothing about a car in the driveway. And there was no indication of heavy acceleration anywhere. If the dogs couldn't smell the path of the kidnapper, if the mother hadn't seen a vehicle, if a car hadn't accelerated quickly, how had the abductor escaped?

Paula repeated it once more. A running shadow. Footsteps in gravel.

"We'll keep trying," Donovan said with a nod.

Vehicles jammed the area: television minivans, reporters' cars, sheriff's department cars, troopers' units with K-9 cages, a precautionary ambulance, and whatever the merely curious happened to be driving. It was late enough that most residents were in bed; nevertheless, the flashing lights had drawn attention.

When the Department of Criminal Investigation's duty agent Jim Bivens arrived, the scene was a mini-light show in the midst of the deep, chilly, moonlit night. Headlights and spotlights shone on the Sims house, on the driveway, on the lawn. Officers lugging Kell lights aimed their beams at anything that moved. K-9 handlers worked their dogs along the edges of Cotter Road, lighting their way with flashlights. TV vans turned on their illuminating power to assist.

Still, when Bivens stepped from his car he was struck by the comparative quiet. Reporters and onlookers waited off the property, a football field away. Paula was on the front porch, encircled by a tiny knot of hushed civilians. The usual mechanical and emotional noises of a violent crime scene were missing. No blaring sirens, no screaming victims, no wailing relatives.

Bivens sought out Frank Yocom, and the two held a quick private conference. Other lawmen stayed out of the way. They knew what was happening. The amiable, rotund county sheriff and the hard-as-nails DCI agent with the Marine Corps tattoo were setting the ground rules.

The position of the Department of Criminal Investigation was a delicate one in cases such as this. DCI would assist only if requested, invited, by the local authorities. After that, agreements had to be reached. Did the local agency wish to relinquish the case, to turn it over to the state? Or was the investigation to be a joint effort? If so, the state's man had to be someone who could work effectively with the chief local official.

Bivens, with fifteen years' experience as a state trooper and another thirteen years with DCI, considered himself a "bullshitter," a flexible, easygoing guy who could get along with any of the locals. And he genuinely liked Frank Yocom. Frank was a good man, a good sheriff. They had worked together before; there would be no problems. The two men set the guidelines quickly. A cooperative effort all the way. Bivens would be responsible for coordination; Yocom would handle the growing number of press people. Then there was the matter of translating ideas into action. Everyone had ideas. Get airplanes. Get helicopters. Get more dogs. Rob Sims offered his suggestions: setting up roadblocks, checking airports, calling the FBI.

"We'll be talking to the FBI in due course," Bivens assured him, "but at this point the investigation is in the hands of Jersey County and the Illinois State Police."

Philip Kocis, the DCI zone commander, had arrived at the scene, as had Wayne Watson and Ken Snider, two agents who lived nearby. Now Yocom ran the story by all the state's men. They followed his gestures as he indicated the front porch on which Paula had stood, the gravel in which she had heard crunching footsteps, the light pole where she had seen something move, the blacktop of Cotter Road to which she had pursued sound and shadow. "But then she couldn't see anything," he concluded.

"What did she *hear?*" asked Bivens softly, his words hanging in the country quiet. "She's running in the rocks, and someone in front of her is running in the rocks. She may not hear his crunching because of her crunching. But when that dude hits the blacktop she's gonna hear a different sound. She's gonna hear a slapping sound. Think about it. If I run down a blacktop, I guarantee you'll hear me running for a long ways."

Perhaps the kidnapper didn't stay on the blacktop, someone speculated. Perhaps he crossed the road and took off. Bivens shook his head. "You're not just gonna take off over strange country in the middle of the night with a baby in one hand and a gun in the other and a mask over your face, take off straight over an open field or pasture or whatever that is out there. You're going to hit the road," he insisted. "She must have heard the slapping feet."

The men looked toward Paula, who sat on the porch, staring into the darkness beyond the house. Should they question her once again, run her through the details to see if she might remember anything else? Or was her condition too precarious? The ambulance attendants had determined that her pulse was rapid, but her blood pressure and respiration were normal. She was in no physical danger. Emotionally she was harder to judge. Her sobs came and went; she was sometimes despondent, sometimes hopeful that the dogs and the ever-increasing number of searchers would find her baby. Investigators decided to risk another interview.

Her voice was a whisper. She was tearful but under control. Rob hovered at her side as she led the men into the house. Like others before him, Bivens was startled by the squeaking screen door. He paused long enough to determine that it was the door's piston cylinder that produced the metal-to-metal screech.

Tense and drawn, Paula pointed out everything in the basement. The easy chair. The bassinet. Her sparse descriptions remained the same. Black shirt. Black mask. Gun.

Investigators had no way of knowing that even as she spoke the words she had chosen, the visions in her head were of other things, of sharp branches silhouetted against the bright moon, of cockleburs clinging tenaciously to socks and sweat pants.

Bivens stepped forward, forcing his presence into the pictures that flashed in her memory. "Tell me what you *heard*," he said. Maybe the squeak of the screen door before the kidnapper appeared?

"No."

Slapping footsteps on the blacktop?

"No."

Anything else? Anything they could put out on the air? Anything at all?

"No." She was barely audible.

It was not the time or place to ask more, not as the pale, whispering young mother sat in the room with the empty bassinet. But Bivens wondered why the couple slept in the damp, musty-smelling basement, why they kept their tiny baby there. Back outside he put the question to Rob. A broken air conditioner, Sims explained, and high electricity rates even if they were to fix it. The basement was cooler.

"What about the FBI?" Rob asked. "Shouldn't they be called now?"

The years had taught Bivens to deal patiently with victims and their families. "We'll take care of it," he replied.

"Did you call for an airplane? Or a helicopter?"

"Just let us take care of it."

"How 'bout a nationwide bulletin? Did you think of that?"

Too many questions always made Bivens uneasy, made him think somebody was trying to find out what he knew, or even trying to pull him off track, to steer him in a different direction.

"Anybody check around the camper over there?" Sims asked.

Bivens found himself staring at the young father in the denim bib overalls. "Look, sir," he said, "you get back to your wife, and if you've got any recommendations, please write 'em down. But I've got a train of thought going here, and you're interrupting it." He watched as Rob Sims wandered back to the porch. His suggestions had been good ones, intelligent and reasonable, more than Bivens would have expected from a devastated thirty-four-year-old overall-clad factory worker. "What's his story?" he asked Yocom.

The sheriff traced Sims' activities for the evening: the exchange at Toy Chest, the rain check for a flashlight at Target, the sales receipt from Venture.

"There's a written record of every stop he made?" Bivens asked.

"That's right," said Yocom. The two men looked at each other, considering the chances of such convenient coincidence.

"Hmph," muttered Bivens noncommittally.

Yocom recounted Paula's phone call to Rob at Jefferson Smurfit and Rob's stop for assistance at the home of his friend, Dave Heistand. He shook his head as he spoke. "If it was me, I woulda come straight home, I can tell you that."

"So he gets through the business district by himself, and

then when he's almost on the open road, where he can really floor it, he decides he can't drive anymore and stops for help?"

"Guess so."

"Hmph," Bivens muttered again.

"Sounds strange, doesn't it?" judged Yocom.

"Yeah."

"What about her crying? Does that sound a little funny to you?" Yocom asked.

"How do you mean?"

"Don't know, exactly," the sheriff pondered. "Listen to her. Just sounds funny to me."

Stella Hyatt stood outside watching officer after officer stumble on the rise in the deck. A man in the dark, carrying a gun and a baby, she wondered—how could he know that step was there? What kept him from falling?

She looked at Paula, who sat crying into a little towel as Rob knelt before her. "It would have been better if I had fought him and not let him take the baby," Paula sobbed. "I'm so sorry I let this happen. I'm so sorry I disappointed you."

"Shh," Rob soothed. "You didn't disappoint me."

She sobbed quietly into the towel again.

Orville Blew rubbed the sleep from his eyes and reached for the phone.

"Are you sitting down?" the voice asked.

"Yeah." Orville, still groggy, wondered at such a strange question.

"Our baby's been stole!"

"Who is this?" asked Orville.

"It's Rob. Our baby's been stole!"

Moments later Orville Blew dialed the Simses' unlisted number. He had begun to believe that the call might have been someone's version of a bad joke. "Did it really happen?" Orville asked. He was hoping he could tell his wife it was just a hoax.

The Blews came immediately from their home in Cottage

Hills, fifteen miles away. Stella watched curiously as they stood in the yard, talking with officers and glancing toward the house, delaying their entrance to the emotional center of the scene until a deputy nodded toward Paula and said, "Your daughter is on the deck." Only then did they begin their slow approach, assisting their adult son, Dennis, who planted himself on the cushioned bench and remained there throughout the night, shoulders hunched, head down, arms folded across his chest. Paula had told Stella that her brother was epileptic, not retarded, but his speech was thick and slow, and Stella could understand why strangers might make that assumption.

Orville Blew, a gray-haired man looking decidedly older than his fifty-seven years, mounted the steps talking about a black market in babies. His remarks jolted Stella, who had met him only once, just a few days earlier. She wasn't sure what she expected from the grandfather of a kidnapped infant, but it wasn't a pronouncement that the baby would probably be sold on the black market.

Nylene Blew surprised her, too. Paula had often mentioned that her mother was a "nervous" person, but the tall, angular woman appeared cool and remote as she hugged her daughter. "I've always been worried about you, way out here in the country," she said.

"Now don't start that," her husband cautioned. She fell silent.

"What about *your* dad?" Stella asked Rob. "Don't you think you should call him, too?"

"No," Paula said, lowering the little towel she held over her eyes. "I don't want him here. When he came to the hospital he didn't even want to see Loralei. I had to *tell* him to go to the nursery. Don't call him."

Rob called his sister instead.

When the dog handlers couldn't find a scent on the driveway, where they expected it to be, they headed to other areas. Ralph Timmons and Tracker crisscrossed the yard. Jim Buysee and Bear went west a half mile on Cotter Road, past the Hyatts' property, until they came to a small hillside

Catholic cemetery. When that route produced no result they went east.

The K-9 officers spoke in hushed tones about the possibility of cult activity, of human sacrifice. Timmons took Tracker through the scattered tombstones of the cemetery. Buysee and Bear worked the fields and lawns on both sides of the road. Nothing.

Mike Donovan and Jud, the "show dog" of District 11, fared no better. Their failure was a special disappointment, for Jud had a reputation for reliability. Together dog and handler had participated in a dozen dead-body searches and in hundreds of live-scent searches. Donovan swore that their success rate was at least ninety-five percent.

Jud sniffed his way across the Sims yard, up and down the driveway, around the pond, searching for the special odor of the microscopic cells that continually fall to the ground from human skin. A running person drops more of them, with greater force. But Jud detected no trail. If the suspect ran across the property, the K-9 handlers agreed, he managed to do it without leaving a scent.

Things were not going well. Except for the slashed screen, investigators were coming up blank, and most of them had a feeling that something wasn't what it should be. Each man saw it a little differently, phrased it a little differently. Some hesitated to phrase it at all. But there was something that disconcerted them, something that said "things aren't right." Frank Yocom was bothered by the sound of Paula's crying. For Jim Bivens, the whole situation was a puzzle. "It just doesn't add up," he confided to another agent. "A lone, masked, armed gunman coming into a rural home, a medium-income home, and absconding with a baby in the middle of the night with no means of transportation. It just doesn't add up."

As the sky began to lighten Yocom and Bivens came together at the edge of the front yard. Their eyes traveled to Paula and Rob Sims on the front porch, now surrounded by Paula's parents and Rob's sister. All of them were focused on the water southeast of the house, where outlines of cattails were just beginning to emerge from the darkness.

"Looks like they're waiting for us to search the pond," Bivens told Yocom. The pond was already on the list of priorities, of things to do as soon as arrangements could be made, as soon as there was sufficient light. Investigators had failed to crack the case in the first crucial hours. Now it was time for slow, careful, plodding police work.

Tracker went home to Wood River, Jud and Bear back to the training seminar in Springfield, all three of them unsuccessful at finding any scent. The heat of the coming sun would weaken whatever smells remained.

Deputies, agents, troopers, and officers were tired, hungry, and discouraged. They had found no clue to boost their adrenaline, no evidence to push them beyond ordinary endurance.

Kocis, the DCI zone commander, joined Bivens and Yocom. It was time to do something, to form a plan, to present a united front to the family on the porch and to the press who had waited all night on Cotter Road. They went over the entire scenario once again, minute by minute, detail by detail, to see if they might have missed anything, if one of them had caught something the others hadn't. It came out the same. Among the three men who conferred in the dawning light there was more than a half century of experience, and they all came to the same conclusion: "Something doesn't sound right."

"But what sounds right and what's true can be two different things." Bivens spoke what they all knew. So there was no choice but to treat the event as Paula Sims said it was.

The investigation into the kidnapping of thirteen-day-old Loralei Marie had begun.

3

A QUIET TENSION GRIPPED THE DEPUTIES AND DCI AGENTS WHO
assembled in the wood-paneled headquarters of the Jersey
County Sheriff. Some who had been at the Sims property
most of the night were still on duty, having gone home just
long enough for a quick shower and a change of uniform.
They recounted the event for their companions, as though
discussing it might make it more sensible. "Strange," they
said as they shrugged their shoulders. "Strange."

Inside the sheriff's small private office Yocom and Bivens
planned the assignments for county and state personnel: the
interviews, the searches, the background checks. Their
misgivings about Paula Sims's story remained suppressed,
at least temporarily. The morning news reported the occurrence as an abduction, and the investigation proceeded on
that assumption.

By 8 A.M. the center of the probe was back at the crime
scene. DCI Agent Ken Snider knocked on doors of rural
neighbors, asking if they had seen or heard anything that
might identify the kidnapper or shed light on his methods.
They had not.

Trooper Charles Yoways and his dog Sergeant were dispatched from the K-9 seminar in Springfield. Not certain what ground the dog teams had covered the night before, Yoways asked where he should begin. The driveway had obviously been searched, but what about adjacent areas, the fields, the woods? Who had been where? Bivens didn't know. Neither did Yocom. The night had been dark and confusing, with each man absorbed in his own task. Only the handlers knew where they had been, and even they might have become disoriented.

Bivens called state police headquarters, where the K-9 seminar continued, to request the return of Mike Donovan and his dog Jud. Headquarters declined, saying that both dog and handler were too tired. Bivens argued the point. Donovan was from his own district, with one of the best dogs in the state, if not the country. He would come without hesitation if he knew he was needed, no matter how tired he was. "Just ask him," Bivens said.

Headquarters was adamant.

"Are you refusing to send help?" Bivens bristled.

Headquarters offered other dogs, fresher dogs.

"Just gimme Donovan," Bivens insisted. "I don't give a damn if he brings his dog or not. I want him to show me what's been searched. Hell, we'll bring in another dog to do the smelling. I don't give a damn what dog he uses."

No, said headquarters. Not Donovan. Not Jud. Another handler. Another dog.

"But another handler won't know what's already been searched, or could have been searched, or should have been searched!" Bivens contended.

In a decision that was to haunt the investigators, headquarters said no.

By 9:40 A.M. troopers Mark Atchinson and Craig Hudson touched down at the Jerseyville airport to pick up Deputy Roger Long, who knew the area and could direct their plane to the crime scene. Atchinson settled the craft in at an altitude a thousand feet above the Sims house and began flying tightly controlled counterclockwise circles, gradually increasing his radius. Hudson operated a thermal ranging device, an infrared camera that scanned the ground below for a spot of warmth that might represent baby Loralei, if she was still alive.

It was admittedly a long shot. Loralei was so little that her body's heat radiation would be minimal and might be confused with that of a small animal. A solid obstruction could easily conceal her proximity. Even the trees, thick with their early summer greenery, could obscure the presence of a two-week-old child.

While the plane circled, Bivens and Yocom walked the grounds. The woods formed an emerald backdrop for the home, then sloped downward to a dry creek bed a half mile away. Early sunlight glinted off the pond, big and irregular, just to the southeast. Exploration was about to begin by the dragging hooks of the Department of Conservation and the divers of the state police Underwater Search and Recovery Team.

Inside the house Paula and Rob Sims were unaware of the pending searches. Bivens was determined to have them off the property before the first probing hook descended into the water. He had once witnessed the reaction of a woman who saw her dead child, impaled on a hook, pulled from the depths of a lake, and it was an experience he would not have repeated.

When the search teams began to unload their equipment at the edge of the pond Bivens sent DCI Agent Wayne Watson to the house to suggest that the time was right for the Simses to travel to Jerseyville to make their official statements. Paula answered Watson's knock on the screen door. "No," she told him as she looked at the boats and the divers. "No, I want to be here when they bring her body up."

But then, Watson reported, her face tightened. She looked shocked at what she had heard herself say. "That's not what I mean," she added quickly. "I mean my baby is alive and I want to be here when they bring her onto the porch."

Bivens and Yocom listened repeatedly to Watson's account. Had they just heard an inadvertent confession? Or a premonition, a mother's dark fear? They looked at the sharp-pointed dragging hooks. They listened to the divers' discussion: Where on the edge of the pond would one stand to toss a baby? How far could a tiny body be thrown?

In Jerseyville, eight miles from her home, Paula sat in Sheriff Yocom's office, ready to give her statement. Gathered to hear her were Yocom, Bivens, and a psychologist sent from DCI headquarters in Springfield. The presence of the psychologist irked Bivens. He needed Donovan and a dog; instead he got a shrink. The psychologist appeared under the auspices of I-SEARCH, a newly founded, newly funded program designed to deal with missing children. The fledgling organization was a popular project for Illinois politicians, including the governor, to champion. What voter could argue with the necessity of channeling the state's resources to find a missing child, particularly one as young as Loralei Marie Sims, one whose grief-stricken mother told of a black-garbed, gun-wielding intruder?

Bivens knew that I-SEARCH had an efficient system to collect and disseminate information; but, more important to him, it was blessed with a substantial budget. Airplanes and diving boats that would quickly deplete the funds of the Jersey County Sheriff's Department and even stretch the fiscal resources of a DCI district would pose no problem for I-SEARCH, and if that meant accepting the presence of an unrequested, unwanted shrink, so be it, thought Bivens. The psychologist remained, more as an observer than a participant, to witness the Simses making their statements.

Paula faced her listeners dry-eyed and quiet. Bivens drew the assignment of asking the questions and transcribing her answers.

My husband Robert and I have been married about five (5) years. We moved to this house around three (3) years ago. This is my first marriage and my husband's second. Our baby Loralei Marie was born June 5, 1986, at Alton Memorial Hospital in Alton.

My husband is presently working the 11:00 P.M. to 7:00 A.M. shift at Alton Packaging Company [the former name of Jefferson Smurfit]. He left for work a little early last night, around 8:30 P.M. He had some errands to run and has to be there a half hour early to relieve the shift before him. I didn't notice anything unusual, I locked the front storm door after he left. Then I went downstairs around 10:00 P.M. with the baby to watch television news. I usually watch the ten o'clock news on Channel 2. I had fed the baby and she was asleep in the bassinet near the foot of the stairs. I was sitting in my easy chair near the baby, I think the weather was on. The next thing I know I saw a man on the steps. I didn't hear a thing. The man was white, wearing a dark ski mask pulled over his head, it had eye and mouth holes. His shirt was a dark T-shirt. He was wearing gloves and had a handgun. He stuck his arm out, pointed the gun at me and said, "Get on the floor, stay there ten minutes or I'll kill you." I laid down on the floor, my head was pointed towards the back door away from the baby. I thought, "What is he doing here, the door is locked." He had the gun in his right hand. I didn't recognize the voice, it didn't appear too young or too old. The man didn't say a word after that, I didn't hear a thing, not even the baby crying. I heard the front screen close, I got up right away, started running up the stairs and as I passed the bassinet I noticed she, the baby, was gone. I ran out the door after the man, I couldn't see him, a car or anything. I could hear what I thought was someone running on the driveway gravel as I was running towards the main road. I ran all the way to the end of the lane. I thought I would see a car or something but didn't. I then ran to my neighbors, the Hyatts, house to have them call the police. I was going to have them call my husband at work but didn't have his number so I went back to our house to get the number. When I got back to the house our dog, a collie was inside by the front door. I called my husband's place of work and had to stay on the line until they could find him. I told him what happened.

When the baby was taken she was wearing a diaper (disposable), white shirt and white with pink trim booties. She has no health problems I am aware of. She was a planned child both of us wanted. We were waiting until we could afford one.

The lake next to us belongs to a neighbor. People are fishing there all the time. I have noticed a young white boy there with no shirt on.

There have been some telephone calls to the house since we brought the baby home. When my husband answers, the person hangs up. He got one today, the phone rang about three times and when he answered no one was there. He asked me who was doing this. He was pretty upset about it at the time. This was after 4, about 4:15.

From time to time the investigators prodded for a clearer answer or a different answer: "Paula, if something happened, get it off your chest now." It was not a time to push too hard; they didn't want to cut off the lines of communication. They wanted her to keep talking. Occasionally she sobbed as she answered their questions, but she pulled herself together and continued. She made half a dozen minor corrections to Bivens's transcription, initialed them, and signed the document.

Rob's statement was shorter, but it enumerated his visits to Toy Chest, Venture, and Target on the way to work and his stop for assistance at the Heistands on the way home. ("I was too nervous and was afraid I might hurt someone.") He told again of the fishermen in the blue Falcon and in the green pickup but was unable to offer any reason that his child might have been kidnapped. ("I have had no real problems at work for anyone to do anything like this.")

The statements did not yield as much detail as the

listeners had hoped they would. Usually witnesses remembered more as they had time to reflect in the hours after a crime. The Simses seemed to remember less.

Efforts to drag the pond were abandoned when the hooks repeatedly became entangled in the vegetation that covered its bottom. After the hooks were pulled in the divers descended. Jack Jackson, James Buckley, and Don Mayer, having established three arc patterns in places where the pond's shoreline offered some accessibility, dived into the opaque water, groping their way through the lush bottom plants. In a "grab and feel" effort they poked and picked deeper and deeper down the pond's slope, following the arcs ever further from the shore. They found nothing in the likely areas, the areas where an object would land if it was hurled from the pond's most easily reachable edges. It was possible that Loralei had been transported to the twenty-foot-deep center of the pond and dumped, but the divers knew they could spend days pawing through the dense underwater growth and still miss her. After four hours they abandoned the effort.

Another K-9 team arrived: Trooper William Rogers and Rocky. "Why didn't they pull Donovan down?" asked one of the handlers as he tried to figure out where to send his animal.

"God damn, that's what I asked for!" seethed Bivens.

Deputies as well as dogs crisscrossed the property as the afternoon heat built; but as a provider of clues, the sunlight was no more generous than the dark.

Yocom couldn't shake the idea that Loralei Marie had to be somewhere on the property. "I just didn't see how that baby could have got away from there. First off, it seemed almost impossible to me for that masked man to have run down that lane. I felt all the time that the baby was there somewhere. That never, ever changed. Not that we didn't consider other things, but the consensus among us was that the baby had to be there."

As the hours passed and the sunlight baked the ground it

became obvious to the searchers that hope of finding Loralei alive was minimal. At less than ten pounds, she would quickly dehydrate in the ninety-degree heat.

Bivens's DCI agents fanned out to check whatever they could. Workers and supervisors at Jefferson Smurfit; clerks at Toy Chest, Venture, and Target; neighbors; friends; relatives; hospital personnel; all were listed for interviews. A phone tap was authorized and installed, in case a ransom call or even a "hang-up" call came in. Cars were stopped on Cotter Road in the hope that a driver who traveled the route regularly had noticed something the night before.

Arrangements were made for yet another exploration of the pond, a sonar search employing equipment sometimes used to locate fish, although it was stretching credulity to believe that the sonar could pinpoint an object as tiny as Loralei in vegetation that had already stymied the dragging operation and the divers. It was a "cover-your-ass–type operation," a one-in-a-thousand chance. If news of the kidnapping was not filling front pages and airwaves, if the case was not so high-profile, if I-SEARCH was not involved, the sonar probe would never have been attempted. But as long as I-SEARCH funds covered the costs, no possibility, however remote its success, would be ignored.

The Federal Bureau of Investigation made its official entry through agents Dale Schuler and Jim Quick. Although FBI jurisdiction was problematic, the organization was there to offer facilities and expertise that might save time if any interstate contacts became necessary.

By Wednesday, June 18, less than twenty-four hours after Loralei was reported missing, seven agencies were cooperating in the effort to find her: the Jersey County Sheriff's Department; the Department of Conservation; the Brighton Police Department; the Illinois State Police and its Department of Criminal Investigation; the FBI; and I-SEARCH.

As the sonar equipment began to arrive on Thursday morning Rob Sims walked to Cotter Road to move his truck. He had parked it across the mouth of the driveway to thwart the curious, some of whom, in the previous evening's twilight, had attempted to glide their vehicles up to the house for a firsthand look at the scene of the crime.

Stella Hyatt was at her backyard clothesline, hanging her wash. "Is there anything new?" she called as she walked to the road.

"I can't believe they're going to waste more time searching the pond," Rob complained. He stood by his truck, focused on a weed that he prodded with his toe. "I know she's not in that pond. I told 'em she wasn't in there."

"When Loralei's found," Stella predicted, "she's gonna be close."

A certainty in her tone grabbed Rob's attention. "Why do you say that?" he asked.

"I don't know." Stella shrugged. "I've just got a feeling that Loralei is not far away."

4

IT WAS THE BUSINESS WITH THE BIRTH CERTIFICATE APPLICATION
that several of them recalled. The father spent a long time
looking it over, studying each line. He asked no questions;
he made no comments; he looked neither pleased nor
displeased. He just perused it, entry by unremarkable entry,
for such a long time that nearby hospital personnel became
aware, then curious, then concerned, and finally amused.
After he nodded his approval one of the nurses glanced over
the medical charts on mother and baby to see if she could
find anything that might have occasioned the father's scruti-
ny. Records indicated a normal pregnancy, a normal delivery, a healthy baby. There was nothing exceptional about
the birth of Loralei Marie Sims.

The infant was remembered by some for her unusual
name and by others for her beautiful red hair. Her parents
were fading from nurses' memories. Most recalled only that
the Simses were reserved, private, and undemanding.

Pamela Colley, the nurse who led Paula and Rob from the
admitting office to the obstetrical floor, found them to be

very quiet. "How many children do you have?" she asked as they rode the elevator. It was a concern to her only because birth order sometimes affected the length of labor.

"It's my first," said Paula.

"And it's our last," Rob added.

Marilyn Quigley, a licensed practical nurse who cared for Paula after her delivery, recalled complimenting the new mother on her pretty daughter. "Thank you," a smiling Paula said in reply. "I've waited five years for this baby."

Martha Beilsmith didn't doubt that she might have made some comment that reflected a special fondness for the little girl with the red hair and alabaster skin. Nurses who chose to tend newborns did so because they liked babies, and this infant was particularly appealing. "I want to take that baby home." Or "She's so pretty I wish she were mine." Or perhaps even "This one's so beautiful that I'd like to steal her." It was the kind of thing nurses said. Just a compliment. She couldn't imagine that anyone would consider it a threat.

It had been near the end of afternoon visiting hours on July 5 when a nurse closed the privacy curtain between the two beds in Room 285 and told Julie Fry that she was getting a roommate. Julie could hear the conversation between the new arrival and the personnel who transferred her from stretcher to hospital bed. She listened for the voice of a proud father but caught only the amiable chatter of nurses and patient. "Gosh," Julie thought, "she's here all by herself."

When the nurses completed their ministrations and opened the curtain between the beds the roommates introduced themselves. Paula Sims looked at the "It's a Boy!" balloon on Julie's bedside table. "Oh, you had a boy?" she asked. "That's what we wanted. What did you name him?"

"Bradley Steven," Julie answered, explaining that the middle name was for her husband, Steve.

"This is Loralei," said Paula later as she displayed her red-haired infant when nurses brought the babies for feeding. "I've always loved that name. When she grows up she can be called Loralei, or Lora, or Lori, or whatever she likes." Paula cooed to the baby as she held the bottle of formula to her little mouth. Julie closed the curtain so she could breast-feed Bradley.

Between the nurses' hourly temperature/blood pressure checks and the telephone calls to relatives and friends the two young mothers chatted. "Is it all right if I smoke?" Paula asked.

Julie explained that she'd had a cold and was just starting to breathe clearly. "I'd rather you didn't," she said.

"I went nine months without smoking," Paula assured her. "A couple more nights won't matter."

At 7 A.M. Julie was awakened by soft sobs. "I'm sorry we had a girl," she heard Paula say. The crying continued on the other side of the curtain as Julie sat up. She couldn't breathe. Her nose was totally clogged; her throat hurt.

"But we wanted a boy," Paula wept.

Julie blinked her irritated eyes and tried to blow her nose. She heard the phone receiver deposited in its cradle. Paula's sobs diminished. On a nightstand between their beds was an ashtray full of cigarette butts.

Paula took a shower, ran a comb through her long hair, and climbed back into bed. At midmorning Rob Sims arrived wearing bib overalls. Julie closed the curtain and turned on her television set to give the Simses some privacy. The combination of Paula's damp, curly hair and Rob's overalls left her with the image of a couple living "in an old beat-up trailer someplace out in the woods."

The staff transferred Julie to a new room and apologized for having housed a smoker with a nonsmoker. She saw no more of Paula until the following day when the Frys and the Simses met at the hospital's "stork dinner," a steak, baked potato, and sparkling grape juice meal honoring new parents. The couples occupied different booths, but the kitchenlike room was small enough that the laughter-and-photography celebration of Julie and Steve was dampened by the quiet of Paula and Rob. After the steak Steve saw Rob reach for a cigarette. Paula stopped him, silently shaking her head.

The next morning, as both women were preparing to leave the hospital, Julie paused at Paula's room. "Good luck with your baby," she called.

"Yeah"—Paula waved—"same with you."

After she was contacted by the Department of Criminal Investigation Julie turned on the television news. Pictures of the Sims home were on every channel. All she could think was that the house looked much nicer than she had imagined.

It had been two and a half years since Paula had worked at National Food; no one there could paint a clear picture for the investigators. A clerk who had spent years working in the checkout lanes with Paula reported that the two of them seldom said more than hello.

A customer service representative said that Paula was short-tempered and had once become angry with a customer over something trivial. She couldn't remember what it was.

A supervisor recalled that another employee had once accused Paula of stealing money from a purse, but she didn't recollect the outcome of the complaint. Her conclusion was that Paula was "strange"; she was unable to elaborate.

Basic facts were in the personnel file: Paula was hired as a clerk-checker earning $3.05 an hour on July 5, 1978, and was terminated from that position, earning $10.55 an hour, on December 13, 1983. She was fired.

Someone, the manager couldn't remember who, reported that she was "discounting"—failing to charge a customer for all the items in the grocery cart. The store had the capability of monitoring each checker's station by means of a hidden camera, and an assistant manager eventually verified the accusation. He caught Paula discounting $200 worth of groceries to $50.

The manager informed her that she was fired; he couldn't recall her reaction.

* * *

The Jefferson Smurfit paper plant was named Alton Box Board when Rob Sims had started work there six years earlier. Some people still called it that. A sprawling mass of black and gray, it sat with other manufacturing concerns along the Mississippi River, twelve miles from the Simses' Brighton bungalow. Above the riverfront, the homes and business of the 30,000-plus Alton residents decorated the hills on which the picturesque community was built.

Rob was hired at the paper plant in September, 1980, after a three-year stint in the navy and jobs with a railroad, a gas station, a lighting fixtures store, and two credit unions.

His Jefferson Smurfit employment file contained a couple reprimands for "excessive absenteeism," one for "unexcused absence," and one for "incompetence or inability," which translated as failure to clean up a work area. Most reports of his job performance were satisfactory.

Rob didn't fit Agent Bivens's definition of a real "shit-disturber," but neither did he seem to be well liked by other workers. Supervisors who were questioned guessed that the employees' negative reactions might be due to Rob's attitude of superiority. He gave the impression that he considered himself smarter, better than the other men.

The investigators' chief interest at Jefferson Smurfit lay in verifying Rob's account of the night of June 17, and that story checked out. Sims had been observed scanning a bulletin board and checking the coal-unloading report.

Were those stops that he would normally make before beginning his shift? No, not necessarily.

Other employees had been watching as Rob listened to Paula's plea on the phone in the steam and power office, took his lunch box to the dining room, went to his locker for his car keys, and left the plant.

Took his lunch box to the dining room? Yes. It was a plastic Igloo container. He dropped it off in the dining room.

Jim Bivens and Frank Yocom pondered the report. The guy's baby has been kidnapped, his wife is crying on the phone, and he takes his lunch box to the dining room? He negotiates the traffic on the main streets of Alton, and when he is almost on the open road he stops to ask a friend to drive him? These were not sensible responses to a crisis, but people in crises do not always respond sensibly. Both investigators knew that. It was a call that could go either way, and it was one they had to make cautiously. Neither of them liked Rob Sims. They agreed that he was argumentative, critical, and arrogant. They also agreed that they couldn't let their feelings get in the way of their judgment. "Maybe this guy is playing a game with us. Maybe he's jackin' us around," Bivens speculated. "But then again, maybe not."

Rob faced a phalanx of reporters in the driveway of his home. "They could have stolen anything I own," he told them. "They could have burned my house down. They could have fired me or sent me to war again, but nothing can compare to this tragedy."

The community grieved with him. Pictures of Loralei were printed by Rob's sister, Linda Condray, and her husband Herb, both professional photographers. The photos appeared in hundreds of business windows in Brighton, Jerseyville, and a dozen other small towns that dot the map of southwest Illinois. I-SEARCH quickly added thousands of posters also bearing Loralei's photo. Loralei's baby face was everywhere, inspiring mothers to special vigilance of their own children and engendering a spate of phone calls reporting sights and sounds that might be, could be, suspicious. "It's probably nothing, but I just remembered—" A whining sound in the woods. A strange car. Some tips were too vague to check. Some, when checked, proved to be nothing.

One tip led to the identification of the fishermen in the "shitty green" pickup who argued with Rob on the Sunday that he brought Paula and Loralei home from the hospital. The two men admitted their presence at the pond and a minor altercation, but investigators were unable to link them to the Simses by anything beyond the squabble.

Everyone speculated about the masked man. "It must be somebody in the market for selling babies," Paula's father told the *St. Louis Post-Dispatch.* "Or maybe somebody who lost theirs and wants another one."

A reward fund was established; contributions flowed in from local businesses as well as private citizens; and the collection was variously reported to have reached $8,000, or $14,000, or $20,000. The exact amount seemed less important than the willingness of the community to do whatever it could.

Two of Paula's high-school girlfriends, June Gibson and Rhonda Scott, organized volunteers to tie pink bows and attach them to safety pins. The ribbons were sold in store parking lots with the promise that the money raised would be added to the fund available for reward or ransom.

Frank Yocom and Jim Bivens watched the proliferation of posters and pink bows with skepticism. Even the accumulating reward fund couldn't overcome their pessimism. They didn't think that information about Loralei's whereabouts was likely to come from the public.

Paula Sims saw TV coverage of the same posters and pink bows. She stood watch on her porch as search after search led nowhere. Those who observed her solitary vigil judged her to be cold and remote, but as she clung to the porch railing she felt herself swirling around the edges of a whirlpool, a vortex of her own creation, being drawn closer and closer to the dark, screaming center. They'll be searching forever, she thought, and I'm the only one who will know.

"We've exhausted every lead you gave us," said Bivens. "At this point we have absolutely no suspects." He and Yocom stood on the Simses' porch on the morning of Friday, June 20. "We're asking you to do this because, statistically, about eighty percent of crimes against victims are committed by someone close to the victim."

"It's just an investigative tool," Yocom added, "something we normally like to use in a case like this."

"Just a process of elimination." Bivens picked up the pitch.

"Let's eliminate the obvious," Yocom concluded.

The two investigators didn't know what to expect when they offered polygraphs to the grieving parents. They were fully prepared for refusal. To their surprise, Rob Sims readily agreed to the tests. "We have nothing to hide," he declared.

The timetable had been carefully prepared. Paula would be asked to accompany Yocom immediately to Jerseyville, where the polygrapher was waiting. Rob would be asked to proceed first to Brighton to "go over a few things" at an improvised investigation headquarters near the Brighton Police Department. The plan would keep the couple separated until each had finished the test and faced the interrogation after it.

Rob accepted the itinerary. Paula nodded, but she seemed less confident when she realized Rob would not be with her. It was Paula's mother, Nylene Blew, who voiced reservations. Bivens and Yocom had not counted on Mrs. Blew's presence when they mapped their strategy.

Someone from the family should go with Paula, Mrs. Blew insisted. It was a suggestion that Paula welcomed. The two women presented a united front: Mrs. Blew would accompany her daughter. Yocom and Bivens exchanged a cautious look. If they objected, they might lose the opportunity entirely, and they wanted the polygraph.

"Now, remember," Rob encouraged his wife as she and her mother climbed into Yocom's car, "you can stop anytime you want. You don't have to talk about anything that upsets you."

Clinton Cook of the Department of Criminal Investigation waited at the Jersey County Sheriff's Department, his polygraph equipment ready to go. He had already framed the "relevant" questions, four of them, that would be inserted in a long list of insignificant queries:

On Tuesday evening, did an unknown white male
    display a pistol in your home and steal your baby?
Do you know where your baby is now?
Did you dispose of, sell, or give your baby away?

Have you falsified or withheld any information to
    police regarding this investigation?

In a precheck interview Cook explained his machine and
told Paula what the relevant questions would be. When he
was satisfied that she understood he started the test.

An hour later Paula was led to the sheriff's private office,
the same office where she had made her official statement
two days before. Bivens and Yocom waited for her there,
along with DCI zone commander Phil Kocis and the
psychologist who had witnessed her earlier interview. They
already knew that, in the polygrapher's opinion, she had
lied.

"Paula," said Bivens evenly, "you took the polygraph as
we requested. Do you know the result?"

"Yes."

"And what is that result?"

"He said I failed it."

"Can you think of any reason the test would come out that
way?"

"I guess I was nervous."

"He's taken into consideration that you were nervous.
You had a precheck and talked about everything, didn't
you?"

"Yes."

"And you understood the questions?"

"Yes."

In an easy move, as though the transfer had been choreo-
graphed, Kocis took over the interrogation. "Well, let's take
this opportunity to clear things up. Here's a question where
he feels that you were lying: 'On Tuesday evening, did an
unknown white male display a pistol in your home and steal
your baby?' Your answer was—"

"Yes. My answer was yes."

"And he thinks you were lying. Can you explain why he
would think that?"

"I don't know. I don't know why."

"Now we don't want to disbelieve you, but we can't
disbelieve our polygraph man either. Did he misinterpret

something? Can you understand why he thinks you were lying?"

"I don't know. I can't understand it." Her voice tightened as though she might cry.

Yocom took his turn. "Paula, if you dropped the baby, if you left her in the car somewhere in the hot sun and she died—"

"If you found her dead in the crib and you panicked," Bivens offered.

"—then we can deal with it," Yocom continued. "But we have to deal with it now."

Paula shook her head. She gasped as she had on Tuesday night, the dry little hiccup sobs.

Bivens took over. "If your baby died as the result of an accident, Paula, the most you could be charged with is concealment, which is minimal. Your only crime would be that you didn't report it, and some people might look at that as an understandable reaction. Is that what happened?"

"No." She lowered her head and shook it dejectedly.

It was a movement that caught Bivens's attention, one that he had seen before when he questioned suspects. To him it indicated that they were giving up. Their crumpling bodies reflected their broken wills and spirits. He watched Paula carefully, expectantly.

In the reception area Nylene sat stiffly, waiting for her daughter to reappear. From time to time she glanced anxiously at the closed door. Paula's dry sobs were not loud enough to reach her.

When Rob arrived he was ushered directly to the room in which Cook and the lie detector waited. He had no chance to talk with Paula, no chance to ask about her test results.

In Yocom's office Bivens was disappointed to see Paula pull herself together. She raised her head and faced her inquisitors. The choreography continued, the lead passing from man to man as the pace and intensity of the interrogation built.

"Paula, you're not being honest with us," Yocom challenged. "If there ever was a time to be honest, this is it." He laid out the possibilities. "If you dropped the baby, if you found the baby dead, a SIDS death or something, let us handle it now. As time goes on this kind of opportunity isn't going to be available. You'll be looking at a murder charge."

Paula's head fell again as the sobs recurred, but once more she steeled her will, raised her eyes, and braved the lawmen. Repeatedly they offered her the "outs" that seemed logical: Did *this* happen? Did *that* happen?

"No." She shook her head. She sobbed breathily.

"But the story you told us just doesn't make sense," Bivens insisted. "It isn't believable. We can't accept it."

"Please tell us where Loralei is, so she can have a Christian burial," Yocom proposed.

The weary investigators were caught by surprise as Paula's cry changed. The breathy sobs gave way to a sound that seemed to Yocom to show "a real, natural hurt." To Bivens it seemed to be a sound that "came from within, not like it was a thing she was supposed to do."

The cry filled the room. It penetrated the door's barrier, grabbing the attention of everyone in the waiting room. It brought Paula's mother to her feet and then to the door. "She's had enough," Mrs. Blew told the investigators as she gathered up her weeping daughter.

"Damn!" uttered Bivens as the women left. "I thought we had her. I really thought we had her."

The first question changed: "On Tuesday evening, the seventeenth, was your baby, Loralei Sims, alive and in your home when you left for work?" The others were the same as those directed at Paula.

"It is the recording examiner's opinion, based on Robert E. Sims's polygraph records, that he is not being truthful when he answered the aforementioned questions," Cook concluded.

Rob's defenses did not crumble as easily as Paula's. He remained calm and collected during the interview, crossing his arms over his chest and shaking his head as he stared, perplexed, at the floor. "I can't understand why he didn't believe me," he said slowly. "I can't think of any reason."

* * *

"It was, it was a normal type of dealing with a crime of this fashion," Rob explained to the press who wondered why he and Paula had been asked to submit to polygraphs. "We, we passed it with flying colors, you know, that would absolutely clear any doubts in their minds of our character."

A pink bow was pinned to the bib of his overalls as he and Paula faced cameramen and reporters in their driveway. Paula, in a light blue T-shirt, laid her head on his shoulder. Her long hair floated over her cheek. "I'm tellin' the truth," she wept. "I know what happened."

Microphones picked up the dry little sobs that had become so familiar to the investigators. Rob patted her arm.

5

"9:45—DISCHARGED TO MOTHER." THIS LAST NOTE ON THE nursery chart at Alton Memorial Hospital was made on Sunday, June 8. Loralei was three days old. On Tuesday, June 17, when Paula reported the kidnapping, Loralei was thirteen days old. Who saw her during the ten days that she lived in the brick house on Cotter Road? Who saw her, and when? These questions were pivotal to the investigation.

Stella Hyatt visited on Monday, June 9, the day after Rob brought Paula and Loralei home from the hospital. So did Paula's mother and father, along with her brother Dennis. That was the day Stella first met Paula's parents. She was at her fruit trees in back of her house, she explained to the investigators; the Blews stopped to say they were glad that she lived so close and that Paula had someone to turn to for advice and friendship. She appreciated their comments, but she wondered why they had not visited more often during the two and a half years that the Simses had lived in Brighton.

Perhaps the arrival of a grandchild presaged the beginning

of a closer relationship, for the Blews told officers that they visited again two days later, on Wednesday evening, June 11, and confirmed plans for Rob and Paula to celebrate Father's Day at their home in Cottage Hills on the following Sunday.

Dave and Linda Heistand reported that they, too, visited on June 11. They had company themselves that evening, but their guests left early, so the Heistands called the Simses, hoping for an invitation to drop by. It was 10 P.M. when they arrived, and Paula looked tired. Loralei was asleep, but Rob went to get her and beamed as he presented her to the visitors. No wonder he's beaming, Linda thought as she looked at Loralei. A beautiful baby, with red hair just like her daddy's.

The Heistands assured investigators that Loralei seemed healthy and well cared for. Linda reported that Paula had phoned occasionally to ask "new-mother" questions: What was "normal?" What was "right?" Why was Loralei sometimes so fussy at night, usually between 9 and 10 P.M.? "Probably just needs a good burp," Linda guessed.

In one of the conversations Paula shared her anxiety about a nurse's comment. "She said Loralei was so pretty she wanted to take her home," Paula told Linda. "Sounded almost like she was threatening to kidnap her."

The Heistands told officers that they saw Loralei only once, but they heard her fussing in the background when Rob called to wish Dave a belated happy birthday. That was on Monday, June 16, the night before she was reported missing.

Investigators determined that the Heistands were the last visitors to see Loralei. They were also the last to *hear* her.

The Father's Day celebration never took place, Paula's parents explained. Paula phoned to say that she and Rob would not be coming. The baby might get too hot in the car or too cold in the Blew's air-conditioned house. Neighbors might stop by. Maybe they would want to hold her. There would be too many germs. Loralei might get sick.

Although it was Paula who spoke the words, Nylene Blew told officers that she felt the message came from Rob. He was overly protective of the child, insisting that the Blews wash their hands before they so much as touched her.

Nylene said she had attempted to convince Paula that the fears for Loralei's health were exaggerated. There was a couple in church who brought their six-day-old daughter to Sunday services with them, she said. There were tiny infants in the grocery stores; their parents didn't worry about germs. Surely Loralei could come to see her grandparents on Father's Day. Surely everyone could eat grilled chicken and pose for precious snapshots.

Both Nylene and Paula cried, but still the answer was the same. "I'm sorry," Paula said. "We can't come."

The Blews offered to come to Brighton instead. There would be no heat or cold to worry about, no neighbors dropping by. "No," Paula said, "Rob wants it to be just us this year."

At the end of the interview the investigators told Nylene of the failed polygraph exams. The tests indicated that her daughter and son-in-law had lied, they explained.

The machines were not accurate, Nylene argued. She had seen a television program about lie detectors, and they were just not accurate. There was no way that Paula could have had anything to do with Loralei's disappearance. Absolutely no way. Not Rob, either.

Investigators suggested that she ask Paula about the test results. "Oh, I could never ask a question like that," she protested. "It would make Paula hate me!"

Yocom and Bivens studied the brief timetable of Loralei's life. She was seen on June 11, by both the Blews and the Heistands. The Blews, denied their Father's Day celebration, planned to visit on Friday, June 20, while Rob was at work. Stella Hyatt was also planning to visit, on Thursday, June 19. The kidnapping was reported on Tuesday, June 17.

Whatever had happened to Loralei, investigators wondered, could it have happened *before* June 17? Was it finally reported only because visitors were coming and there could be no further delay?

"But the Heistands said they heard a baby fussing when

Rob phoned," said Yocom, puzzled, "and that was on the sixteenth."

"Could have been a recording," Bivens said. "Anything's possible."

A tape recorder was one of the things investigators wanted to look for. The approach was carefully planned, just as it had been with the polygraph. Bivens assured the Simses that care and consideration would be shown. The searchers would not tear the house apart.

Since the couple had already admitted to "casual" use of marijuana, Bivens wanted to remove that as possible grounds for their objection. "If you've got a little bit, just tell us now and we'll handle it." Legal technicalities were not a priority; he wanted permission to search. Mike Donovan and his dog Jud stood by. So did crime scene technician Dee Heil, Jersey County State's Attorney Lee Plummer, and Sheriff Yocom.

There were no drugs in the house, Rob said. "Go ahead and search." But the investigators wanted more than that. They wanted Rob and Paula out of the house, away from the property. Their ploy was the same one they had used to get Rob out of the way during Paula's polygraph, the need to "go over a few things" at the temporary headquarters in Brighton. Two female DCI agents were waiting for Paula. The FBI was waiting for Rob. Fresh people, a change of personalities.

Bivens watched Paula look to her husband for a cue. "It'll be all right," Rob told her. "But remember, you don't have to say anything if you don't want to."

Mike Donovan brought Jud across the redwood porch and through the squeaking screen door. "Dead body," he said. Jud had been trained on putric acid, a foul-smelling substance with an odor similar to that of human decay. Donovan sometimes buried jars of it as a training exercise for the dog. "Dead body" was Jud's signal to seek out that odor. Donovan removed the harness and let him go.

Bivens and Yocom waited outside, hoping that some of

their questions would be answered. Could the baby have been lying dead in the house when authorities were first called to the scene on June 17? Could she have remained hidden there for two days while the dogs searched outside? If so, would Jud be able to pick up some trace scent now, a week later? Might her body still be there, tucked into some box, or corner, or hole? The Simses hadn't been told that the dog would be searching for a body, and they weren't allowed time or opportunity to remove anything once they had given permission for the search.

Donovan watched as Jud worked his way from room to room. Crime scene technician Dee Heil stood by with camera and notebook, ready to document any finding. Along the perimeter of the kitchen and dining room Jud sniffed. Around the edges of drawers and doors. Through closets and cupboards. Nothing. Down the stairs to the basement, where the air turned cooler but hung with a musty dampness. Past Loralei's empty bassinet.

"Dead body," Donovan repeated. Jud circled the basement family room, the bathroom, the bedroom. Again nothing. The dog headed back upstairs. Donovan could feel the temperature rise as he followed.

Only the garage was left. Donovan opened the door, snapped on a light, and sent Jud in. "Come here!" he called to Heil. "Look at this." In the center of the garage stood an old car. Around it walls and benches displayed an impressive assortment of new tools. Socket sets, a drill press, a band saw. More noteworthy than the tools themselves was the precision of their organization. They were laid out in logical order, aligned, *arranged.* Every tool was clean. There was no mess, no sawdust, no metal shavings. "There's gotta be ten or fifteen thousand dollars worth of stuff here," Donovan judged.

Jud worked his way quickly and easily around the garage. He stopped at his handler's feet as though to ask "What now?" Donovan opened the front door and signaled the men waiting outside. Yocom and Bivens entered, along with state's attorney Lee Plummer.

"Nothing, huh?" Yocom patted Jud's head.

"I can't believe those tools," Donovan marveled. "Damn garage is like a hardware store." Bivens nodded; he and Yocom had already seen the tools. They were ready to initiate their own search. They wanted to look for a tape recorder. They wanted to check out the garbage disposal. Beyond that they didn't know what they were after. Something, anything that could give them a clue about the case that had baffled them for the past seven days.

They had followed every lead, however insubstantial. They had read and reread every interview report. They had speculated, imagined, and reconsidered. They had watched the reward fund rise and the posters proliferate. And still they had nothing. Nothing but a gut feeling, which Bivens refused to call a gut feeling. "A gut feeling is amateur. It was a gut feeling *based* on a lot of things."

They also had the polygraph exams, but those would be inadmissable if the case went to court. The results were not even helpful in dealing with reporters, for the press had accepted without question Rob's assurance that both he and Paula had passed "with flying colors." Various relatives had since repeated the remark, which appeared in some form in every newspaper story and on every television broadcast.

Yocom had phoned Bivens when Rob's "flying colors" statement first hit the 6 P.M. newscasts. "Did you hear what that son of a bitch said?" he asked. Bivens had to wait until 10 P.M. to hear it for himself. The press had never asked Bivens or Yocom about the polygraph results, and neither man could see much to be gained from introducing the subject at the daily news conferences Yocom held, so the failed polygraphs remained the investigators' secret.

Bivens and Yocom stood in the Simses' kitchen, studying the knives in a cabinet drawer. Yocom looked to a nearby electrical switch. He reached over and flipped it on. The blades of the garbage disposal whirled. He turned it off, worked his fingers through the drain opening, and felt around the interior of the drum. The Simses' plumbing emptied into a septic tank. The tank could be drained, but that would be an extreme measure. Maybe later.

Jud returned to the search, sniffing drawers and doors that

the men opened. One drawer yielded a supply of detective magazines, neatly stacked and arranged by date. Bivens glanced through the titles of the articles, remembering the suggestions Rob had offered a week earlier, suggestions that hinted of some knowledge and sophistication.

Another drawer contained photographs of Paula, nude, pregnant, sitting on a three-wheeler. Yocom shook his head. "My God. Shows you how weird they really are."

Bivens smiled. He had developed real respect for Yocom during the frustrating week they had spent on the case. Yocom's knowledge of Jersey County was remarkable, and his authority there absolute. But the two men had different views of life. "What's kooky for one person is normal for somebody else," Bivens said. He returned the pictures to their drawer.

A packet of photos. A stack of detective magazines. A garbage disposal in working order. It wasn't much reward for a morning's effort in the sweltering house.

"Did you ever take your dog through that area?" Bivens asked, wiping the sweat from his forehead. In the house the ceiling fans had created some air flow. Outside the midday sun baked down with only a whisper of breeze to offer relief.

Donovan shaded his eyes with his hand as he looked at the wooded hillside that dropped down behind the backyard. "I didn't search it, but somebody else might have."

"Dammit," muttered Bivens. "I wish to hell we knew who had been where."

Donovan took Jud to the edge of the yard where the trees afforded some shade. The dog needed to cool off. A plastic bucket lay on the grass. Donovan rinsed it with water from a garden hose, filled it, and brought it to Jud, giving him an appreciative, almost comradely pat on the back. It had been a long day already, and it was just 12:30. Jud gulped the water, splattering Donovan in his eagerness. "Easy, boy." The dog looked up but quickly lowered his head for another assault on the bucket. Before his tongue could reach the water Jud froze. He faced the wooded bank that dropped off steeply from the grass of the yard. He raised his nose high, sniffing first to one side, then the other. Donovan recognized the action. Jud was wind-scenting. The breeze had brought him a hint of something, and he was locating, categorizing. It could be anything, an animal, a drug cache. Anything.

"Find it," Donovan commanded.

Jud started down the hill, his body low and tense, his nose raised. Thirty feet from the edge of the yard he stopped and crouched. His huge front paws pressed the ground alternately but didn't advance. His nose was low, working in short horizontal motions across the scant breeze. He made a noise deep in his throat, not a whine, not a growl, not a bark, but a special noise to tell his handler that he didn't want to go any closer.

"Stay," said Donovan. Jud's noises ceased, but tension gripped his muscles. Donovan called to Bivens. "Get Yocom! And somebody from crime scene!"

Bivens came to the edge of the yard. "Why?"

"He's got it," said Donovan, watching Jud.

"What?"

"The body. He's got the body." Donovan spoke quietly.

"Bullshit."

"Look at him. He's got it."

Donovan started down the steep bank. The leafy ground cover was almost a foot high. He walked just past the place where he had allowed Jud to stop. Nothing. He looked back at the dog, whose nose held steady, pointing in the direction of his find. Donovan moved the undergrowth with his foot. There it lay, a small brown skull. "It's all over now," Donovan sighed.

Bivens knelt to look at the discovery. "Shit, I think your dog found a groundhog." He moved his head to view the skull from another angle. "Well, wait a minute—"

Yocom's bulk had slowed his descent of the steep bank. "What is it?"

"I don't know," said Bivens.

Yocom circled and knelt on the other side. He bent to put his nose within inches of the skull.

"What the hell are you doing?" Bivens asked.

Yocom sniffed. He rose slowly, his face reflecting both his distaste and his certainty. "It's human."

"Oh, come on, Frank. Dead meat is dead meat."

"It's human."

Yocom spoke through the frame of the screen door. The screen, with its jagged slash, had gone to the crime lab. "Could we talk to you?"

Rob and Paula, returned from fruitless interviews in Jerseyville, sat in the dining room with Paula's father, Rob's sister, and an area minister. "Come on in," said Rob.

Yocom and Bivens stood silently for a second after they entered. It was never an easy announcement, no matter what the circumstances. "We think we found your daughter."

"Is she all right?" Paula rose from the table. "Where is she?"

"We found skeletal remains in the woods back of the house." Bivens made the situation clearer. "We think the remains are human. We think it's your baby."

Paula sank into her chair. "Oh, no," she sobbed. Rob seemed too stunned to speak. He patted Paula's arm.

Mark Johnsey cleared the ground around the skull, cutting away every leaf and vine, picking up each twig. The removal of the greenery revealed more bones. Johnsey inserted each in a latex glove and tied the glove's open end. He staked the glove to the ground at the spot where the bone had lain. A small red flag marked the top of the stake.

The bones were tiny and brown, stained from body fluids. They were difficult to see, for they matched the color of the earth. Even Johnsey, a forensic anthropologist from the state police crime lab, an expert in the identification of skeletal remains, had a hard time. The movement of the leaves above his head produced dancing shadows on the ground. He had to look carefully, to move slowly.

From the distribution of the bones Johnsey concluded that an animal had been eating the remains, dragging the body down the bank as it chewed. He cordoned off a large rectangular patch of hillside where the brown fragments were concentrated. That would be his domain, his responsibility.

Outside the rectangle a dozen officers organized to search the wooded embankment. They set out through the woods, looking for any remnant of the clothing Loralei had worn, or for a grave in which she might once have been buried. Pushing back vines and leaves, they traveled through the dense underbrush, the fallen logs, the trees.

The tiny booties would be difficult to spot. The diaper could be in shreds. The white undershirt might be caked with dirt. A mound of earth? A hole? A tiny garment? The men traversed the woods until there was not enough light to continue. They found nothing.

In the rectangle that he was determined to explore himself Mark Johnsey set up a grid. To anchor it he chose a tree that was less than a hundred feet from the sliding glass doors of the Sims basement. He measured the area into squares and assigned each a number. The divisions would allow him to notate the location of any discovery.

He worked until twilight and returned the next morning. When he finished, the twelve-foot-by-twenty-nine-foot rectangle was bare ground. The greenery had been supplanted by dozens of red-flagged stakes, each securing a white latex glove.

A spot of stained and stinking earth indicated the site of original decomposition. The spot, coupled with officers' failure to find a grave, led to the conclusion that the body had never been buried.

What was left of Loralei Marie Sims lay on the ground, each piece encased in white latex. One glove contained the skull; others a piece of jawbone, a section of arm, vertebrae. Tissue stuck to some of the bones. A patch of red hair clung to the skull.

6

ON JUNE 24, AS JOHNSEY WAS CLEARING THE HILLSIDE RECT-angle and men were combing the woods, Yocom, Bivens, and DCI zone commander Phil Kocis prepared to face the press. They expected to hear questions about the polygraph results and Rob's "flying colors" statement. The quandary was how to handle the answer. "I can't contradict him," Kocis said. "It's against our policy to comment on an investigation."

"Well, by God, I can," fumed Yocom. "They flunked that critter one hundred percent, and I'll be damned if I'm gonna let him walk around saying they passed it."

Reports of the press conference were carried on the early evening broadcasts. A week earlier, when people had first learned of the masked intruder, the little victim had been anonymous. Now she was Loralei Marie, the baby face on the posters in every store window; Loralei Marie, the pretty infant for whom they had donated money and worn pink bows. The news that her bones lay on a hillside brought genuine sadness to many. The announcement that her parents had lied on polygraph tests roused anger and indignation in everyone.

Among the first to feel the swing in public sentiment were Paula's high-school friends, June Gibson and Rhonda Scott, who stood in store parking lots offering the pink bows they had made and asking for contributions to the reward fund. As the investigators' announcement hit car radios the generosity and sympathy of shoppers disappeared. People who drove up were "real angry, real ugly." Animosity that had once been directed at a faceless, nameless kidnapper was aimed instead at the long-haired young mother whose sobs had been captured by TV cameras, at the bearded young father who had patted her arm, and, to some extent, at the young women who sold the pink bows. June and Rhonda gathered their ribbons and went home.

Rob and Paula Sims made no comment to the press. On Wednesday morning, as Mark Johnsey continued to indicate the discovery of bone fragments with red-flagged stakes, the Simses packed some clothes, locked the house on Cotter Road, and moved to the home of Orville and Nylene Blew, Paula's parents. Later in the day two female DCI agents, along with Jersey County State's Attorney Lee Plummer, traveled to the Blew home. Orville Blew met them at the door. Paula did not wish to speak with officers, he said. Neither did Rob. Neither did the Blews. Shortly afterward prosecutor Plummer was informed that any further contacts with the Simses should be made through their attorney, Gage Sherwood.

The discovery of the skeleton filled the regional papers on Wednesday morning. Coverage featured the already-familiar image of Rob and Paula standing in their driveway, her head resting on his shoulder.

At a greeting card shop in the Jerseyville mall Gisela Rasp picked up her phone. She had recently seen the couple in the photo, she told Sheriff Yocom. The woman had come into her store carrying a pretty red-haired baby. "What's the baby's name?" Gisela had asked as she lifted the blanket. The infant was sleeping, its eyes half closed.

"Loralei," the mother had replied. Gisela said she remembered the name, for it was a German name, unusual in Illinois, and she was German. She had watched as the mother left the shop and joined a bearded man. It was the couple who now appeared on front pages and on television screens, she told Yocom.

The date of the incident fascinated investigators. Saturday, June 14, the day before Father's Day. If a fear of germs prevented the Simses from taking Loralei to visit her grandparents, why would they take her to a mall? Why would Paula allow a stranger to lift the baby's blanket?

Or was Gisela Rasp mistaken? Was she one of the odd ones who offer tips and suggestions whenever some case garners an unusual amount of publicity? Bivens stopped at the card shop to meet her. He took along another agent to verify his judgment. They thought she sounded convincing.

The card shop incident was only one of the mysteries that plagued the investigators. Why was Loralei's body denied even the meager protection of clothing? There was no blanket, diaper, shirt, or booties. Someone had stripped her.

Was her body just tossed down the bank? The distance from the edge of the yard to the site of decomposition was little more than thirty feet, easily covered by a good throw. Or did someone carry her into the woods and deposit her? There were no footprints, but the undergrowth was heavy.

If her body was in the woods, why hadn't the dogs detected the scent? Mike Donovan was positive he and Jud had not searched the wooded hillside that first dark, confusing night. Other handlers were less adamant. They remembered being further back, in the creek bed; they weren't sure about the hillside. "It's hard for a dog handler to tell you where he's been," Donovan explained to Bivens and Yocom. "So much zigzagging." Maybe the body had been there all the time, and the searchers had just missed it.

"We should have had the same dogs, dammit!" Bivens again cursed the Springfield decision that had denied

Donovan's speedy return. "I can't believe it. Some guy in charge of a damn dog program making a major decision on my case!"

"Should have had a K-9 coordinator," Donovan agreed.

"That sticks in my craw," Bivens fumed. "Now we'll never know. Was that baby in the woods from day one or not?"

A week later the Simses put their Brighton property on the market. Their attorney said the sale was prompted by sad memories and by Paula's fear of staying alone in the isolated house while her husband worked midnight shifts.

Rob and Paula returned to Cotter Road on several successive summer evenings, but Paula didn't enter the brick bungalow. She just couldn't, she told Stella Hyatt. Not yet. The two women talked while Rob packed.

There were questions that Stella had to ask, questions that she pondered on nights when she couldn't sleep, nights when her head was filled with the sound of Paula's pounding and the vision of an empty bassinet. "What about those polygraph tests? The sheriff says you and Rob flunked them."

Paula nodded. "That happens sometimes when people are under a lotta stress. Our attorney said so."

"I'm not saying you did anything wrong, Paula," Stella said slowly, "but if I had failed a polygraph test, I'd ask for sodium Pentothal, or anything they could give me, just so that everyone would know the truth."

Paula could have told her neighbor that she and Rob had already taken two more tests, tests arranged by their attorney and administered by a private St. Louis polygrapher. She could have told Stella that Rob had passed those tests, but not without admitting that she herself had failed both of them. Instead she said, "I volunteered to be hypnotized. I don't know what else I can do."

Stella chose the phrase carefully. *"Whoever did this,* I hope they get as strong a punishment as they can."

"You mean even the death penalty?" Paula asked.

"Whoever did this deserves to die," Stella pronounced.

When Paula returned the next evening she held fast to the theory that the bones were not Loralei's. "Somebody's baby died, and they left it on the hillside and took Loralei as a replacement."

"That doesn't make any sense," Stella disagreed.

"Well, the police think we did it, and that doesn't make any sense either," Paula contended. "We wouldn't be dumb enough to put her on our own property. You'd have to be crazy to do something like that." Then her eyes filled with tears as she abandoned the argument. "I wonder if she was alive when the animals started eating her," she said as she wept. "Did they eat her alive? Did she feel them eating her?"

"Don't think about that," Stella admonished as she herself gave way to tears. "Don't let that thought be in your head."

It was difficult to determine the cause of death when so little remained. It was difficult even to establish a positive identification. X rays verified that the skeleton was human. Mark Johnsey, who picked the bones off the hillside, estimated the child's height at twenty to twenty-eight inches, its age at one month or less. Race and sex were impossible to determine. The county coroner could find no "obvious damage" to the skeleton. There was no skull fracture or other apparent injury that would have caused death.

In mid-July, three weeks after the remains were found, a forensic dentist who studied X rays of the jawbone concluded that the tooth buds were consistent with those of a thirteen-day-old child. He could not say the jawbone was Loralei's, but he pointed out what seemed apparent to most people: The remains were found in back of the Sims house, and there were no other infants reported missing.

Nevertheless, the effort to positively identify the body continued. Sheriff Yocom requested blood and hair samples from Paula. Taking a nurse with him, he collected the evidence from her at the office of the attorney she and Rob had retained. Jim Bivens flew the samples, along with the skeletal remains, to Atlanta. There Allo-Type Genetic Testing compared bones, blood, and hair, looking for a match in the immunoglobulin allotypes.

The laboratory's procedures were predicated upon the fact that virtually all of a baby's immunity is inherited from her mother. A child does not begin to develop her own immune characteristics until she is well beyond the newborn stage. Therefore, thirteen-day-old Loralei's genetic makeup would directly reflect Paula's immunology.

In a report issued at the end of August, ten weeks after Loralei disappeared, Allo-Type concluded that there was a probability of 97.2 percent that Paula Sims was the mother of the child whose skeletal remains had been examined. "Paula Sims is approximately thirty-six times as likely to be the mother of the child as a random white."

Through their attorney, Gage Sherwood, the Simses disputed the conclusion that the dead child was theirs. A probability of 97.2 percent left room for doubt; it meant that 2.8 percent of other white women shared a genetic makeup that matched the baby's as closely as Paula's did. If the statistics were applied to the regional population, 2.8 percent could include thousands of white women of childbearing age.

Bivens authorized further tests. Another two weeks went by while Allo-Type performed them. The new studies established Paula's maternal relationship to the child to a certainty of 99.75 percent. The Simses' attorney announced that Rob and Paula accepted the result.

Loralei's bones were mailed back to Jim Bivens in a shoe box. They were claimed by her parents and buried in an undisclosed location at the end of September, three and a half months after her disappearance.

On a day when no one was watching, Paula Sims stood at the back door of the brick bungalow she had fled in mid-June. The house had been sold.

"Rob left me there to clean, to pack up the last of our things. I was by myself. It was the last time I was gonna be there.

"The thought kept going through my mind, go down there, go down there. And I did."

She walked to the edge of the lawn, where the wooded hillside dropped sharply. Tucked into the spreading greenery was a strangely precise barren patch, the rectangle where Mark Johnsey had carefully picked up each tiny bone. The leaves of fall were beginning to float down. Soon they would cover the naked earth.

"I stood at the top of the hill. I could see the area that was cleared. There was markings from the police, little tags of some kind, something colored."

The day was warm and clear, but Paula shivered, for the visions that flashed in her head were moonlight and black branches, cockleburs and crunching leaves, the damp earth-odor of night.

"I had been tryin' to make myself forget. But then I stood there and I remembered it. It pushed into my brain. I wanted to get away, but I couldn't make myself move. I just stood there—I don't know how long—until it passed. I said my good-bye to Loralei, and I walked back to the house. I told myself over and over that nothin' like that could ever happen again."

Jersey County State's Attorney Lee Plummer explained repeatedly to the persistent press and the waiting public that he lacked the proof necessary to bring charges against the Simses. Investigators had nothing but circumstantial evidence. Loralei's body was found close to the back door of the Sims house, and Paula's story seemed implausible, but that wasn't enough for a conviction. The polygraph results were inadmissable. Plummer's explanations didn't deter reporters. They called Sheriff Yocom regularly to ask if there were any new developments.

For six months the Simses lived with Paula's parents and brother in Cottage Hills. In January, 1987, they purchased a modest older home a few miles away, on Washington Avenue in Alton, Illinois. When Jim Bivens learned of their new location he phoned Tony Ventimiglia of the Alton Police Department to tell him that the Simses were in his jurisdiction. "Great," sighed Ventimiglia. "That's just what we need."

In March of 1987 Paula and Robert Sims were called back to Jersey County to appear before a grand jury. No new evidence had surfaced, and there was little hope of charges being filed, but Frank Yocom wanted to give it one last try. Maybe they would say something different, something incriminating.

Agent Jim Bivens delivered the subpoenas to the Simses' newly purchased house, for their move to Alton placed the couple in Madison County, out of Sheriff Yocom's reach. Rob stepped to the porch to accept the documents. He couldn't understand why he and Paula would be subpoenaed, he said slowly, shaking his head. "What can we say that we haven't already said?"

In front of the grand jury the Simses said nothing. They invoked their Fifth Amendment rights and refused to testify.

In September, 1987, a Jersey County coroner's inquest officially declared that the cause of death of infant Loralei Marie Sims was "undetermined." The insurance carrier for Rob's employer paid the full value of the policy that had been automatically issued at Loralei's birth; the Simses received $100.

By that time Paula was pregnant again.

Her friends and family members were joyful. It was what she needed, they assured her. It would ease the heartache of the past. It would give meaning to the future. She returned their smiles and acknowledged their encouragement.

But in the silence of her new house her smile faded. She stared at herself in a mirror, gathering the visions that floated before her and pushing them into a dark corner of her memory.

"It won't happen again," she vowed. "It won't. It won't."

II
Paula and Rob

7

La Plata, Missouri, was a town of neat white bungalows. The ground was gently rolling, the lawns were trimmed, and in summer there were flowers, pansies and petunias and roses. The street noises of a larger community were missing; kids' voices carried from blocks away, signaling afternoon fun.

In the 1960s, when Orville and Nylene Blew settled there, La Plata had three grocery stores, two doctors' offices, a furniture store, a Laundromat, a weekly newspaper, and a population of 1,600. The business district was built around three sides of the town square, where a bandstand stood ready for civic celebrations or children's games of hide-and-seek. There was a Saturday night movie, seventy-five cents for adults, fifty cents for kids. If the citizens needed anything more, they had only to travel thirteen miles north to Kirksville, the nearest "big town."

La Plata was a farm community, mainly, but Orville Blew was an employee of Amoco Oil; he worked on the pipeline that cut across the prairie. Orville came to town in 1966 with his wife Nylene, a tall, handsome woman who was strangely frail, at least in her own eyes. She was sometimes hit with a despondency she couldn't explain. "I don't know what's wrong with me," she told neighbors with a shake of her head and a laugh tinged with desperation. Occasionally she felt so bad she took to her bed for a day or two, until she could face the world again.

One of her worries was her son Dennis, who had contracted measles when he was nearing age three. Shortly after that he had begun to exhibit sudden small seizures, and his movements showed a lack of assurance and control. His parents took him from one specialist to another; doctors eventually agreed on a diagnosis of epilepsy, but no treatment brought relief.

Nylene blamed herself for her baby's problem, sure it was caused by something she had done or something she *should* have done. Doctors tried to reassure her, but she couldn't shake a nagging guilt, a feeling that she had somehow failed as a mother.

At the time Dennis's symptoms were noticed the family's second son, Randy, was a year and a half. He was a cute child, outgoing, mischievous, and dark-haired. He looked like his mother.

Paula Marie was born when Randy was two. She was a quiet, golden-haired daddy's girl.

Paula was in the second grade when the Blews first rented a house in La Plata, coming from a small town not far away. A pretty child, she did the things little girls do: took piano lessons, joined the Girl Scouts, giggled with her friends, romped with her dog, and posed for pictures in fancy dresses her mother had sewn.

The Blew children were enrolled at the local elementary school, a low, sprawling building sitting atop a slope next to the meadow of gravestones and half-dozen private mausoleums of the community cemetery. There were more than thirty students in Paula's grade, and everybody knew everybody else. Paula and her new girlfriends played house in any family garage that offered space, rode their bikes through the quiet streets, and had secret meetings in a backyard treehouse.

Occasionally Paula's brothers, Randy and Dennis, and their friends headed for the basketball court by the Presbyterian church. Sometimes the girls went along to watch. If they were lucky, the boys let them play. Paula was good at basketball, tall and quick and aggressive.

Dennis's seizures increased in intensity and frequency as he grew, but the Blews were determined to offer him the normal activities of boyhood. Orville volunteered to coach the baseball team; both his sons played on it.

In his studies Dennis did well. Books were a refuge, an area where his abilities were equal to those of other boys. If a seizure struck him during the school day, the principal phoned Nylene, who picked up her son and took him home to rest.

Both Paula and Randy were protective of their older brother. They knew how to take care of him when the sudden attacks hit, and they allowed no one else to tease him, although they themselves sometimes did. Their childish cruelty hurt, and Dennis retaliated in any way he could, hitting Randy, pulling Paula's hair, or stomping on her bicycle.

During the summer La Plata's youngsters looked forward to warm days at Santa Fe Lake. Paula and her friends met at one house or another and walked along the railroad tracks to the water. The route took them through the railway overpass, where they often lingered to write something silly or romantic or insulting on the concrete. After that they swam most of the day.

When the Blew children were old enough they began to spend a week or two every summer with their paternal grandparents in Chillicothe, Illinois, a vacation that young Paula learned to dread. "My grandma stated in front of me many times that her favorite granddaughter was Barbie. I could understand that, because Barbie was the first. But Grandma seemed to rub it in: Barbie was so cute, and

Barbie did so good in school, and Barbie was so good in this and that. I got sick of hearin' it. Someone would come over and Grandma would talk about Barbie, and I would be right there, and she would never say nothin' about me."

Whatever rejection she felt from her grandmother was a minor problem; her dread was concentrated in the behavior she came to expect from Grandpa. He was a retired railroad worker, always home, waiting for a St. Louis Cardinals or Chicago Cubs game to be televised. While he waited he turned his attentions on Paula. "I remember waking up, and the man would be on me. And that's hard when you're real little. That's a lot of weight to get out from underneath. I'd still be in bed in the morning, and he'd come upstairs, and there was no way out up there unless you wanted to jump out a two-story window. I'd say, 'I'm gonna call for Grandma!' And he'd say, 'You go ahead. She's gone. She went to the store.'"

The molestation stopped short of penetràtion. "I would just work on gettin' away from him, 'cause he couldn't chase me."

Each escape left her waiting to face the danger again. "My brothers would be out with friends they had made, and I would be helpin' my grandma around the house, and all of a sudden she'd say she was goin' to the store. And I would say, 'I wanna go, too.' But she'd say, 'I'm just gonna run to the store to get one thing. I'll be right back.' I was petrified."

Grandma's absence meant Paula had to stay out of Grandpa's reach, but distance did not protect her from the sight of him, his fly open, his penis exposed. "I told him, 'I'm gonna tell Grandma on you.' He said, 'She won't believe you.' I said, 'Yes, she will.' He said, 'No, she won't.' And he always used to try to give me money. Later on I finally got through my mind what he was doin' that for. I thought, I'm not no prostitute."

Paula concluded that her best defense was a locked door. "I ended up lockin' myself in the bathroom many times." But Grandpa's insistent knocking and rattling of the door-knob were terrifying, and sometimes, as she cowered in a corner, the door's barrier seemed too weak to stand. "That's when I climbed out the bathroom window."

Even Grandma's presence in the house was not sufficient to deter the old man. "I'd be sittin' watchin' TV, and my grandma would be in the kitchen. She couldn't see the bedroom door from the kitchen, but I could see him. He'd be in there doin' strange things to himself. I'd just get up and go in where my grandma was."

Paula kept silent about the attacks. "How was I supposed to go to my grandma, me just a little girl, and say, 'You know what Grandpa's doin'?' I'd be embarrassed to say that, plus how hurt she'd be, denyin' it, not facin' it. She never saw him do it. It was just my word. And she never really cared for me anyway.

"My dad would have been the one to talk to, I guess. My dad would have believed me. He would have known I wouldn't lie about something like that. But I couldn't tell him. I just couldn't."

The molestation, which began when Paula was in grade school, continued for several summers, coinciding with a transition in her behavior that was noted by her friends. "Something definitely changed in Paula about fifth or sixth grade," one remembered. Raised with two older brothers, Paula had always been a bold little girl, knocking down wasps' nests with a broomstick and dashing for the safety of the house, slamming the screen door just in time to save herself from being stung; but she became more brazen. She began to sneak cigarettes; she dared her girlfriends to try a beer; she walked through a local store now and then to see what she could pick up, just little things, a lipstick or some gum, and displayed the pilfered item as a prize and a challenge.

With the passing summers her transgressions grew more serious. She had just entered her teenage years when she and two local boys were caught throwing rocks at semitrailers traveling across the railway overpass. A highway patrolman spoke with her parents; baffled and upset, they grounded her.

Punishment in the Blew household was administered by Orville, who spanked a wayward child with his hand or a strap, depending upon the seriousness of the offense. Paula invariably put her rigid arms over her bottom in protection. "Move your hands," her father warned, "or they'll get hit."

The Blew youngsters were not an easy trio to control. Randy was assertive, clever, and arrogant. He tended to "mouth off" in school, getting himself in trouble with teachers. Paula was quieter, earning As and Bs without trying too hard, but she liked to tag along after Randy, and her rebelliousness grew as steadily as she did. Dennis's seizures worsened each year. His deteriorating physical abilities confounded him, and when the frustration became insurmountable he bit his hand or kicked whatever was within range. His mother regularly purchased plaster of paris to mend the holes in the walls.

Orville Blew was sometimes away for a week at a time working on the pipeline, and the responsibility for the children fell to Nylene, who found them to be more than she could handle. "Wait till your father gets home!" she warned repeatedly. When Orville arrived on a Friday afternoon she gave him a kiss and a hug, then launched a litany of the children's offenses. "They all need lickings," she advised.

"Now wait a minute," he protested. "I just got home. You want me to ruin the weekend by starting it out with punishment?"

When Paula became a seventh grader she joined Dennis and Randy in the building shared by La Plata's junior high and senior high students, a solid-looking three-story structure with a basement. Classes were spread over all four floors. In the new environment Paula's ties to her girlfriends loosened. She preferred the company of her brother Randy, a ninth grader. He was a "decent" student and a good athlete, although his tendency toward mischief turned belligerent at times. Some local parents considered him a troublemaker, but his peers thought of him as handsome, popular, and fun. Once in a while his insolence put him in the principal's office, and his parents were summoned for a conference. Teachers discovered that Orville Blew was quick to stand behind his son.

Paula, like Randy, was athletically gifted. A reputation for being "sticky-fingered" followed her to high school, but she managed to stay out of trouble with the principal. She enjoyed softball and was a star on the junior varsity basketball team, agile and determined, her long golden hair flying as she ran. Randy played center on senior varsity, and both teams had consistent winning records. Dennis watched from the sidelines.

Nylene's existence was tied to her home and her children. She was a tidy housekeeper when she wasn't "feeling bad," but recurrent and inexplicable dark moods continued to plague her, descending like a fog and leaving her, for a day or two, incapable of managing the demands of life. "I'm just impossible," she apologized to those who knew of her problem. "Somebody should take me out and shoot me."

If her gloom lifted while Orville was home for a weekend, they went "honky-tonkin'," an evening of dancing and a drink or two in nearby Kirksville. On her good days Nylene was cheerful and capable. She sewed, she planted flowers, she cooked a good hot supper for her family every evening. When she baked she often sent Paula to the elderly neighbors next door, John and Uldene Jackson, with a plate of cookies or a couple pieces of cake. Paula always stayed to talk. "She was a beautiful girl," the Jacksons thought, "healthy looking and beautiful."

As high school progressed Paula spent more and more time with her brothers. Her old girlfriends were leery of her. She was too much of a "tough cookie," somebody they didn't want to tangle with. They saw her now and then, sitting in a car parked at the town square, a beer in one hand and a cigarette in the other, ready to slip one or both out of sight if the wrong person appeared. And if a girl found something missing from her locker, she was likely to say, "I know Paula took it."

In 1973, when Paula was a freshman, a new boy appeared in town. His name was *Evan Dow, and his family came from the East. He spoke with an "accent," and he made fun of the small-town ways of his classmates, shaking his head and saying "you turkey" every time one of them amused him. He pronounced the word "toikey," and they quickly turned the label around and proclaimed it his nickname.

Evan struck up a friendship with Randy Blew. Both boys were juniors when Evan arrived, and both were judged to have a "wild streak." Evan didn't have Randy's athletic prowess, but they shared an insolence, a rebelliousness, that made them likely companions. And because Evan was with Randy he was also with Paula, for Paula was always with Randy.

Paula, Randy and Evan gravitated to drugs, joining a group of teenagers, a bigger group than most La Plata citizens realized, who experimented with liquor, pot, and pills. Paula's girlhood friends talked about the change in her. Sometimes her eyes looked glassy, they thought, and sometimes "she didn't act quite right," but none of them saw her take anything, and she continued to be as quick and strong as ever on the basketball court.

The Blews warned their children about the dangers of drinking and drugs, but Orville was often away, and Nylene, left to supervise three difficult teenagers, either did not recognize the extent of Randy's and Paula's drug use or felt powerless to do anything about it. She sometimes noticed that a few of her Valium were missing, and occasionally she wondered how Dennis's pills had been used up so quickly, but when she confronted Paula and Randy they steadfastly professed their innocence.

High school boys regularly gathered in the mornings at the Pool Cue, and they were back again after school. Girls did not often enter, although Paula was known to hang around, following Randy and Evan. When the boys weren't playing pool or pinball they were a few blocks away at the Tasty Freeze, where they could park their cars close enough to share conversation through open windows, pass beer cans and joints under cover of darkness, and impress the girls. Randy was usually at the center of any gathering, cracking jokes and enjoying his own popularity.

When things got boring someone would invariably say, "Hey, you wanna go run 'em?" Then the crowd would head to the straight, flat stretch of road that passed the cemetery, and the boys would try their cars and their skill. CB radios helped them keep track of the local police.

Dennis often begged to go along. Sometimes Randy took him, but Dennis wanted to join the fun, to be part of the drinking and the driving, and that was prohibited by the medication he took. Warnings could not dissuade him from a can of beer or a drag on a joint. Randy found it easier and safer to leave him home, even though that meant enduring his wrath the next day.

Nylene required that the children stop at her bedroom door after an evening out, to check in and say good night. They complied, but there were nights when Paula wasn't sure she would make it to her mother's threshold to smile and wave before she collapsed on her own bed.

After his graduation in the spring of 1975 Randy took a step toward independence with a factory job in Illinois, where he lived with relatives. Dennis checked into a St. Louis hospital, where specialists operated on his brain to see if they could alleviate his increasingly frequent seizures. Paula divided her time, visiting both brothers. She sat with Randy on an Illinois hilltop, the two of them blissfully stoned, marveling at the beauty of the greenery before them. She comforted her mother when doctors said there was nothing they could do to help Dennis.

Randy came back to La Plata and found work with the Santa Fe Railroad. A girl he had dated for two years had moved to Arkansas, and socially he was at loose ends. He lived under his father's roof but chafed at the restrictions still applied to him. Dennis was home, too, his physical deterioration making it impossible for him to consider either college or a job. Someone had to be with him constantly; usually it was Nylene.

Dennis had grown to be a large man, almost a head taller

than his father and thick around the middle. His attacks came without warning, and sometimes he fell and hurt himself before anyone could reach him. The responsibility for his care contributed to Nylene's nervousness. She became tense and brittle, anxious and demanding. Neighbors said, with understanding nods, that she was "high-strung."

As Paula reached her junior year she was still a standout on the basketball floor and still Randy's frequent companion, although he was no longer in high school. When she wasn't with Randy she was with Evan, for they had become "promised," a step short of engagement. He was her first sexual partner. Whatever she needed to know about intimacy and birth control she learned by experience; it was not a topic she could discuss with her mother.

Her drug use continued and, when Evan dropped her off just in time for her midnight curfew, she could barely call a cheerful "I'm home!" before she stumbled to her own room to pass out or vomit. She kept a plastic wastebasket close to her bed and tried to stifle the sounds of her own body, sure that her parents could hear her nighttime retching; but drugs were a subject the Blews didn't know how to handle, and they dealt with the problem by ignoring it.

The situation might have grown worse, for hard-core narcotics found their way to La Plata. Paula, however, had been terrified of needles since childhood, and Randy recognized the dangers of escalation. As Evan Dow's drug use progressed and theirs did not, both friendship and romance cooled.

Randy bought a used Camaro Z28 with his railroad earnings. He drove it fast, despite warnings from his father. In the spring of 1976 he was overhauling the car with the help of Mike Buck, a longtime friend, classmate, and fellow basketball player. While his car was out of commission Randy drove Mike's car or hung around the Pool Cue or the Tasty Freeze.

In the early evening of Saturday, April 10, after a day of beer drinking and aimless driving with Mike, Randy came home for supper. When he left the Blew house again Dennis begged to go along. "No," Randy said, "not tonight."

Dennis's frustration and bitterness overflowed. It was a beautiful spring evening, and both his brother and his sister were going out. They could drink, they could drive, they could dance, they could date, while he could only sit at home with his parents. He cursed in futile anger as Randy walked out the door.

At the town square, toward which teenagers gravitated, Randy's buddy, Mike Buck, met a friend who offered him a motorcycle ride. Mike climbed on the bike, leaving his car keys in his ignition, as he always did.

With his Camaro still in disrepair Randy walked to the square, just a few blocks from the Blew house. He slipped behind the wheel of Mike's car and went for a spin around the familiar streets. He met Paula, driving the Blews' car, on the road that passed the square. He motioned her to stop. "Where you goin'?" he called. She could barely hear him above the music that was blaring from his radio.

"I don't have much time," she yelled. "I'm supposed to meet some friends."

"You got a joint?" he asked. She nodded. She had pills and pot in her purse. "Come on," he said, grinning. "Let's take a ride."

A few miles away Evan Dow's father stood with a companion at the side of the road, adjusting a piece of farm machinery. The roar of something oncoming startled them. It flashed by so fast that Dow turned to his companion and asked, "Was that a car?"

"If it was," his friend answered, "it was goin' too fast for me to tell what color it was."

The accident happened near the cemetery on a stretch of road that runs straight and almost flat, a stretch that Randy knew well from drag racing. On a gentle rise in the road's surface at the southeast cemetery corner he sideswiped an oncoming car.

A woman standing on her porch watched as the car in which Randy and Paula were speeding jumped the shallow ditch, smashed into a tree in her front yard, and burst into flames. Had it not been for the tree, the car would have hit her porch.

Paula opened her eyes to see fire erupting around her. "We gotta get outa here!" she shrieked, pounding on her jammed door. "Randy! We gotta get outa here! Randy!" She shook him, but he slumped over the steering wheel, his arms hanging heavily, uselessly. In desperation she climbed over his limp body, threw her weight against the driver's door, and climbed out. Flames leapt higher as she struggled to pull him from the wreck. Soon there were others, pushing her out of the way, clustering around her brother. She didn't understand why they were pounding on his chest. She didn't know that she was screaming. As the crowd grew and emergency equipment began to arrive she ceased to understand anything.

Her face bloodied, Paula was placed in the front seat of an ambulance. She turned to look at the sheet-covered stretcher in the back. "Who's that?" she asked.

Five members of the family riding in the other car were injured. The only fatality was Randy, whose skull was crushed. He was nineteen years old.

At the Blew home the elderly Jacksons from next door and some other neighbors were gathered, just an informal drop-by visit on early Saturday evening, when Orville Blew received a phone call telling him there had been an accident. He left immediately. The Jacksons stayed with Nylene, who was too upset to do anything but lie down.

Paula was taken to the Kirksville Osteopathic Hospital, where she was treated for facial fractures. Yet when she returned to school three weeks later she had no visible scars. Her facial bones had been restructured from inside her mouth. Classmates looked for evidence of the accident in her appearance but saw nothing. The difference they noticed was something internal, something that few of them could put into words. It was more than sadness; they had expected her to be sad. But she was gone to some silent, tortured place that had no emotion, no name. The change in her, they agreed, was "drastic."

Whatever remained of Paula's relationship with Evan

Dow crumbled in the aftermath of the accident. "You should have stopped him," Evan admonished. Evan's blame fed the guilt she already felt. She drank more beer, she smoked more pot, she got a ticket for driving eighty-one miles an hour. She was mad at herself. She was mad at God. She dared Him to take her, as He had taken her brother.

8

AMOCO OFFERED ORVILLE BLEW A NEW POSITION, A RECLASSI-
fication from "pipe liner" to "deliveryman." The change
meant an opportunity for a considerable amount of well-
paid overtime, overtime that could build a healthy retirement fund. It also meant that he could be home every night.
The only disadvantage was the job's location; it was in
southern Illinois, far from Randy's often-visited grave.

Paula promised her parents she would make a fresh start
when they moved. No more drugs. No more drinking. A
new group of friends.

On her first afternoon in the newly purchased house in
Cottage Hills, before the boxes were unpacked, a boy named
Kent knocked on the door. He had once lived in La Plata,
where his father had worked with Orville on the pipeline.
He had come to show her around, he said, to point out some
of the local sights, to introduce her to some of his friends.

The friends he introduced were the friends she had left
behind. Pills and pot were readily available; beer flowed
freely. Her resolve to go straight didn't last out the day.

A week later June Bland found Paula in a park, playing a solitary game of basketball and throwing a Frisbee to her dog. It was the animal that brought them together as much as anything, for June was short and had no particular athletic talent. A black and white Border collie, the dog was named Rush; he was the latest in a long line of pets that Paula had raised, and he was, in her mind, the best. He could grab a Frisbee from the air as easily as she could sink a basketball.

Paula and June quickly discovered that they lived just a block apart, that they were the same age, and that they shared an inclination to push the limits of authority. At Civic Memorial High School their last names, Bland and Blew, put them in the same homeroom.

"Who's that?" asked June when she noticed Randy's picture on the Blews' bookcase.

"My brother," Paula said, looking sadly at the photo. "We were inseparable. But we were real wild. We did some heavy partyin'."

June had done some "heavy partyin'" herself and considered Paula's beer and pot pretty tame. "The wreck slowed me down," Paula explained.

June became a regular visitor at the Blews' house on Virginia Avenue, for her own home did not offer her much stability or security. Her parents had divorced after twenty-two years of marriage, her mother had moved out of town, and she argued too often with her father and her sister. The Blews welcomed her and invited her to dinner night after night. "They treated me like I was one of their own," June remembered.

It was in the school cafeteria that Paula said a tentative hello to Rhonda Henson. Both girls, at least in the milieu of a large high school, were quiet and reserved. Civic Memorial was not actually in Cottage Hills, where the Blews lived, but in Bethalto. The communities of the southern Illinois region flowed together with nothing more than signs to mark their boundaries, and the school picked up students from throughout the area. It was large and crowded and, in the fall of 1976, on double sessions. The cafeteria was noisy, and Paula and Rhonda seemed to be outside its active flow. "I just knew from the minute I saw her, from the minute we sat down and started talking, that I liked her," Rhonda said. "And I was really shy. I wouldn't go out and say hi to the first person I saw on the street. But I always genuinely liked her."

Rhonda learned of Randy's death when Paula took out a wallet and showed her his picture. "That's my brother," she said. "He was killed." Rhonda did not discover until later that the accident had injured Paula as well.

Rhonda, June, and Paula formed an unlikely trio, for June was brash and outspoken, a "brassy blond," while Rhonda was calm, careful, and sometimes withdrawn. Paula was the catalyst that held the threesome together, bridging the personality gap between the extremes.

She and June had the same English class; occasionally the teacher would dismiss them early, and they would sneak a cigarette in the bathroom. Rhonda joined them but worried that they'd all be caught. "Paula was a hell-raiser," Rhonda said. "So was June. June would just as soon fight with you as look at you. In school I'd be thinking, 'Oh, you guys are gonna get us in trouble.'"

As upperclassmen the girls attended classes from seven-thirty until noon; sophomores and freshmen filled the building in the afternoons. Because of the schedule, many of the seniors had jobs, and the days seemed rushed. The camaraderie and closeness offered by La Plata were notice-ably absent, even for a girl who had dropped most of her childhood friends by the time she reached high school. Paula played softball but never won athletic recognition at Civic Memorial. By the time she came, as a senior, the roles of athletes and achievers had already been claimed by others. She didn't try to break into the ranks. The school was so large, and its schedule so hectic, that most of her senior classmates were unaware of her existence.

Paula's interest in learning was minimal. She cared more about the afternoons, when she spent her time drinking beer and riding around with Kent, who became a friend but not a boyfriend, or talking and smoking pot with Rhonda and June.

The girls graduated in the spring of 1977. Paula had a senior picture taken but didn't bother to put it in the *Spectator,* Civic Memorial's yearbook.

Her father introduced a young man who worked at Amoco, a polite, clean-cut, well-dressed, all-American guy. He was handsome, tall, and athletic. He was obviously right for her. His name was Randy.

Their first date was for a concert. She took some pot in her purse, hoping he smoked. As the music began a joint was passed down the row, not an uncommon occurrence in the seventies, and Randy took a hit. So did she. She relaxed and dug the pot out of her purse.

Their second date was for dinner and a movie. Afterward she told her parents she didn't plan to see him again. "But why?" they asked.

"I dunno," she said with a shrug.

"Paula," her mother protested, "he's perfect. He plays basketball. And tennis. What's wrong with him?"

"Nothing's wrong with him," she replied, and in truth she could find no flaw. Maybe that was the problem; he was complete as he was. He didn't need her. "Just no spark," she said. "That's all. Just no spark."

Paula couldn't seem to focus on what she wanted out of life. She talked about moving to Peoria and getting a job at the Caterpillar factory. She worked for two months as a cashier at Central Hardware but quit abruptly when she could take no more from a supervisor who was always "riding" her. She toiled for a week on a Christmas tree farm but walked away from the job and never bothered to pick up her paycheck.

Her parents urged her to settle down, to choose a direction, to find an interest.

Together she and June enrolled in a keypunch program at Lewis and Clark Community College. They began enthusiastically, seeing in their classes the promise of independence

and prosperity. Both of them bought cars. Paula had a blue
'69 Maverick and took good care of it, planning to use it
eventually as a down payment on another car. June wore out
a Torino and then a Pinto and rode with Paula when her
own vehicles were gone. They waxed their cars in the Blews'
driveway, listening to tapes on Paula's cassette player. Little
River Band was a favorite, along with Queen, Foreigner,
Bob Seeger, and Styx. Paula stopped her waxing whenever
she heard the introductory notes of Styx's "Lorelei." Sometimes she and June sang along.

> *When I think of Lorelei*
> *My head turns all around.*
> *As gentle as a butterfly,*
> *She moves without a sound.*
> *Lorelei, let's live together,*
> *Brighter than the stars forever.*
> *Oh, baby, forever!*

"If I ever have a little girl," Paula said, "I'm going to name
her Lorelei."

Paula and June were frequently together, even outside
their keypunch program, for they had no boyfriends on the
scene to keep them busy. They partied with various friends,
but Paula never seemed to make a special connection with
any of the young men she met, and June was determined to
remain true to her navy boyfriend, even though she complained bitterly that he never wrote to her.

The two girls considered themselves "hippies." They
went to St. Louis rock concerts whenever they could afford
it; they drank beer and smoked marijuana. "But nothin'
else," June said. "Beer and pot, that was it." Beer was
available in eight-ounce four-packs, "little Pabst," and they
never finished all the cans. "Back then everything was so
free," June remembered. "If cops pulled you over, they just
poured the beer out and said, 'Hit it. Go home.' We had
really good teenage years."

June came to think of herself as a near-member of the

Blew family. She and Paula took Dennis to the park, bringing a lawn chair for him. He "blanked out" now and then, but they could handle him. June "baby-sat" for him if Paula and her parents were busy.

As Dennis's dependence had increased, so had Nylene's tension. She smoked restlessly and repeatedly resolved to quit, but she borrowed cigarettes from Paula whenever her resolution weakened. She made an issue of things that others considered unimportant and got on the nerves of those around her. Paula kept peace by acquiescing to her mother's demands or by staying out of the way. As Paula and June walked out the door Nylene's complaint followed them: "You don't know how I feel. You don't understand."

When Paula drove to Missouri to see relatives June went along. Paula grew quiet as they detoured through the sadly familiar streets of La Plata. She stood by Randy's tombstone and looked to the southeast cemetery corner. "Right there"—she pointed—"that's where it happened."

Although they went to business classes throughout fall and winter, neither June nor Paula took the challenge seriously. They often shared a joint as they drove to the campus. Being high, they assured each other, wouldn't impede their keypunch ability. They didn't find the work difficult until they came to a business machines course in which students were expected to master several pieces of equipment on their own time, with the help of an instruction manual. The lack of direction unnerved them. "A big old room full of typewriters and machines," June sighed. "We just couldn't believe we had to take this in order to be a keypunch operator." When the course ended the girls were disappointed to discover that no one was waiting to offer them jobs.

With their keypunch plans dashed they were excited to learn, in the summer of 1978, a year after they had graduated from high school, that National Food was hiring checkers. Both applied, but June had never been good at math; only Paula was hired.

Paula was happy with her new job, and initially she gave it her concentration and effort; but as she became accustomed to the store's routine she returned to old habits, smoking a joint in the car on her way to work, something to relax her, to mellow her out, to get her ready for a day of customers. As the months went by she became more audacious. She smoked on her break in the employee bathroom, afterward spraying perfume into the air to disguise the odor of marijuana. On occasion she carried a little bottle of whiskey and added it to the Pepsi she drank. She was sure that neither the pot nor the liquor diminished her ability at the cash register; on the contrary, they made her calmer, friendlier.

She had no complaints about her salary. It was more than enough for her needs, since she was still living at home. She bought a new car, a Dodge Arrow. Her father advanced the money, and she paid him back within a year. Amply supplied with everything, she could offer no reason for shoplifting, even to herself. Items she had once pilfered in La Plata, gum and candy, gave way to more expensive things, jewelry and perfume, and to articles that were more difficult to steal, jeans and sweaters. The relative of a friend showed her the ropes: how to choose the department, how to watch the salesclerks, how to get the merchandise out of the store. Paula was good at it.

Her parents never questioned her bulging closet. They assumed that she was spending her paycheck on clothes. Soon there was so much in her dresser drawers that she wondered why she continued to steal. She had everything she wanted, certainly more than she needed.

When she was caught she wasn't taking anything large or difficult, just a tiny pair of baby overalls, something she should have been able to slip into her shopping bag in an instant. As the police officer took her arm she handed her car keys to June. "Come pick me up," she said. She didn't want the police to look in the car. It was full of things she had stolen during the day's "shopping" excursion.

At the station she was so scared that she refused to give her name until officers threatened to throw her into a cell with a disreputable-looking man. She was relieved that the police didn't do a strip search; if they had, they would have discovered that she was wearing two pair of jeans, a stolen pair under her own.

The following morning she made a court appearance and paid her fine. She told her parents nothing about the incident, but the experience left her chastened. It ended her shoplifting.

The little overalls Paula had tried to steal were for Rhonda's new son. Rhonda had disappeared from the trio when high school ended, for she had delivered a baby a few months after graduation. Paula and June phoned one night just to ask how things were going. When they learned that her newborn boy was seriously ill they visited, and once the contact was reestablished they knocked on her door regularly and held her hand through long night vigils, knowing nothing about medicine but promising each other that the baby would be all right.

With Rhonda a wife and mother, things were never the way they had been in high school. The girls were not a trio anymore. Both Paula and June liked Kenny Scott, Rhonda's new husband, but Rhonda's marriage made them conscious of the lack of romance and commitment in their own lives.

Paula planned her ideal future and shared visions of it with June. "She was a very particular person, and she was very private. She was never one to tell you she was on her period or she's got cramps or something. She was always very private about that. But she talked a lot about her dreams. She wanted a husband and kids. She wanted everything to be just right, you know. She wanted to have no worries. She wanted a nice home, nice car, even savings. Even savings," June emphasized. "That was her dream, to marry and to marry forever."

June's dream centered on her navy boyfriend, who frustrated her by failing to call or write. As his communication waned she grew increasingly despondent until she called Paula, crying, saying she had taken sleeping pills she'd found in the medicine cabinet. Paula ran the block to June's house, pulled her to her feet, and kept her moving. June wasn't sure how many pills she had taken, and neither girl had any notion how potent the capsules might be. Paula stayed for twenty-four hours, forcing June to walk, then letting her rest. She refused to leave until she was sure the danger was past and there were no more pills in June's house.

When they talked about the incident later June and Paula tried to laugh. "Stupid," they agreed. "Really stupid." But both of them could see that June's desperate, angry act reflected a lack of purpose in their lives. They had no plan. They had no sense of direction. They were just marking time, waiting for something, or someone, to come along.

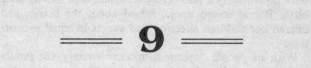

9

ROB SIMS'S LIFE WAS UNSETTLED WHEN HE MET PAULA. THERE had been a time when his sense of direction seemed strong, when he appeared to be headed toward college and a career, like his older brothers; but that evaporated not long after he left Alton High School in 1970.

Being overshadowed by his brothers was a lifelong problem for Rob. Both Jerry and Tom Sims did well in high school; both worked their way through college and established themselves as professionals; both brought pride to their parents. "Everything was aimed at the two older boys," said a source with close ties to the family. "The two younger kids [Rob and his sister Linda] were just sort of there."

As children, all four of the Sims offspring, like their mother, were fat. A steady supply of cookies and ice cream from Bernie Sims's kitchen accounted for the problem. The Sims boys took control and escaped the burden of obesity in their high school years; the Sims women were never able to shed their excess pounds with any permanent success, although various diets were optimistically attempted.

Rob and his siblings grew up in an unassuming household. Their father, Troy, who taught elementary school, was a man curiously removed from the day-to-day upbringing of his own children. "He was never really involved with the kids," judged a family observer. "He was unable to see their problems because he was concerned about his own."

It was their mother, Bernie, who raised the three boys and Linda, who was one year younger than Rob. Another girl, born prematurely a year before Rob, had died shortly after birth. Bernie stayed home, fussed about the house, and offered her children affection and sweets in equal proportion.

With six people dependent upon one salary, the family had the necessities but few luxuries. They lived on the financial edge, turning to relatives to borrow money when they faced major expenses.

A tight budget was nothing new to Troy Sims. He had grown up in a family that was hard pressed to survive. His father was killed in a farm accident, leaving his mother to do the outdoor work, assisted by an older son. Troy, barely past the toddler stage, was left in the care of a sister not much older than himself who put him in a closet whenever he became too much for her to handle. Bernie's background was more affluent but not without its quirks; her father proudly displayed a Ku Klux Klan membership certificate on his wall.

The Sims family came to Alton in the late 1950s, when Rob was seven, so that Troy could work for a nearby school district. The district's evaluators soon discovered they had hired a disorganized instructor with no lesson plans, workbooks, or corrected papers. In 1961 Troy received a letter threatening him with dismissal if he didn't shape up. The notice apparently had its intended effect, for after that evaluators saw significant improvement in his preparation and class conduct. Everything seemed to be under control when he suddenly submitted his resignation in April of 1963. Two weeks later his teaching certificate was suspended for "immorality." He was out of the classroom for six weeks while the "immorality," its exact nature unspecified in school records, was remedied. In January of the following year his right to teach was reinstated. An official noted, "Mr. Sims has been under treatment and I have now signed statements that he is considered cured."

Those who heard whispers of the misbehavior frequently disbelieved what they were told. "Must be some other Sims," they said, assuming that the Troy Sims they knew was too mild-mannered, too much a family man, too *normal* to be the subject of such a charge.

At gatherings of relatives the problem was tacitly acknowledged but never openly discussed. Rob was eleven at the time, old enough to be aware of the turmoil and to pick up, consciously or unconsciously, the attitudes reflected by a father whose "immorality" involved improper conduct with a girl.

Despite the skeleton in his family closet, Rob moved toward a responsible adult life. After high school he began part-time work at Laclede Credit Union, a job which came to him through the manager, Harrol Cannedy, a man for whom he had mowed lawns and done odd jobs. Rob's assignment at Laclede was to do whatever needed doing—filing, answering the phone, emptying wastebaskets, running errands. It was a good job, particularly for a student with an undistinguished academic record. Rob (who was known as Bob in high school) earned As in shop and architectural drawing classes, but basically he was average, ranking 350th in a group of 706 seniors. His extracurricular activities centered on playing the tuba in band and orchestra. Some of the popular students regarded him as a "nerd."

The Laclede job was flexible enough to allow Rob to continue working while he took a year of classes at Lewis and Clark Community College. When summer vacation rolled around he added more hours at the credit union. A similar pattern of work and study began his sophomore year, but he dropped out after a month of classes to accept full-time employment at Laclede.

His new position was an occupational step up. Rob's duties were similar to those of a bank teller, helping customers with deposits, withdrawals, loans, and check cashing; but dropping out of college cost him his draft deferment, a serious consequence to a young man at the time of the Vietnam war. A year later, as he faced the possibility of being drafted, he chose to enlist in the navy.

*Terry Davidson grew up in Brunswick, Maine, in a house just eight miles from the Brunswick Naval Air Station. On a chilly night in February, 1973, her friend *Evelyn phoned and begged her to accept a blind date. Since Evelyn's navy boyfriend didn't have a car, he usually persuaded another sailor to give him a ride to her house; that left Evelyn the task of finding a date for the driver. Terri had declined previous invitations, but on this night Evelyn was insistent. "Well, okay," Terri agreed.

An hour later a lime-green '69 Ford truck pulled up. "Rob Sims, Alton, Ill." was emblazoned on its side. The red-haired driver had a neatly trimmed beard and intense eyes. Physically he wasn't imposing, only an inch taller than Terri's 5'8", but she liked his looks, and he seemed polite enough. The foursome piled into the truck and headed for the Enlisted Men's Club at the base. "So, what would you like to drink?" Rob asked Terri as they sat down in the bar.

"A screwdriver," she blurted, the only drink she could think of. It was four days before her sixteenth birthday.

They talked for an hour or two, Terri trying to act sophisticated while she twirled a strand of her long, light brown hair. Rob smoked Marlboros, told her about Illinois, and asked questions about Brunswick, her family, and her school. He really seemed interested, although she couldn't imagine that there was much in her life to interest anyone. She told him about her two older sisters, both moved out and living on their own, and about her seventeen-year-old brother who had died after an illness. His death had left her mother so overcome with grief that, even two years later, she just wasn't there for the little problems Terri had, the day-to-day concerns of a teenager. Rob nodded. He was sympathetic and attentive.

Terri was impressed. Here was a man almost five years

older than she was; he was from a different state; he was in the navy; and he was interested in *her*.

The evening ended with no definite plans for a second date. There was some talk about snowmobiling the next day with Evelyn and her boyfriend. Terri said she might come. Rob was noncommital, too. Both of them showed up.

Soon Terri was spending all her free time with Rob. Her mother had always said it was wise to meet and date a lot of boys, but Terri didn't agree. If she found a guy she liked, why should she bother with anyone else?

He was nineteen, she told her parents. That sounded better than twenty. The deception worked for two months, until April, when Terri mentioned that Rob would be celebrating his twenty-first birthday. "He's turning *twenty-one?*" asked her mother. "What happened to twenty?"

By then it was too late to object. Terri was obviously happy. She found Rob easy to be around. He was comfortable. He made her feel safe. He wasn't pushy as far as sex was concerned. They parked and petted, but he didn't pressure her to "go all the way" until she felt she was ready.

Most of their time together was spent in the green truck, just driving around. Rob bought a bottle or two of Boone's Farm Strawberry Hill wine, and they drank it while the eight-track played their favorite tapes, John Denver's "Sunshine on My Shoulders," Bread, and Gary Puckett.

He didn't talk much about the navy, except to grumble about his superior officer, a chief who "had it in" for him and was always "on his back." His days were spent typing schedules and logs, he told Terri, and he was sick of all the "niggers" he had to deal with.

For Terri, Rob's companionship supplied the closeness she didn't have at home. He quickly became her strongest emotional connection. When he began to show signs of possessiveness she was glad. She secretly rejoiced that he became aggravated if she looked at other men. She thought it was funny and endearing that he was peeved if she noticed a particularly nice car or truck driven by someone else. The wrong remark could make him sullen, so she was careful. She concentrated all her attention on him.

For Rob, the relationship was an early example of a pattern he would repeat: He found a younger woman of at least average ability and promise, a girl with some immediate pain or void in her life; then he stepped in to fill the emptiness. As he would in later couplings, he quickly established himself as the center of Terri's existence and became the dominant force in her life.

When he spoke of marriage she was ready to listen. He gave her an engagement ring for Christmas, ten months after they had met. She was just sixteen, a high school junior, but she could see no reason to hesitate. She was sure she had found what she wanted. When Rob's squadron was sent on a five-month deployment to Spain she became even more certain. She couldn't believe how much she missed him. He sent her a doll costumed as a bride; it was the most romantic gift she could imagine.

They were married the following July, four months after she turned seventeen. Her parents had to be persuaded to sign a permission form, since she was under legal age. The ceremony was conducted by a justice of the peace; Terri wore a long, pink flowered dress; Rob wore his white uniform. Only eight guests attended: Terri's parents, her sister and a boyfriend, and Rob's two brothers and their wives. Afterward they all went out to dinner.

It was the first time Terri had met other members of Rob's family, and she was relieved to find that his brothers, Jerry and Tom, were friendly. Jerry, a pathologist, had a tendency to "talk above" her, but Tom was fun. He was nearer Rob's age and had shoulder-length hair; Terri thought he looked like Jesus Christ. Tom's wedding gift reflected his work as a medical illustrator; he presented the newlyweds with two large framed drawings of matching human eyes. With no time or money for a honeymoon, Rob and Terri spent their wedding night in the apartment they had rented a few days earlier.

It wasn't until they lived together that Terri became fully aware of Rob's penchant for order and cleanliness. He was neat, she knew, and he took good care of his truck, but she almost laughed the first time he stood at the kitchen counter and checked the toaster tray for crumbs. Then she realized he was serious.

Terri's classmates were impressed with her sudden devotion to housekeeping. Her friend *Sandra marveled at the immaculate condition of the apartment. "This place is so *clean!"* Sandra said repeatedly. "I could eat off your toilet seat!"

Sandra was less impressed with the demeanor of Terri's new husband. When the two girls tired of sitting around the apartment on a Saturday afternoon, Terri walked outside to persuade Rob to take them somewhere. "I wish we could do something," she sighed, leaning on one fender of the truck while Rob polished the other. "Maybe take a ride or something. We're bored."

Rob considered the hint. "If you're bored," he replied, "go back inside and wash the windows."

"I can't believe he said that!" Sandra exclaimed when Terri told her of the suggestion. Sandra was even more amazed when Terri took out a bucket and went to work.

Terri accepted Rob's demands as part of the bargain she had made. "If you're married, you're supposed to be Betty Crocker," she said with a shrug.

Occasionally Rob's standards surprised her. When they purchased a secondhand washer and dryer he phrased his expectation as a question: "Now, you *are* going to clean these every time you use them, aren't you?"

"Clean them?" she asked. "Wash the washing machine?"

"That's right," he said.

A few weeks later he scowled as he noticed residue near the machine's bleach dispenser. "What's this?" he asked.

"Gee, I don't know," she lied. "I just cleaned it yesterday."

Terri didn't object to the duties, the requirements. She didn't object when Rob rationed her tobacco supply, doling out ten cigarettes in the morning and saying, "Here. That's all you get." She did object to the pound of marijuana brought to the apartment by one of Rob's friends, a navy buddy named *Jake. They would all be arrested, she told them. Rob laughed.

Terri knew that Rob smoked pot (he had told her so), but he never lit up in front of her until after the wedding. It took some persuading to get her to participate, but she found her first joint a pleasant surprise. The drug lowered her inhibitions and increased her sexual appetite; pot became a ritual of the young couple's life. They got high every evening, just the two of them.

Occasional discord marred their first months together, but usually the disagreements were trivial and the battles verbal. There was only one physical confrontation. It was at the end of the shouting, as she rummaged through a closet to find a coat so that she could leave. "That was my way to fight, to just get out," Terri explained. "I couldn't stand the tension when the fight wasn't over but the words were done."

She was tossing garments on the floor, searching for the one she wanted, when Rob slapped her. "I deserved it," she told herself afterward. "I was flippin' out. Nothing else would have brought me to my senses. I deserved it."

A second deployment sent Rob's unit to Bermuda, and Terri was so lonely that she visited a navy chaplain to beg for her husband's return. High school classes occupied her days, and a job at a hospital, where she laid out food trays for patients, filled her evenings; but she lived for Rob's daily letters, which ended with a series of postscripts. One was invariably "pill and pack," a reminder to take her birth-control pill and to smoke no more than one pack of cigarettes a day.

By the end of his hitch Rob had reached the rank of yeoman third class. He complained bitterly about the navy, and his superior officers were apparently displeased with his outlook. Although there was no disciplinary action on his record, he was deemed ineligible for reenlistment "due to his negative attitude."

There was never any doubt that he would return to Illinois. His job at the credit union was waiting, as federal regulations required. He bought a Pontiac Bonneville to tow his truck, which had persistent engine problems, and he and his young wife said good-bye to Maine.

Troy and Bernie Sims welcomed Terri, but she felt awkward nevertheless. She was only eighteen. She was living with her in-laws, whom she had just met. She didn't know her way around the area. She was totally dependent.

It was hard for her to make conversation with Troy, Rob's father, a slight, reticent man with straight gray hair and a receding hairline. Terri wondered what it would have been like to grow up with a father so quiet and remote. She tried to imagine Troy Sims throwing a baseball with his sons. The picture didn't fit.

Rob seemed closer to his mother, who called him "Bob" or "Bobby." When he was younger, she told Terri, she had called him "Bobby Blue Jeans" or a sweet, nonsensical variation, "Jobby Bean." On schoolday mornings she had roused him with little songs.

Wilma Bernadine Sims, called "Bunny" by her husband and "Bernie" by everyone else, was short and obese, at least 250 pounds, Terri guessed, maybe nearer 300. Her weight made it difficult for her to move. A trip to the grocery store was as much as she could manage. Afterward she had to put her feet up to ease her aching legs. Her house wasn't as clean as it used to be, she told Terri apologetically. There was dust where there had never been dust before. It was just too hard for her to get around. Troy seemed embarrassed by his wife's weight. He listened silently as she talked of her problems. "He's always telling me to cut down," Bernie confided to her new daughter-in-law. "But look, Terri," she added, showing the meager amount she had put on her plate, "this is all I have for lunch."

Rob's sister Linda, who lived with her parents, was heavy, too. A year younger than Rob, she had a brash manner, a pretty face, and long hair that she bleached honey blond. Her life seemed solitary. No girlfriends visited; no boyfriends called.

Terri was glad when she and Rob found a tiny but

affordable apartment on the second floor of a brick house. Rob made it clear that he didn't want her to work. Her job was to take care of the home, as his mother did. Supper—meat and potatoes—was to be on the table when he walked in the door. "Look," he stipulated one evening when he discovered she had neglected to sew a button on a shirt, "I spend eight hours a day on the job. I expect you to spend eight hours a day cleaning and taking care of things around the house."

He was back on his own turf, Terri realized, where he felt confident enough to call the shots. She, on the other hand, was insecure and homesick. She did what was expected of her, but the tasks in the tiny apartment didn't keep her mind occupied. She began to watch soap operas, putting on pounds as she sat in front of the TV.

Part of the problem was the pot. In addition to smoking every evening, as he had in Maine, Rob now smoked in the morning as well. When he lit up he wanted her to participate. He gulped the smoke into his lungs and held out the joint. "There's a high going to waste here," he argued if she shook her head.

The drug affected them in different ways. "When he smoked," Terri said, "it was like speed. 'Let's wash the car. Let's listen to some music.'" To her it was a sedative. Afterward she wanted only to eat or relax. While Rob dashed off to work or to run an errand she sat at the table and finished the doughnuts.

He wasn't happy with her weight gain. "You better not get as fat as your sister," he warned. It was always her sister that he chose as a negative example. He never mentioned the obesity in his own family.

Terri lobbied for permission to find a job, something to keep her busy, to get her moving, to help her lose weight. "I can't sit and watch soap operas all day," she complained. "I want to go to work."

"I don't want my wife to work," he said.

"Then at least I want a dog for some company," she argued, figuring he would have to give in to one request or 'the other. Rob wasn't enthused about a pet, but she persisted. A dog or a job. Maybe both.

A job might be a possibility, he conceded, but only if she could find one that allowed her to see him off to work in the morning and to have supper on the table when he arrived in the evening. And to be home on weekends.

She wondered if he was setting her up for failure; where would she find a job like that? She pored over the newspaper ads, looking for waitress positions with limited hours. At the same time she scanned the columns for a dog.

The one she found was free, a mixture of cocker spaniel and German shepherd. She took it home and bathed it; she wanted it looking good and smelling sweet when Rob saw it. It was still wet when he arrived. He cast a disapproving eye on the matted, shivering creature. "Ugly," he pronounced, but he let her keep it. He named it Jake, after his navy buddy. Jake had been ugly, too, he said.

Three days after she got the dog Terri found work as a waitress at a steak house. The job nearly met Rob's requirements. On Fridays she wouldn't have supper ready, but if she hurried, she could be home in time to greet him at the door. A job and a dog. Things were looking up, she told herself.

The improvement was temporary.

═══ **10** ═══

THE WOMEN AT LACLEDE CREDIT UNION WEREN'T PLEASED AT Rob Sims's return. It was hard for them to put a finger on the reasons for their aversion. "Just his attitude," they said to *Gayle Allard.

Gayle had been hired during Rob's absence, to take over his teller duties. Four of the seven women at Laclede had stations in the front office, behind the counter. Since Gayle was new, and since she was the only one who didn't already harbor a dislike for Rob, she was assigned the position nearest his; their desks faced each other. Gayle thought Rob seemed nice; quiet, but nice. His slouching, hunched-over walk made him look older than he was, but he was well-groomed, wearing neat slacks and sport shirts.

Gayle and Rob followed the same schedule for their coffee breaks and lunches. As they became better acquainted he offered to teach her to play hearts; they took out a deck of cards in the employee lunchroom whenever there was time.

Gayle was in her mid-twenties, slender, dark-haired, striving for independence, and living on her own in an apartment on Eighth Street. When an apartment became vacant in the building next to hers she told Rob about it. She knew that he and Terri were looking for more space. They moved in.

"Give me your phone number for Terri," Rob said one day. Gayle hesitated; she was by nature cautious and private. Only half a dozen people had her unlisted number. She wasn't sure how much she and Terri would have in common, for Terri was just a teenager, and very quiet; but she could understand that the girl might be lonely, having come to southern Illinois from Maine and knowing no one in the area. Besides, Rob had been pleasant and courteous during the few months she had known him. She gave him the phone number.

Gayle saw Terri occasionally as they were coming or going from their adjacent buildings, and at Rob's invitation she stopped once or twice at the Simses' apartment. She wasn't comfortable there. The air in the living room was so thick with sweet smoke that her eyes watered. At first she thought it was just incense. Then she figured out it was marijuana. She was relieved that Terri never called.

Office camaraderie began to strain as time passed. Gayle noticed Rob didn't get up from his desk to wait on customers as often as she did, and he made a fuss about typing loan applications and change-of-address forms; he considered that "women's work." Rob, in turn, grumbled that it was Gayle who didn't do her share at the counter. He said she was lazy.

Dissension increased when Rob was given duties as an assistant collector. He sent out past-due notices, contacted debtors to request payments, and occasionally arranged for a repossession agency to pick up an automobile. The additional responsibilities made him feel he shouldn't have to wait on people at the counter. But Gayle contended that she had special duties, too.

Some days Rob didn't bother to answer her "good morning." He enjoyed making a show of his temper, letting everyone know if he was peeved. When he had trouble with his manual Royal typewriter he took off his shoe and hit the keys.

Sometimes his hostility was roused by a phone call from his mother. If he was told that Bernie Sims was on the line, he fumed. After the call he slammed down the receiver and announced his complaint: "I wish that woman would leave me alone." Other times he was even more adamant: "I hate her."

The women in Laclede's front office soon realized that Rob's mother was not the only woman he disparaged. One personal habit seemed to indicate his contempt for all of them. He was frequently flatulent, and he made no apology if he tainted the air of those around him. When one of the women got up courage to let him know she was offended, he grinned and shrugged.

Gayle became convinced that Rob's flatulence was deliberately induced when, on more than one occasion, she saw him open and devour a can of great northern white beans. "Why do you eat beans?" she demanded, her annoyance and disgust apparent.

"I like beans," he replied with a smile.

Rob sometimes had lunch at an inexpensive café with eighteen-year-old *Gary Tomlin, a young man who had been hired at Laclede while still in high school and later promoted to full-time duties, just as Rob had been. "Rob was tight with a buck," said Gary. "He was always bitching about money." But Gary saw that Rob could afford marijuana. And a truck. And a motorcycle, a Honda 450. And a new car.

The car was a four-cylinder Mustang, bright red inside and out. When it arrived it was, briefly, his pride, but he quickly discovered it didn't have the "pickup," the power, he wanted. It was soon gone, replaced by a Tempest. To the Tempest he added a Chevy; the Chevy was replaced by a Thunderbird.

Rob let Gary and everyone else know that he was looking for a new job, something that would pay better. He told Gary that he didn't like working with the women, but he claimed that, before he went in the Navy, he had been intimate with all but one of them. "He said there was only one that he didn't fuck, and that was because he didn't have any rubbers with him and she wasn't on the Pill. But he had her in the backseat stripped down naked, and she was just begging for it." Gary didn't bother to ask if the credit union's married women were included in the tally; he assumed that the story was no more than wishful lust, but he found it odd that Rob bragged of intimacies with women who clearly disliked him.

The calls began on a Monday evening in early November. "Hello?" said Gayle Allard. "Hello? Hello?" There was no reply. She hung up the phone and rejoined her elderly neighbor on the couch. They were supplied with popcorn and sodas, ready to watch *Gone with the Wind*. It was the first time the movie had been scheduled on TV.

As the opening credits concluded Gayle's phone rang again. Her impatient hellos went unanswered. The strange, wordless calls persisted throughout the evening, turning the on-screen romance into a farce of interruptions.

During the remainder of the week the calls continued, a bombardment of them, each delivering only silence. There was no heavy breathing, no off-color suggestion, just an emptiness that echoed until Gayle hung up.

Illinois Bell offered to put a "trap" on the line, a process that might ascertain the number from which the calls originated, but warned that such contacts often turned out to be from someone familiar. It was not likely that this determined harassment was coming from a stranger, particularly since her number was unlisted.

Gayle signed the papers authorizing the trap and prepared to follow instructions, which, in 1976, before Touch-Tone had become common, required that she dial the number seven on her rotary dial phone while the caller remained on the line. If she could complete the dialing while the connection between the two phones stayed open, electronic equipment would determine the source of the call.

With the trap in place Gayle answered the phone, listened

to the familiar silence, and dialed the seven, hoping the numbers would circle back to their starting place before the caller hung up. When the last click of the dial was replaced by the hum of a broken connection she told herself, "Next time." But the next time was no different. She dialed as quickly as she could, but by the time the circle returned to its home position the caller was gone.

Night after night the ringing continued. Gayle dialed faithfully, holding her breath as the numbers spun into place. Sometimes she forced the circle backward, trying to shave a fraction of a second off the time. When she finished a dial tone signaled her failure.

She considered disconnecting the phone or requesting a new number, but either choice meant that she would never know who was badgering her. Only a few people had been entrusted with her number—just her family, a couple close friends, and a few coworkers from Laclede. She didn't want to believe that any of them were suspect, but whoever it was, she wanted to know.

In the second week of the battle the attack opened on a new front. Gayle came home after work, pulled an envelope from her mailbox, and unfolded a white paper on which letters cut from a magazine spelled out "Be Careful." When she walked outside the next morning she discovered a broken antenna on her new car.

An Alton police officer listened to her story but wasn't convinced that all the events were connected. Broken antennas were not uncommon, he said; teenage vandals were usually to blame. He wrote a report on the incident but offered little hope of being able to do more than that.

The third week brought a continued barrage of phone calls, and another envelope as well. The white paper was the same, the letters were pasted as before, and the warning varied only slightly: "Watch Out." The next day her car tires were slashed.

This was not random vandalism, she insisted to a sergeant who was assigned to the case; she had been targeted by someone. The sergeant, a middle-aged, fatherly man, agreed. "Have you spurned a boyfriend?" he asked.

"No," she said.

"Can you think of anybody who might do this?"

"There's a guy at work," she began. "We don't get along very well." But when she heard her accusation she couldn't let it stand. "I don't know if he would do anything this crazy," she added.

But then peculiar things began to happen at Laclede Credit Union. A Twinkie that Gayle was saving for a coffee break disappeared from her locker; its remnants turned up in her desk drawer, crumbs and cream smeared over her papers.

Another day her lunch bag was flattened, smashed as though someone had repeatedly and furiously stomped on it. Without naming names she showed the battered sack to the manager. Probably a practical joke, he said.

The third message in her mailbox had a sense of immediacy that Gayle hadn't felt in the first two. The letters, looking incongruously cheerful in their glossy, bright colors, spelled out "Someone Is Watching You."

It was a possibility she could not deny. He's in the building across the lawn, she thought, and he could be at his window right now, laughing as he sees me read this. The phone rang as she opened her door, and a quaver in her "hello" exposed her helplessness. She was too upset to dial the seven; she dropped the receiver on its cradle and stared at the colorful threat in her hand.

The warning words echoed ominously the next morning as Gayle looked at her car. It was her treasure, a copper-colored Ford Elite, the first brand-new car she had ever owned. It had survived the broken antenna and the slashed tires with its newness intact, but now scratches ran the length of its side, a series of deliberate scratches, not the kind that would result from an accident. He *was* watching, she *knew* he was, and she was determined not to let him see her cry. She held her head high as she returned to her apartment to call the police.

It had to be Rob Sims, she told the sergeant. It was impossible not to suspect him. He had her phone number. He was within arm's reach of her desk drawers and her office locker. He lived in the apartment building across the lawn, giving him quick and easy access to her car.

"Has he said anything to you?" asked the sergeant. "Has he made a pass at you? Has he made any threats?"

"No," she replied. "It's just that he's always *there,* wherever I am. At work, at home, everywhere."

"But that's exactly where he's supposed to be, isn't it?" asked the perplexed officer. Proximity did not warrant action, he explained. He needed evidence. "Maybe you'd feel better if you got a gun and learned to use it," he suggested.

"I could never shoot anybody," Gayle protested.

Instead she carried a baseball bat whenever she left her apartment, and she advised friends not to visit. "I won't answer the door," she said. She had become a prisoner in her own home, and even there she was unable to escape the endless, nerve-shattering ringing of the phone.

"Keep dialing," said the sympathetic voice at Illinois Bell. "We're trying."

When Gayle arrived at the office she had to study the multicolored mound on her desk before she knew what it was, or rather what it had been. Nothing important or valuable, just a yarn teddy bear, a fluffy pom-pom creation that a friend had given her. It looked as though it had exploded. There was nothing left but a pile of string. She sat before the tangled mass, her head in her hands, as Rob walked in. "Goddamn!" he said. "What happened here?"

She gathered the yarn and walked to the lunchroom, two of her coworkers following behind. "It's him," Gayle said. "I know it's him. I know it!" Other women in the office agreed with her conclusion, but the sergeant was right; there was no real evidence. Rob was, if anything, more than usually polite, smiling blandly as their paths crossed throughout each day. He was always where she was, but that was where he would naturally, reasonably be.

Sometimes Gayle's anger and frustration mounted to the point where she couldn't continue to sit across from him, seeing the benign smile behind the red beard and hearing his low, droning words as he spoke on the phone. She picked up her typewriter and carried it to a far corner of the counter.

Gayle learned to steel herself whenever she saw the block printing that addressed a new mailbox threat, but nothing could have prepared her for the contents of the final envelope. She gasped as she looked at the *Playboy* centerfold. A gorgeous nude woman, but her breasts were gone, hacked away by jagged cuts, and her pubic area had been ravaged by slashes. What was left of her body lay incongruously across the pages, seductive smile, smooth skin and long legs, their implied invitation contradicted by the desecration of her sexuality. The pasted-on prophecy stopped Gayle's breath: "This could happen to you."

Her mother insisted that she take the threatening messages to the postmaster. Together they presented the evidence: the envelopes, the colorful letters glued to white paper, the mutilated centerfold.

The postmaster could offer nothing but concern, for the careful block printing on the envelopes gave no clue to the writer's identity. The postal service would attempt to follow up, he said, but identification of the sender was "a long shot."

Gayle considered herself at war. She could have disconnected the phone, but dialing the seven was her only weapon. She could have stayed with her parents, but she rejected any move that connoted retreat. She intended to fight, even if fighting meant frustrated dialing and cautious inspections of her car and her desk drawers.

With both home and workplace under assault, her only comfort was in escape to some neutral ground. She tried to keep busy with other women from the office, going to dinner, watching a movie, or choosing Christmas presents, but eventually she had to go home.

As she approached her apartment building at the end of an evening's shopping the black spray-painted letters seemed to leap from her door: "FUCK YOU." She froze on the sidewalk, her holiday purchases clutched to her chest.

The stakes had been raised. He had come to her door to

deliver this message. He had abandoned the buffer of the postman, had relinquished the remoteness of the telephone, had stepped away from the public acts of vandalism and come to her threshold.

And then a terrifying realization took root in her mind: he might have pushed *beyond* the door. He could be inside, behind a couch, under a bed, in a closet, waiting to do to her what he had done to the woman in the centerfold.

She went to her neighbor's apartment to call the police. "It has to be him," she told the sergeant. "He heard us talking at work. He knew we were going shopping. He knew I'd be coming home late."

When officers had gone she covered the offending words with newspaper and lay through the hours with her baseball bat at her side, alert to any sound of intrusion. In the morning she waited until she saw him leave before she rubbed out the spray-painted letters with steel wool.

In the sixth week of the reign of terror, on an evening just before Christmas, Gayle's phone rang once more. She anticipated the silence and prepared to dial the seven. Instead she heard the sergeant's voice. "You were right," he said. "It's a phone listed in the name of Robert Sims."

When Terri saw the officers coming up the walk her first concern was for the marijuana. There was a supply in the apartment, as always. She made sure it was hidden before she opened the door.

She was arrested and charged with making two harassing phone calls. If Rob had been home, he might have been arrested, too, for the police had no way of knowing which of them had done the dialing.

Terri considered confessing her willing effort to aid Rob's retribution against the "bitch" at work, the woman he hated. It required only a few seconds each time she passed the phone to call the number he had provided. At nineteen, she had chosen to think of the daily dialing not as harassment but as sophisticated mischief, a stealthy ritual that pleased her husband, a shared secret that united them.

She considered telling the officers that she knew about

some of the vandalism done to Gayle's new car. That couldn't be classified as mischief, of course; she didn't know how to explain that things had just spiraled out of control. She considered all kinds of explanations during the ride to the police station, but in the end she kept quiet. She didn't think anyone would understand; she didn't understand it herself.

"I don't know why I did it," she sighed, even after she had had years to consider. "I guess I did it because he told me to. I can't think of any other reason. I didn't think for myself in those days."

So Terri told the police as little as she could. She simply admitted that she had made the two calls the phone company had managed to trace. From the Alton jail she phoned Rob, who was at a dinner meeting of the Illinois Credit Union League. Rob asked Harrol Cannedy, his boss, who was there also, to lend him a hundred dollars. "Sure," said Cannedy. "What for?"

"To bail my wife out of jail," he replied.

The next morning Terri faced a judge. She made the two calls, she said, because she found a phone number on a piece of paper in her husband's pocket and wanted to know whose number it was. She was fined $102.

Gayle Allard knew better. Not all those calls, those long silences. Not for weeks and weeks. Those calls were not from Terri, trying to identify a phone number. That made no sense. The mutilated picture in the mail. The spray-painted vulgarity on her door. All those things done to her new car. The Twinkie smeared in her desk. Terri hadn't done that. "It wasn't her," Gayle said. "It was him."

But there was nothing she could do to prove it. Terri had taken the blame for the two calls that officially existed, and that was that. The Simses still lived next door. Rob's desk still faced hers.

Gayle spent the Christmas holidays with her parents and looked for another apartment. At work, things were more complicated. She had a good job, and she didn't want to leave it, but Rob had worked there longer, and, legally, he had done nothing wrong. "Why did you have her *arrested?*" Harrol Cannedy, the Laclede manager, asked Gayle. Rob had explained it all to him, he said. Terri was just young and insecure. She found the phone number and figured Rob might be seeing another woman. Rob wasn't responsible; he just had a crazy, jealous wife.

Gayle told Cannedy about the weeks of phone calls, the trap on her line, the vandalism. He said there could be two sides to the story, and he didn't want the problem to affect the work of the office.

Gayle couldn't report back to her desk. She couldn't sit across from Rob, believing that he had made the calls, that he had vandalized her desk and her car and her door, that he had sent her a threatening, mutilated picture—especially when the boss seemed to blame *her,* rather than Rob, for the emotional upheaval. She asked for a two-week leave of absence, without pay, while she looked for another job.

But other women in the office who had witnessed her six-week, day-to-day drama were not satisfied with the outcome. One of them interceded, and Gayle received a phone call from a member of Laclede's board of directors. With no real expectations she told her story in complete detail.

To Gayle's relief, Laclede gave Rob a choice of quitting or being fired. He quit, but he managed to leave with a reference from Cannedy, a reference good enough that it got him a job with Olin Credit Union down the street.

11

ROB AND TERRI MOVED TO PIERCE LANE IN NEARBY GOD-
frey, to a house that was rural and secluded, surrounded
by cornfields teeming with mice. Terri insisted on getting
a cat.

The remote location increased her loneliness. Evenings
and weekends Rob expected her to be at home, yet he paid
little attention to her. He worked on his cars, accumulating
tools to refinish their exteriors and adding a '57 Ranchero to
his ever-changing inventory. She cleaned so much and so
often that, years later, she would shake her head in disbelief.
"I can't emphasize the cleaning too much," she said. "It was
the *most* important thing to Rob."

The steak house frequently called, requesting that she
work a weekend shift. Each time she said, "No, sorry," until
a Saturday when the manager asked her to work just four
hours. "I can't keep saying no to these people," she explained to Rob, who was tinkering with a car. "You'll be out
here all day anyway." When she came home he met her at
the door, giving her a silent, hard stare until she handed him
the $35 she had made on the short shift.

Her earnings were regularly contributed to their joint funds, but she didn't share the checkbook. She never saw Rob's paycheck and didn't know exactly how much he earned. They did the grocery shopping together; if she needed money for anything else, she had to ask for it. But she didn't ask; she knew Rob would say they couldn't afford it, whatever it was. Nor did she ever give him less than the total she collected in salary and tips; he would have recognized the amount as too little.

Sometimes she thought about the things she didn't have, the clothes and little luxuries. When Rob's sister Linda asked her to be matron of honor at her wedding, Terri wore her own wedding dress, long and pink. With it she wore brown lace-up shoes; they were the only dress shoes she owned.

Linda had lost her excess weight and was slim and pretty when she married Herb Condray, a teacher-turned-photographer who was a couple decades older and had children nearly the age of his bride. Terri was surprised to observe how well Herb got along with Troy Sims, his new father-in-law. The two men enjoyed a camaraderie that she had never seen between Troy and Rob.

Terri had to laugh when she saw the wedding photos. There she was, in a long pink dress and brown shoes. She looked like a middle-aged housewife, not a nineteen-year-old.

For her twentieth birthday she hoped for something lovely, something romantic, a pretty sweater or a bottle of perfume. From her husband she got a hot-dog cooker. From his parents she received a hamburger press.

She was unhappy with Rob's view of her, the view that was reflected in his gift, but she understood that it wasn't the way he saw just her; it was the way he saw all women. "Women had their place," she explained. "They had their purpose. Clean the house, cook the meals."

Sex was something they didn't discuss. If Rob had any sexual fantasies, he didn't share them with her, and she didn't share hers with him. "It was to do, not to talk about," said Terri.

They were on different wavelengths in other areas, too. Terri was increasingly unhappy about Rob's use of marijuana, which was especially heavy on weekends. "It was wake up, roll over, grab a joint. Shower, eat breakfast, smoke a joint." If they planned to go somewhere, Rob wanted a hit before they left. "No, wait," he said as they were about to go out the door. "Let's smoke a joint first."

"It really began to get to me," Terri explained. She blamed the marijuana for her weight gain, more than twenty pounds in the two years she had lived in Illinois. Rob continued to warn her not to get as fat as her sister. She didn't tell him that she had already passed her sister by four pounds.

The disco classes would eventually stand out in her mind as the beginning of the end. Disco was the hot new craze in 1977, and she wanted to take lessons one evening a week. Rob refused to join her. In earlier years that would have ended her plan; but Terri signed up anyway with another waitress from the steak house, a divorcee in her late twenties. In the class they were a "couple," taking turns dancing the man's part. Rob let her know what he thought of the arrangement.

After one of the lessons the two women went to a bar where they drank enough that Terri had to gulp black coffee before she considered herself able to drive. She headed home, wondering what Rob might say, but when she looked at him, sleeping soundly, she realized she no longer cared what he said.

Terri waited until the end of February, just after her twenty-first birthday, before she broached the subject with Rob. She mentioned the possibility of a trial separation, and the discussion was calm. He asked if she wanted to go back to Maine or stay in Illinois and try to support herself. She chose Maine.

To those who asked, Terri explained the marriage's problems in nonaccusatory terms. "We just outgrew each other," she said, always adding that it was a trial separation, that she and Rob hadn't come to any firm decision. She tried to be reasonable, to balance the pleasures and the pain of the past three and a half years. Two months after she left she phoned Rob. "I guess we should go ahead with the divorce," she said.

He filed the papers in June, 1978. She received a second-hand Pontiac and a few household items. He kept five older cars, a camper shell, most of the furniture, and a 380 Beretta. He agreed to repay three credit union loans totaling $5,100; in view of his accepting responsibility for the debts, she requested no alimony.

When the decree arrived Terri was shaken by its finality. She wasn't sure she had done the right thing. She phoned Rob, trying to determine if he was having second thoughts, too. He didn't say much about his feelings, but that was not unusual. He seldom spoke about emotions.

She attempted to find out more from his family. His sister Linda reported that he didn't seem to know "what to do with himself." His mother said he had been "devastated" by the divorce. Their reactions encouraged Terri to propose a reconciliation. "Should we give it another try?" she asked Rob.

"Yeah," he answered, "maybe we should."

He met her at the St. Louis airport at 10 P.M. on a fall evening. There were no commitments, no absolutes. The plan was to take it week by week, to see how things went, to talk, to try to work out their differences. But Terri had come on a one-way ticket. It was all she could afford.

She felt something when she saw him, although she wasn't sure what it was. She had lost weight and hoped he would be pleased, but he didn't mention her figure.

When they got to Pierce Lane Terri was amazed at the changes. A water bed stood in the area that had been an enclosed porch. A lighted aquarium separated porch and living room. It didn't look like the same place she had left six months earlier.

In the morning she discovered the changes went beyond

the furniture. Within an hour after they awoke Rob announced that the reconciliation attempt wouldn't work. "What do you mean?" she asked. "How do you know? I just got here."

"I didn't know what I wanted," he said matter-of-factly, "but now I'm sure. It's over."

"But we haven't even talked," she protested. "What about our plan, taking it week by week?"

"It won't work," he pronounced. "It just won't." He walked out, leaving her bewildered in the isolated house that had once been her home.

She looked through the drawers and closets she used to clean, searching for a clue to the changes. Tucked in a cupboard she found the writings of another woman, notes addressed to no one, just thoughts on paper, an unbound diary.

When Rob returned, Terri asked questions. Was there someone else in his life? And if there was, why had he committed to a reconciliation, even a tentative one? Why had he agreed to her return, encouraged it?

Rob didn't want to talk. He dressed carefully, as though he had somewhere important to go, and left her alone again in the house.

The next day the pattern was repeated. Rob went off to work in the morning and to some unknown place in the evening. "Talk to me," Terri begged as he left. "Show me a little sympathy. Don't do this."

"I was confused," Rob said, standing at the door. "I didn't know if it would work. I can see now that it won't. So just leave. Get out."

But she had no way to leave, unless she managed to start one of the cars that sat in various stages of repair. And she had nowhere to go, for she had never formed any close friendships in the area. She had no choice but to be there when he returned. "Get out," he said again, slowly and quietly. "You're a fat hog. Get out."

Terri called Linda, Rob's sister, and asked for help. She stayed with Linda and her husband Herb while she pulled her shattered emotions together and hoped that Rob might come by for a rational discussion.

She never saw him again.

The notes abandoned in the cupboard were written by Pamela Johnson, a young woman who had begun dating Rob shortly after Terri got into the Pontiac and drove to Maine for the "trial separation." Pam and her infant son Justin lived in a duplex on Spring Street, next door to Acie Miles, a friend Rob had known from his youth.

Justin's father had walked out when Pam was four months pregnant; she shared the duplex with another young woman, depending on public aid to support her child. When the roommate left and Pam couldn't handle the rent by herself, Rob suggested that she live with him. Her first job upon moving in was to help him pack up some of Terri's belongings. Rob said that his marriage had fallen apart when he caught his wife in an affair with a black man, a man whose car he had repossessed while doing his job as a collector at Olin Credit Union.

He wasn't happy with the job at Olin, where he was hired after he left Laclede. He told Pam that the work was too dangerous, that someone had taken a shot at him when he tried to repossess a car. He told Gary Tomlin, his former coworker at Laclede, that he didn't get along with his bosses at Olin and detested all the "old biddies" in the office. In late summer, 1978, he quit.

Little comment was made on his departure at the time it took place, but within weeks a discovery triggered rumors which floated from employees at Olin to employees at Laclede. As was common practice, Olin offered loan applicants the option of insurance that would take over payments of their loans in case of disability or death. The insurance company made such payments directly to the credit union. Rob, who worked in collections, was one of the employees who handled these transactions. He received the insurance company checks, endorsed them with the credit union stamp, and applied them to the proper accounts. But for a brief period prior to Rob's departure, Olin employees learned, just a portion of the insurance payments were credited to the debtors' accounts. When disabled debtors received past-due notices and asked why the insurance company had not covered their payments, the misappropriation came to light. An office search turned up deposit tickets which verified that debtors had been credited with only part of the money they should have received, leaving some $4,400 missing.

Rob denied any wrongdoing, and whatever explanation he gave to management was never shared with the employees at Olin. Officially, the credit union said nothing. Employees were bonded, so there would have been no problem in recovering any missing money; but there was good reason not to report such an incident. By handling the matter quietly, credit union officials could avoid drawing attention to lax security measures and paying increased premiums on their bond insurance. Details of the story passed from one employee to another, and even from one credit union to another, but never became public knowledge.

After he left Olin Rob found work with the Illinois Terminal Railroad. Pam Johnson, who had set up housekeeping with him, discovered that he was perpetually in need of money but believed his explanation: He was stuck with paying off Terri's many charge accounts.

Rob and Pam led a quiet life. She stayed home with her baby. They seldom had company; they never had parties. As always, Rob smoked pot and worked on his cars, fiddling with the engines and using Q-Tips to dab paint on any exterior imperfections.

Sometimes Pam laughed at his strange ways. If she yelled out to the garage to tell him he had a phone call, he never hurried. He sauntered to the house, washed his hands in the bathroom, dried them carefully, and only then picked up the receiver. It was a good thing that the calls were always from his friend Acie, she told him. No one else would wait that long.

Rob and Pam visited Acie and his wife on occasion, but usually they were home together, just the two of them, plus baby Justin. Sometimes Rob let Pam know that he resented the amount of time she spent with Justin in the evenings, playing with him and putting him to bed. "He's a little baby," she protested. "He needs attention. What am I supposed to do?"

More contention centered on Justin's visits to his paternal relatives. Pam insisted that the little boy's father and grandmother had a right to see him. Rob objected, and Pam was sure his objections were grounded in jealousy. "There's no reason to be jealous," she told him. Nevertheless, he was always sullen when she and the baby returned.

She faced a similar reaction whenever she went dancing. It was something she liked to do, and Rob refused to join her, so she went with her sister. "Who did you dance with?" Rob asked when she came home. "Was it a fast dance or a slow dance?" His admonition was always the same: "The only reason a man dances with a woman is because he wants to go to bed with her."

On a weekend morning in the fall of 1978, a few months after she moved into the Pierce Lane house, Pam woke to find that Rob was gone. In the kitchen she discovered her panties tied to the handle of the refrigerator door. She called Acie's house, where she could usually find Rob if he wasn't home. "What's going on here?" she demanded.

Rob said that he could tell by the smell of her underwear that she had been fooling around with someone.

"If you don't trust me any more than that, this relationship will never work," she told him. She packed up baby Justin and found refuge with Kay Hanks, an outgoing woman who rented a huge church-owned house. Kay, a beautician, considered herself "Mom to half of Madison County," and her home was always filled with people—her own four sons, their girlfriends, her stepchildren, and a variety of others, some of whom she met at the Trio Lounge, where she occasionally commandeered the women's restroom and gave haircuts to the boys at the bar. One of Kay's boarders was moving out, so Pam and little Justin moved in.

It was just after Pam vacated the Pierce Lane house,

leaving behind her unbound diary, that Rob told Terri "maybe" they could give it another try.

Immediately after the abortive trial reconciliation with Terri Rob began dropping in at Kay Hanks's laid-back boarding house to see Pam. It hadn't been hard for Pam to become part of Kay's "family." She was twenty-two, the same age as Kay's eldest son, and she was subjected to the same advice and scolding Kay gave her own children, advice often served with a Bible quotation on the side.

When Rob appeared on the scene he, too, was quickly accepted by Kay's free-flowing household, for he was quiet and no trouble to have around. He talked about cars with Kay's sons; he played with little Justin; he let Pam know that he still cared.

Kay listened to his problems. Most of his complaints were about how "dirty" Terri had treated him. She left behind a pile of bills, he said, and she was trying to claim four of his old cars. He asked Kay if he could transfer the car titles to her name until he got everything worked out. She agreed. She had no way of knowing that the Sims divorce had been finalized months before and that Terri had no interest in taking Rob's old cars.

Laying the blame on Terri obscured the real reason for Rob's financial difficulty. He had accepted complete responsibility in the divorce settlement for $5,100 in loans, and he had spent money on a water bed, an aquarium, and other "home improvements." His problems with Laclede and Olin made it unlikely he would find a similar job in any other financial organization. His $6.90-per-hour job at the railroad paid less than he was accustomed to, less than he needed. He soon got out from under the credit union loans by filing bankruptcy. The transfer of titles to Kay protected the automobiles, not from Terri, but from bankruptcy court, a circumvention of the system he had picked up in his experience as a collector.

When Kay lost the lease on the big church-owned house Pam Johnson had to find another place to live. She took young Justin and went home to her parents for a time, but in the fall of 1979, a year after she had found her panties tied to the refrigerator, she moved back in with Rob.

This time they were serious about making it work. Rob supplemented his railroad work with part-time jobs at a Conoco station and a lighting fixtures store. He proposed, and Pam picked out an engagement ring. She considered them to be a family, but when Rob was arrested a few weeks later, in November, 1979, for stealing screwdrivers from a hardware store, he told her nothing about it. He paid $115 in fines and court costs and kept the incident to himself.

Three months after she returned to Pierce Lane Pam left again. On an evening before Christmas she asked Rob to watch Justin, who had just turned two, while she went to a discount store for a last-minute round of holiday shopping. When she returned Rob told her that the toddler had fallen near the wood-burning stove in the living room and had hurt himself on the bricks underneath it. Justin was asleep, and Pam thought no more about the incident until morning, when she removed his diaper. The marks on his bottom didn't look as though they had come from a fall. She dressed the child quickly and took him to Kay Hanks. "What does this look like?" she asked, showing Kay the welts.

"Looks like somebody whipped him," Kay replied.

Rob continued to visit Kay, who followed the biblical admonition of "judge not" and said nothing about the marks on little Justin's bottom. Kay was surprised to see how "shook up" Rob was by Pam's second and final departure, and she offered what consolation she could. "You'll get over it," she advised. "Everything works out eventually."

It was at Kay's house that the lives of Rob Sims and Paula Blew converged. Paula and her friend June Bland liked to tag along with June's cousin, Jennifer Sheppard, when she visited her old friend Kay. Kay's house buzzed with activity, and there were always young people around for the girls to talk to. There was beer and, behind closed bedroom doors, there was pot. Sometimes Rob Sims was there. June and

Paula didn't pay much attention to him, for he was older than they were by seven years, and a little hard to get to know. Usually he was talking cars or playing cards, but now and then he joined them for a joint in one of the bedrooms.

June and Paula met Pamela Johnson, too, for she continued to visit Kay, often bringing little Justin with her. It angered Pam if Rob arrived while she was there. She figured that when he saw her car outside he ought to drive on by. "Why don't you fix him up with Paula?" she said to Kay. "Then maybe he'll leave me alone."

In early 1980 Rob arrived at Kay's house while Jennifer Sheppard was visiting; it was a day she didn't have June and Paula in tow. "I've got an extra ticket," he said, speaking of an upcoming rock concert. He sounded lonely.

"Ask Paula," the women suggested. They knew that she wasn't dating anyone special. "She works at National Food," Jennifer told him, "and if you don't want to phone her, you can just stop in the store and talk to her at the check-out counter."

And that's what he did.

=== 12 ===

Rob and Paula attended the Missouri River Festival, an outdoor rock concert. They swam with friends at Gillespie Lake. They went to a German celebration in St. Louis. They drank a pitcher of beer and danced at a local bar.

"How old is he?" Paula's mother inquired.

"Twenty-eight," Paula said.

"Twenty-eight!" Her mother's tone implied disapproval. "Has he ever been married?"

"He's divorced."

"What does he do for a living?" asked her father.

"He was just laid off from the railroad." She didn't tell them that he had been working part-time at a nearby "head shop," a store that sold drug paraphernalia.

The Blews weren't pleased when Paula announced that she and her new boyfriend were planning to spend a couple days camping in Missouri. "He's not right for you," her mother said. "He's too old." Her father agreed.

Paula went anyway. She and Rob slept in a tent or, when it rained, in his old van. He "tried something" the second night; she rebuffed him. He said he respected her for being the kind of girl who would say no.

"Do your parents like me?" he asked.

She felt the relationship should be built on honesty. "No," she admitted, "they don't."

"What's the matter?" he bristled. "Don't they think I'm good enough for you?"

"Nobody would be good enough for me," she said. "I'm the only daughter. I'm the baby. Nobody would be good enough."

Rob turned sad when he talked about his marriage to Terri. She'd had an affair with a black man, he told Paula. It was the same story he had given Pam, but the account acquired new details. Terri had cleaned every penny out of their joint savings account, Rob said, and had used the money to buy her black lover a Harley-Davidson. "She was nothing more than a whore. When I kicked her out she went crazy." He said she had broken the windshield on his Ranchero, cut its tarp with a knife, sliced its tires, and taken a shot at him. "She woulda come crawlin' back to me if I let her. But if she woulda come, I woulda kicked her." He turned away, his face set in anger.

Paula was touched by his misery. "I could see how much she had hurt him. I could see how much pain he was in. I knew he had some problems, but I thought it was just from the divorce he'd went through, that he was hurt emotionally. And I knew he had bad feelings a little bit toward his family because they didn't treat him like he thought he should have been treated as he was growin' up, because he wasn't wanted."

His parents had hoped for a daughter, Rob said, to replace a baby girl who had died earlier. They didn't welcome another boy, especially one who wasn't as smart as his older brothers. As a child, he complained, he got hand-me-downs. He had to have a paper route to earn money to buy himself shorts, undershirts, and socks. If there was anything left over, he saved it to buy toy cars.

He needs help, Paula thought; he needs to be cheered up.

His entire persona was a challenge to her: the defeated posture, the long-suffering pose, the sad, faraway look in his eyes, the heavy silences when he didn't want to answer a question. She would make him happy, she decided, or at least less unhappy.

She didn't pretend he was perfect. He dressed badly, in pants that were too short and shirts that didn't match; but that was because he was out of work and low on cash. He was negative about many things, finding fault and casting blame; but that was because he had been hurt by the world. And even if she didn't quite love him the way he was, she would love him as he would become, after she had changed him, after she had molded him into "Mr. Right."

There was never any real proposal. Talk of marriage and children began gradually, casually. She said she wanted a boy and a girl. He said he did, too. She said she had already picked out their names, Randy and Loralei. He said that sounded good to him.

The Blews grew more and more apprehensive about the deepening relationship. "He's too old," her mother cautioned. "He's been married before."

"I don't like a man with a beard and a mustache," her father warned. "He's hiding something."

Even when Rob found a job they weren't placated. "He's not right for you," they told Paula. "He's just not right."

Employment at Alton Box Board (the former name of Jefferson Smurfit) was considered a good deal in the industrialized southern Illinois area. By the time Rob started work there in September, 1980, he and Paula were close enough that he named her beneficiary on his company insurance policy.

The factory's structures sprawled near the riverfront, not far from Laclede Credit Union, where Rob had once worked. The distance between the two employers, however, was the distance between white collar and blue collar, the distance between lunching at a restaurant and carrying an Igloo container into the factory dining room. Rob's brothers, his role models, were men with college degrees and respected positions; he had not planned to end up in a paper plant.

Rob surprised Paula with an engagement ring for Christmas. It was nothing spectacular, a single small diamond. She didn't want anything bigger; she was afraid she might lose it.

The Blews renewed the arguments they had been offering unsuccessfully for months. Each objection they raised made Paula more determined. "I'm gonna marry him," she vowed.

"You'll be sorry," her mother declared.

"He's not good enough for you," her father protested. "Can't you see that? He's not good enough for you, Paula."

When their pleading had no effect they tried coercion. "We won't pay for the wedding," they announced.

"That's fine," she shot back. "You don't have to. I got my own money."

June and Rhonda, Paula's high-school friends, were surprised when they learned of her wedding plans. Not that they didn't expect her to marry eventually (marriage was the goal of most girls they knew), but their contacts with her had ebbed. Rhonda was caring for her frail child and working into family life with her husband. June, after the sleeping-pill fiasco, had gone to live with her mother in a nearby town while she tried to get her life together. With Rhonda busy and June gone, Paula's tenuous support network had evaporated. Rob Sims stepped into her life and became her focal point.

Once again he had found a younger woman with an emotional void in her life. It was a pattern he had started five years earlier when he met sixteen-year-old Terri, who was struggling in the emotional vacuum of her brother's death and her mother's grief, and continued with twenty-one-year-old Pam, who was trying to raise an infant after her boyfriend's departure.

It was a pattern he would perpetuate even after his name, and Paula's, had become notorious.

"Will you be my matron of honor?" Paula asked Rhonda. The request brought the two young women back together, and the faded friendship rebounded as they discussed their dresses, the ceremony, and the reception.

In the face of the inevitable the Blews relented. "I'll make Rhonda's dress," Nylene offered.

By the spring of 1981, when Paula was finalizing arrangements, June's life had taken an unexpected turn. Her navy sweetheart, whose absence and failure to communicate had driven her to the sleeping pills, had come home. "I got pregnant in March and got married in April," she explained. On Paula's wedding day June was penniless. Her returned boyfriend, now her husband, had been unable to find a job; she was working as a shampoo girl. She had no money for a wedding gift, no money to buy herself something to wear. She stayed home.

The wedding was held on May 2, 1981, at a Baptist church whose minister did not know Paula or Rob but who thought they seemed to be sincerely in love. Dennis, Paula's brother, was Rob's best man. The reception took place in the church basement immediately after the ceremony.

"It happened so fast," Rhonda said. "She met him. She got married. And everything was fine. For a while."

"We got into our first argument on our honeymoon," Paula recalled. "We went to Daytona Beach. We were gonna go swimmin' and enjoy ourselves. I got on my bathing suit, and he said, 'Where do you think you're goin'?'

"I said, 'We're gonna go swimmin', aren't we? The ocean's right out there.'

"He said, 'You're not leavin' this room in a two-piece bathin' suit. I told you to buy a one-piece.'

"I said, 'I got a one-piece in my suitcase. I'll put that on.'

"Then he said I couldn't leave there without puttin' on shorts over my one-piece. He didn't want nobody lookin' at me, that's what he said. He wasn't about to let nobody look at me. I married him. I was his.

"But when we got back to the room he wanted to take a picture of me in my one-piece bathing suit, *without* any shorts on, but wearing his cowboy hat. And I refused. So we got in an argument."

There were more arguments after the honeymoon, usually about the Blews. Rob objected to Paula's visits with her parents; their failure to welcome him into the family was not forgotten or forgiven. "They're history," he told Paula. "You married me."

He agreed to visit his in-laws only on special occasions, and he made the guidelines clear to Paula: "We're going to stay an hour. And *you* say it's time to go. Don't make me be the one to say it." Determined to avoid contention, she kept an eye on the clock and, at the prescribed time, announced, "Well, we gotta get goin'."

His family was treated with equal reserve. "They never gave a damn about me," he explained. "I'm the black sheep. Jerry's a doctor and Tom's an artist, and I'm stuck working in a factory." When a birthday or holiday made a visit mandatory he forewarned Paula, "Don't ever be left alone with my dad. Don't let him hug you. Don't let him touch you."

As family ties loosened the newlyweds built a life apart. An answering machine screened their calls. Rob might pick up the phone if he heard the voice of his friend Acie, but few others got his attention. As long as Rob was in the house Paula let the machine take messages from her family; she called back when she was alone, after he had gone to work. She visited alone, too, and disguised the fact by leaving for her job a little early or coming home a little late. "I started lyin' to him so I wouldn't have to face the consequences. He didn't want me to see my family. He talked about my mom terrible. And they went out of their way to be nice to him, after we got married, but he treated 'em so bad."

If he discovered one of her furtive visits, his temper exploded. "He was jealous of my parents. One time he chased me, and I locked the door on him. He said, 'Open that door!' He was cussin' me out.

"And I said, 'If you hit me, I'm gonna leave you.'

"He said, 'Open up this door.'

"I said, 'You promise you're not gonna hit me. I'll leave you if you do.' I opened the door, and he stood there and looked at me, and then he turned and punched a hole in the wall. We just hung a picture over it.

"He told me later, after he got high, he said, 'Did you mean that?'

"I said, 'I meant it. If you ever hit me, I'll leave you.'

"When I look back on it, I wish he woulda hit me."

Paula said little about Rob's extraordinary housekeeping demands. She couldn't complain to her parents, for they had warned her not to marry him.

She told friends that she and Rob were in no hurry to have children. There were things they wanted to do first: purchase a house, take some vacations together. As long as both of them were working—Rob at the paper plant and Paula at the supermarket—the modest dreams were real possibilities.

They purchased three-wheelers and spent weekends riding at Flat River. Rob was cautious and protective of his machine, which was outfitted with special hand grips and mag wheels, so gussied up those who saw it began to call him "Hollywood Bob." Paula, on the other hand, was daring, searching for rugged terrain, climbing the steepest hills. After she had braved a challenging trail with other riders she found him sulking back at the campsite, furious that she had outshone him. "Cut it out," he demanded, "or we're going home."

The Simses' comparative affluence separated them from Paula's old friends. Rhonda and June had babies to consider. They couldn't afford the things that Rob and Paula could, and they felt the disparity even if they didn't speak of it. "Rob and Paula had snowmobiles and other adult toys; they had things you don't get if you have children," Rhonda explained. "In our minds they were well off while the rest of us were struggling."

Behind the appearance of prosperity, however, was a couple surviving, as Rob's parents always had, on the financial edge. The "toys" they enjoyed and the marijuana they smoked stretched their budget to its limits. They had what they needed, but they lived from paycheck to paycheck.

Rob earned good wages at Jefferson Smurfit, but he hated his job. The factory was dirty, he complained, overrun with cockroaches. He was stressed out from trying to keep track of the many gauges at his work station, especially since other men slept on the job and left all the responsibility to him. He faced possible danger from asbestos within the plant. He aggravated his bad back by pushing bales of paper. As his complaints escalated his record accumulated notations of "excessive absence."

He applied at Shell and Explorer. Orville, trying to mend the rift in the family, attempted to get him a job at Amoco. He wasn't hired. The best he could do was rotating shifts at the paper plant, a routine that left him weary and disgruntled.

Paula worked flexible shifts also. Sometimes her hours coincided with Rob's; sometimes they didn't. The schedule allowed her some independence, in terms of both money and time. She earned more than $10 an hour, and although nearly all of her salary was used to cover joint expenses, she had a small savings account. She could squeeze in short visits with friends and family on her way to or from National. As long as she was clever, Rob didn't know.

A few new friends came into their life, people like Dave and Linda Heistand, who ran a local water bed store. Sometimes they met for a card game or a barbecue on a weekend evening.

The marriage settled into a routine. Rob and Paula bought a house, conveniently located for both his job and hers, but soon decided the purchase had been a mistake. The basement was wet, and the property line didn't run where they thought it did. Months of persistent objections were necessary before the bank rescinded the contract and refunded the down payment. They chose instead the secluded bungalow near Brighton, in Jersey County.

Paula was fired just as they were about to move. "I tried to help out somebody that was in a big bind. Her husband was laid off, and they was on food stamps. I got caught at it. It was okay with Rob. He said he didn't care. We was talkin' about having a baby, and I was gonna quit anyway if I got pregnant."

She told her friends the truth about her firing but lied to her parents. She had quit, she explained to her mother and father, because standing at a cash register all day was too hard, especially in light of a severe leg cut she had suffered in a childhood swimming accident.

Paula picked out the Jersey County bungalow. Its privacy and rusticity pleased her, even though its location would increase her distance from family and friends. "I thought I'd be able to handle the situation, 'cause Rob would be goin' to work, and then I could be myself while he was gone. I'd be able to talk on the phone; I'd be able to have people over. And when he was home I'd have the pot, I'd have the marijuana, so I could tolerate it. And I thought as long as I had that, and as long as I had him leavin' regular to go to work, I would be okay. I would be okay, don't you see?"

══ 13 ══

"THIS IS A DANGEROUS PLACE FOR KIDS," SAID PAULA'S MOTHER the first time she saw the Brighton home. "Look at that pond. They could drown."

"Rob will put a fence up," Paula assured her. "This will be a great place for kids."

The new house placed Paula fifteen miles from family and friends. She no longer made a daily journey to work, so she couldn't sneak a visit as she was coming or going. The trip to Brighton required a dependable car, and neither Rhonda nor June regularly had one. The Blews came only when specifically invited, which was seldom. Rob's mother and father almost never came, for Bernie Sims's health and appearance had deteriorated to the point where she rarely left her house; "tent" dresses failed to camouflage her obesity, and moccasins could barely contain her swollen feet. Once in a while Rob's sister Linda stopped by, but Rob and Paula had little contact with aunts, uncles, and cousins in the Sims family. When some occasion brought everyone together Paula was subdued and reserved. Family members judged her to be "plain" and "mousy."

Paula no longer had any money of her own. Her name was on the joint checking account, but Rob gave her only one blank check, to be used in case of an emergency. When she drove to Alton or Cottage Hills to see friends or family he grumbled about wear and tear on the car and the high cost of gasoline. If she complained about her isolation, he reminded her that she had chosen the location.

Her duty was to keep the house spotless inside and out, to plant a garden, to cook his dinner, pack his lunches, wash his clothes, and listen for his arrival. Her companions were the pet dogs; there were Brittany spaniels first, but they proved too noisy, barking at whatever they heard in the woods. They were replaced by a collie, Shadow, who was quieter.

Rob gave Paula a BB gun for Christmas so she could shoot stray dogs that foraged on the property, but her fondness for animals prevented her from using it. The owner of the adjoining acreage suggested that she take aim at the muskrats that abounded along the edges of the pond, but she didn't like to do that either.

One day Rob took a shotgun to a muskrat; he returned to the house immediately, visibly upset. "I killed it," he said. "I haven't killed anything since Vietnam."

"You had to kill somebody in Vietnam?" Paula asked.

"Yeah, either kill or be killed," he explained. "I didn't want to do it, but I had to. My best buddy got blown away right in front of me."

He told her of Vietnamese kids with hand grenades who had to be shot before they threw their grenades and killed his entire unit. "He was just a nervous wreck after he shot that muskrat," Paula recalled. "He said, 'I've gotta smoke a joint.'" She didn't know he had never been in Vietnam.

Sometimes they went camping or to stock car races. They seldom ate at a restaurant. They never attended movies. Marijuana was the only thing certain to get them out of the house. "He was so tired when he worked," Paula said. "When he had days off he wanted to stay home, unless we went somewhere to get some pot." Occasionally they were invited to a party, a mellow, beer-drinking, joint-smoking gathering at the home of friends.

She smoked daily, as much as he did, and preferred to scrimp on groceries or forgo a dental appointment rather than allow the supply to run low. Marijuana was a budgeted expenditure, their chief form of entertainment.

While smoke drifted hazily around them Rob shared his idea of Utopia: "I'd like to be on a deserted island, me and you, and have a supply of pot that never runs out. That's all I want."

As their connections with family and friends waned Paula and Rob became, in the judgment of many, "loners." For weeks and months it was just the two of them in the house at the end of the long driveway, the fussy, malcontented factory worker and his once-spirited wife, living a clouded version of the American dream.

Rob organized his tools and tinkered with his cars but, as far as Paula could tell, didn't accomplish much. "Him and his cars, oh! They never run, they just sat there and rusted. When we mowed the lawn I had to help move 'em. He hooked 'em up with a chain to the truck while I steered 'em. And then he would jump on me 'cause I didn't turn the wheel just right. I didn't get the car exactly sittin' in the right spot in the yard. It had to be just so, not an inch forward or an inch back. Finally he would say, 'Just go inside. I'll do it myself.'" She did, anxious to avoid an argument; she was certain that the neighbors, a hundred yards away, heard the fighting.

"He used to tell me I was stupid. That started shortly after we got married, just about little piddly stuff. He'd say, 'You're *so* stupid.' Then it got to be his IQ compared to my IQ. He said, 'What's your IQ?'

"I didn't know what my IQ score was, and he laughed at me. I told him, 'I think it's about ninety.' You see, I thought a hundred was the best. That was before he told me what his was.

"He said, 'Well, you *are* stupid. That's an illiterate person.' He said his IQ was 130, genius level.

"I said, 'Well, at least I have common sense.'

"He said, 'What's that supposed to mean? Are you saying I got no common sense?'

"I said, 'I didn't say that.'

"He said, 'Well, shut up. Just shut up.'

"After a few years I got to believin' it. When something would go wrong, something I did, I'd say, 'Well, I'm stupid.'

"And he'd say, 'You sure are.' "

On the bad days, the solitary, lonesome days when she thought about leaving, she remembered her stupidity. She remembered that she had been fired from the only real job she had ever had. She remembered that her parents had warned her not to marry him.

Stella Hyatt was turning over the soil in her spring garden the first time she met Paula, who passed by on her way to the mailbox, accompanied by Shadow, the collie she introduced as her "baby." A few days later Paula tapped on Stella's front door. "Hi," she called. "Are you busy?" The two women spent the afternoon in Stella's kitchen, talking about their houses, their gardening, and their needlework.

After that Paula made frequent appearances, their timing determined by Rob's schedule. If he was working days, she came two or three times a week and stayed until she or Stella glanced at the clock and noticed that they had talked another afternoon away. "I think she must be a very lonely person," Stella told her husband. When Rob rotated to swing shift or graveyard shift Paula's visits were curtailed. If Rob was home, she was home.

Paula never invited Stella to return the afternoon visits. At first the lack of invitation seemed odd, but then Stella grew accustomed to the routine. She waited for Paula's knock on the door and enjoyed having her young neighbor sitting in her kitchen, just like the daughter she had always wanted.

It was difficult for Stella to form an opinion about Rob. He never visited, but when he learned that the Hyatts were rebuilding a collapsed retaining wall he drew plans for it and helped Marvin Hyatt haul railroad ties. The most Stella could say was that he seemed to be a good neighbor, someone who minded his own business and expected others to do the same.

His desire for seclusion was apparent. A "Private Drive" sign went up at the end of the lane soon after he moved in, and he consistently refused to let fishermen hear "his" side of the pond, although the water was actually on someone else's property.

It was equally apparent that Paula didn't share his desire for isolation. If Stella mentioned teenage gatherings that had been part of the lives of her sons, Paula wanted to hear all the details. "Your kids must have been so happy," she said. When the topic turned to relatives assembling for the holidays, Paula's response was wistful: "I wish things could be like that for us."

The absence of family in the lives of the Simses was evident to Stella. Rob's mother was physically unable to do anything but watch TV and read magazines, Paula said, and lack of activity had caused her to become so grossly over-weight that Rob didn't want to look at her. "I have to *make* him go to see her," she confided.

Her own mother couldn't be burdened with any problems, she explained. "I can tell you things I can't tell my mom," Paula said to Stella. "My mom is just, well, nervous."

For Paula, the good days were the days when both she and Rob stayed blissfully high. "He had two different sides to him. When he was high, which was ninety-nine percent of the time, he was okay. Mostly he worked on his cars. I was thankful when he was out there, 'cause then I didn't have to be around him. I didn't have him on my back."

When they planned a trip throughout the southwest she rolled joints for days before their departure. They smoked even as they climbed down the trail into the Grand Canyon. The pot, combined with beer and *asti spumante,* her favorite wine, kept them placid and affable. They argued only about the driving. He said she traveled too fast; she said he drove "like an old lady."

"He's a good provider," Paula said whenever Rhonda or June asked about her marriage. They kept in touch by phone, but the calls were infrequent.

"When you gonna have some babies?" June demanded. "You're gettin' too old. You better be havin' some babies."

In the spring of 1985, when Paula turned twenty-six, the Simses agreed that it was time. Paula talked things over with her doctor, who advised her to stay off birth control pills for six months before attempting conception, just to be sure there would be no residual ill effects on the baby. She kept a chart of her temperature to find her most fertile days.

"We're trying to start a family," she confided to Stella.

"What do you want?" Stella asked. "A boy or a girl?"

"We'd like to have a boy first," Paula said.

"Well, you know the old saying," Stella cautioned. "You have to take what you get."

As Rob and Paula were trying to bring a new life into the world Rob's mother, Bernie, was leaving it. "When she got real sick, toward the end, Rob would go see her every day. It was a total change, because before that she would call and cry and want him to stop by. She begged me, 'The next time you're in town, please, please.'

"And I could only say, 'Well, I'll tell Rob.'

"But he said, 'Forget it. I'm going to make them suffer the way they made me suffer. They want me now, but when I was little, when I wanted them, where were they?'

"On her deathbed he started feelin' guilty about how he had treated her. That's when I was almost sure I was expecting, because I was startin' to feel real queasy. I said, 'Let's tell your mom.'

"He said, 'No, we're not sure you're pregnant. I don't wanna tell her when we're not sure.'

"I said, 'Don't you want her to know before she passes?'

"And he jumped all over me. He said, 'She's not gonna pass. She's not gonna die. She's gonna make it.'

"On her deathbed she called him 'Bobby Blue Jeans.' He started cryin'. He said, 'I know she's gonna die. I don't want her to die.'

"But she passed. I was with her right before she went. She was scared." Bernie died in October, 1985, and was buried in a coffin selected to accommodate her large size.

Her death affected Rob enough that he loosened the strictures on Paula's visits to her parents. He said she could make the trip to Cottage Hills whenever she wanted.

"But that didn't last long. He was gettin' ready to go to work one day, and he said, 'What are you gonna do today?'

"I said, 'I thought I'd go see my folks.'

"He said, 'You just seen them a couple days ago.'

"I said, 'Well, I got everything done around here, and they'd like to see me. My mom would like me to go shopping or something.'

"He said, 'No, you were just there.'

"I was upset. I said, 'But *you said* you weren't going to keep me from my parents anymore.'

"He said, 'No. You're staying home. I'm gonna call later and check on you.'"

She caved in to his demands. "I let him run my life. I despised that. After the years it just got worse and worse, and I despised it worse and worse. But I just went along with it. I knew when he was gone I could pretty much do my own thing, but I still had to answer to him. I thought I had to live like that. And then, too, I always thought things was gonna get better."

It was a baby, she believed, that would change things. A baby would make the difference.

Stella could tell by Paula's smile that the visit to the doctor had brought good news. "You're pregnant, aren't you?" she asked.

"I sure am!" Paula beamed. Her head was filled with plans. "We'll take the baby camping with us," she said. "And isn't it a good thing that the school bus runs right by the house?"

Pregnancy lessened Paula's isolation, for doctor's checkups gave her an excuse to travel again. She always stopped to see June, who discovered a few weeks later that she herself was pregnant. Talk of baby preparations highlighted each visit. Paula told June about the Lamaze classes that she and Rob attended. She described the stroller Rob had purchased, and the automatic baby swing. The crib came from Rob's father; it was the one that had been used by Rob and his brothers and sister.

The diapers, powder, lotions, and bottles were checked by Stella Hyatt, who was at last invited to the Sims home, at an hour when Rob was at work. The house looked as Stella knew it would, cozy and neat, and the supplies were abundant. She could think of nothing else that Paula should buy.

Names had been chosen, Paula said. A boy would be Randall Troy, Randall for her brother and Troy for Rob's father. A girl would be Loralei Marie, Marie because it was her middle name, and her mother's, and her grandmother's; Loralei (with a slight variation in the spelling of the song title) because it was what she had always wanted to name a daughter.

"I wish you'd had a boy like Rob wanted. Do you know how much this girl is gonna cost you? A boy, you can put a pair of shorts on him and let him run. Girls are real expensive." Although she should have expected it, Paula was hurt by Troy Sims's reaction to his new granddaughter.

"Come on," Paula said. "I'll walk with you down to the nursery. You'll see how beautiful she is."

Everyone else who visited agreed that she was indeed a beautiful child. Her hair was red; her skin was creamy; her eyes were bright blue.

Paula wasn't sure how she was supposed to feel after giving birth. She assumed her reactions were normal, although she couldn't sleep for more than an hour or two at a time. She couldn't eat. She couldn't stop smoking, even though she had assured her hospital roommate that she would abstain. "Even in the hospital I was so nervous. I felt like I was just goin' a hundred miles an hour. Had all these things I wanted to do. I was on the phone constantly, sharin' my great news. I was just so happy, and so excited.

"My mom said, 'Paula, you need to calm down. You're too wound up.'

"And I said, 'Well, I'm *happy!* I got this beautiful baby. I'm just so *happy!*'"

Rob drove his wife and infant daughter home in his new silver Jeep, traveling so slowly that a trail of cars behind him honked their horns. He had placed a "Baby on Board" placard in the Jeep's back window.

The Blews visited. Paula let her brother Dennis hold Loralei for a few minutes, sitting beside him as he cradled his niece.

"That was a dumb thing to do," Rob said after his in-laws had gone. "He could have had one of his fits. He could have dropped her."

Other friends dropped by. "Don't pass her around," Rob warned Paula. "She's not a piece of meat."

Stella Hyatt came, bringing a delicate infant dress. Rob was somewhere on the floor above when Paula deposited Loralei in Stella's waiting arms. When he came halfway down the stairs his reproachful look was enough to make her reclaim the infant and place her in the bassinet.

"Did you tell her to go in the bathroom and wash her hands first?" he asked as soon as Stella had gone.

"No," Paula admitted.

"Well, then her hands weren't clean, Paula," he scolded. "She could have pulled a weed on her way over here. She could have petted her dog. You don't know what she touched."

Father's Day had been planned even before Loralei's birth, grilled chicken at the Blews' home. On Friday Rob said no. The temperature was too high; the baby would become overheated in the Jeep.

"But my parents have air conditioning," Paula argued.

That would be too cold, he said, especially after the baby had ridden in the hot Jeep. "Do you want our baby to be sick? Then go ahead, take her to see your parents." Paula canceled the festivities.

She called friends for hints on baby care. Was she doing things right? Were Loralei's reactions normal? "I kept thinking, I need to do this, I need to do that. She needs to be fed. I was keepin' an eye on the clock. They said at the hospital, feed her every three hours. If she cried, I picked her up immediately. I was just so nervous. I wanted so much to be a good mother, and then I thought I wasn't gonna be a good mother."

She worried that something might happen to the baby. She studied articles on crib death and crept to the bassinet, watching intently until she saw Loralei's chest rise and fall. If she detected no movement, she laid her hand on the little torso, feeling for a heartbeat.

Her fears kept her awake at night. The thought of food made her sick. She returned gratefully to the marijuana she had given up during pregnancy, but even that didn't assuage her anxiety.

Her tears flowed, about anything, about everything. A mishap in the kitchen or a memory from La Plata. An argument with Rob or a tender moment with Loralei.

Between the worrying and the weeping something intruded, something so dark and obscene that she could never admit it was present. She pushed it away and crammed other concerns in its place, bottles and burping and baths, the right things, the proper things for a young mother to think about.

But it came again when Rob had gone grumbling back to the paper plant, when she wandered through the rooms of her quiet house, when there was no one around to stop her and she could not stop herself.

14

STELLA HYATT OFTEN STOOD AT HER KITCHEN WINDOW, TRANS-
fixed on the brick bungalow at the end of the lane. Another
family had moved in, but Stella couldn't erase her memories. Sometimes she stared so long that her husband Marvin
became concerned. The polygraph results haunted her, for
they confirmed her misgivings about Paula's story. She had
to agree with Sheriff Yocom and the townspeople who knew,
in their hearts, that the truth of the empty bassinet had not
been told. Over and over Stella traced the afternoon conversations she and Paula had shared. Maybe there was a
comment she had missed, a hint that should have told her
something was wrong. Maybe she had misjudged everything, she told Marvin. "Maybe Paula was just trying to stay
afloat."

The six months that Rob and Paula spent with the Blews,
making their headquarters in the basement family room,
took a toll on everybody in the household. "My mom has
always got something wrong with her," Paula said. "That's

just my mom. She's never feeling good. I guess that's why her and Robert never got along, because they're so much alike. My dad even said that one time. They're both complainers. But my parents really tried. They were nice to Rob."

Paula promised Orville and Nylene that she would give up drugs once and for all, and for a couple months she kept her word. Rob, too, swore off, and they rid themselves of much of their drug paraphernalia. Before long, however, they returned to their familiar "weed," using a pinch-hitter, a small wooden box that held one hit and also contained any smoke. The device enabled them to use pot in the Blews' basement without alerting Orville and Nylene. Paula felt she needed drugs more than ever, something to take the edge off her pain, to build a hazy shield over her memories.

On a day when she baby-sat for Sammy Condray, the son of Rob's sister Linda, she discovered a bottle of Valium in a kitchen cupboard. She pocketed a few and felt better just knowing the pills were there, in case she needed them.

She frequently visited June, who lived just two blocks away. June gave birth to her own baby girl, Whitney, and Paula cried as she held the infant. "I don't have one of my own anymore," she said.

In midwinter, after six months with the Blews, the Simses bought a two-story white frame house just a few miles away, on Washington Avenue in Alton. It was an attractive old house with an angled roofline that gave it a whimsical storybook quality. Inside, a circular stairway added to its charm. The natural seclusion that had marked the Brighton home was lacking, but the price was right, and the location was as close as they could hope to get to Jefferson Smurfit.

The Simses set about making the house more private. Within days a five-foot chain-link fence outlined the lawn, and the gate in front had a padlock. In a rear corner that adjoined the schoolyard the chain link was augmented with redwood for even more separation. A deadbolt was added to the front door, and a drafty wood-and-glass back door was replaced with one made of steel. In the backyard a dusk-to-dawn lamp similar to the one that had illuminated the

Brighton driveway was installed. Neighbors watched the changes without comment. Most of them had no idea who had moved into the house.

The few friends and relatives who entered observed more improvements. New draperies supplemented the venetian blinds on the front windows, and reflective film was applied to other windows, film that inhibited the view of anyone looking *in* but did not interfere with the vision of anyone looking *out*. There was a loaded .25-caliber pistol atop a tall chest in the dining room.

The precautions didn't surprise those who knew of them. They thought Rob and Paula were behaving exactly as a couple would if their child had been kidnapped. By the time the alterations were complete, the house was an island of isolation on a busy street.

And the Simses were expecting their second child.

On a weekday afternoon Paula stopped at her parents' house and glanced at the television, where Oprah Winfrey's guests, a panel of young mothers, were discussing the despondency that had descended upon them after the births of their babies. "What's that about?" Paula asked.

"Sit down and listen to it," Nylene suggested, patting the couch beside her.

Paula joined her mother long enough to hear the talk of mood swings, loss of appetite, sleeplessness. As a tearful young woman spoke of visions of killing her infant Paula rose abruptly. "Why don't you find something decent to watch?" she asked.

"Things like this happen," Nylene said.

Something in her mother's tone struck a nerve. "Not to me," Paula announced as she headed for the kitchen. "Change the channel. Get that crap off the TV."

Rob reminded her each day to take her prenatal vitamins. He told her to get out of the kitchen when the microwave was in use. He said she couldn't scrub the bathtub because fumes from the cleanser might hurt the baby.

The obstetrician explained that the fetus hadn't "flipped

over" as it should have and ordered a sonogram to determine if it was in breech position and might require cesarean delivery. The sonogram confirmed his suspicion but offered no indication of the child's sex.

"Turn, please turn," Paula said as she rubbed her stomach. The thought of being cut terrified her. A second sonogram was done in her third trimester to determine more accurately the age of the baby. It was still in breech position, but this time the picture was more revealing. "There's no guarantee," the doctor said, "but it looks like a boy."

The Simses set up barrier gates at the top and bottom of their circular stairway, decorated a bedroom as a nursery, put a baby monitor beside the crib, and bought some clothes for little boys. A cesarean delivery was scheduled for February 8, but Paula's labor began early. She was admitted to the hospital on February 1, during a snowstorm. The doctor surprised her by asking, just before her anesthetic was administered, if she wanted her tubes tied. "Rob and I never talked about that," she said; she declined.

Randall Troy was a healthy red-haired baby. Everyone called him Randy. The Simses' vigilance after the delivery, like the security features added to the new house, perpetuated their stance as wary victims. They declined to announce Randy's birth in the local paper. They turned down the offer of a complimentary picture from Alton Memorial's "stork lady." They asked the hospital staff to keep their newborn away from strangers at the nursery window. "Father requests visitors to not view baby unless they are with him or his wife," a nurse wrote.

Paula told Rob about the doctor's offer to tie her tubes. "Why didn't you?" said Rob. "You should have."

"We never even talked about it," she protested.

"Well, I don't want no more kids," he announced. "I'm gonna get fixed."

"No," she said, "don't do that. Wait until Randy is six months old. I wanna be sure he's gonna be all right."

* * *

150

The Simses were elated when they brought their baby home. Even Rob, a natural pessimist, was full of cheer. He had a son, and a hospital pastor had spoken with him, assuring him that God's love and protection went with the child.

"Paula," he said, "I feel real good."

"Great!" she responded, surprised at his positive energy.

"Nothing's going to happen to Randy," he said. "We're gonna watch him grow up. We're gonna watch him graduate. We're gonna watch him get married. We're gonna have grandkids. Randy's gonna be okay."

"Yeah, he is," she agreed, expressing a certainty she didn't quite feel. "Everything's gonna be all right."

By the time June visited two days later Paula's confidence had an overlay of desperation. "Nothin' is gonna happen to this little baby," she pledged. "Nobody's gonna hurt him. I got a gun, and I know how to use it."

"You can't be livin' like that," cautioned June. "You gotta let your guard down and enjoy your baby." If the comment about the gun was for June's benefit, it was unnecessary; she fully believed the kidnapping story.

"Paula's really worried that something terrible is going to happen to the new baby," June told her husband. "I tried to convince her that nothing like that could ever happen again."

Rob's pleasure in his son altered his attitudes, at least temporarily. He said that friends and relatives could visit. He agreed to attend church with Paula and the baby. He gave her permission to visit her parents whenever she wished.

To a degree he fulfilled his promises. He made fewer objections to visitors, but his concerns about cleanliness made guests, and Paula, uncomfortable. "He had these hangups," she explained. "I had to tell people, before they come in, to take off their shoes. They had to wash their hands. They couldn't come in the house if they was the least bit sick. They couldn't smoke, of course. Finally people wouldn't come over if he was there. They was so uptight. And I was so uptight. I was a nervous wreck."

Rob insisted on fixing the baby's formula himself. "He didn't think I knew how to do it," Paula said. "Or I might get it contaminated with germs from my hands. I knew I was supposed to wash my hands, of course; I'm not stupid. But he didn't think I was smart enough or careful enough. He pretended he was doin' it to help me. 'Here, I'll help you. That way I'm contributing something.' He always washed the formula can off, the whole thing. And every time, he washed the can opener. I was allowed to wash the bottles and boil the nipples, but then he'd say, 'These nipples aren't clean. Boil 'em again.' He just had this thing about being clean."

Rob's attempt at harmony lasted several weeks, weeks that were crucial to the survival of his son, weeks when Paula made a secret, silent pledge as she smoked the joint that started her day: "Nothin' bad is gonna happen to Randy." The dark thoughts were with her again, but they were tempered by the unusual "niceness" from her husband and by her determined belief that his improved attitude portended a better future for all of them.

Randy was protected also by being *Randy*. He carried the name of the brother Paula had lost, the brother whose death made her feel painfully guilty, even though common sense told her the accident was not her fault. Certainly she could not twice bear the blame, real or imagined, for the loss of *Randy*.

The new Randy needed all the protection possible, for he was a difficult, colicky baby. He cried for no reason that was apparent, and his wailing sometimes seemed interminable. Paula asked her mother for advice, but Nylene had none to offer; she had found the tasks of motherhood formidable, almost beyond her endurance. "I don't remember," she said when Paula asked questions. "I don't know what you should do. I don't know how I made it."

The times etched in Nylene's memory were the frightening times. "She just remembers the falls, things like that," Paula said. "She's got 'em written down in the baby book.

She's got all the diseases written down, the measles. She's got when I fell on the concrete and busted out a tooth. She remembers when Dennis and Randy used to try to stretch me between 'em. She remembers when Dennis got me or Randy out of the crib and come walkin' in with one of us. She was petrified. She remembers all those things."

Paula devised her own methods for quieting little Randy's cries. She turned on the vacuum cleaner, for he could sometimes be comforted by its noise. She put him in his baby swing, letting the motion rock him to sleep. She turned on the stereo and danced with him, humming in his ear. But on an exhausting day, when all the tried-and-true methods failed, she forgot the pledge that she made each morning. "He was cryin', and I tried all the things that always could comfort him. He wasn't hungry. His diaper was clean. I had rocked him and just everything. Everything. Everything that I knew to do. I walked with him and sang to him, and he still cried. And then I laid him down, and I yelled at him."

The words she shrieked betrayed the act she had once committed, the act that she had sworn never to commit again: "Shut up, or I'll kill you, too!"

As the threat rang in her ears she grabbed her screaming infant and cradled him in her arms. "I'm sorry, Randy," she wept. "I'll never hurt you. I promise. I promise. I promise."

Rob's pledge of more company and fewer restrictions faded as spring arrived. A single visit to church two months after Randy's birth marked the end of his efforts to make Paula happier. "One day I said, 'I'm going over to my parents after you go to work.'

"And he said, 'You was just over there the other day.'

"And I said, 'But you said I could go over there as long as I had stuff done around here.'

"He said, 'No, I changed my mind.' So there went that down the tubes."

She had seen it happen before, with the promises he had offered after the death of his mother. They were back to their usual routine.

* * *

Both June and Rhonda were surprised when Paula, in a semiregular phone call, said that Shadow had been put to sleep. "But why?" they asked.

"Arthritis," Paula said, explaining that the collie, unable to manage the circular stairway, sat at the bottom of the steps and whimpered. When the arthritis was compounded by intestinal problems Paula called a veterinarian, and Rob loaded the dog into his truck for a final trip.

Paula never told Stella Hyatt that Shadow was gone. She sent birthday and anniversary cards, using her parents' return address even after she had moved to Washington Avenue, as Rob instructed. ("I don't want nobody just dropping in whenever they feel like it.") Occasionally Paula phoned Stella to tell of Randy's progress. "Do you mind if I call you?" she asked.

"No, of course I don't mind," Stella answered.

"There's no one to talk to here," Paula said. "I don't know any neighbors. I'm so lonely. I miss coming down the hill to see you." Stella could tell that she was trying not to cry.

"Paula, you can come see me anytime you want to," Stella soothed. Paula sobbed but forced a deep breath and regained her composure. Their talk turned to the subject of babies. "Paula, I have to say this." Stella was hesitant.

"Yes?"

"About Loralei. You know what the police suspected."

"Yes."

"When this new baby goes to the doctor, any marks on him, anything that could possibly be suspicious, you may as well make up your mind that you'll get a call from a social worker."

"Rob and I talked about that," Paula said.

"I just want you to be prepared. When he falls and gets a bruise you make sure you tell the doctor what it's from."

"I wish I could come and talk to you," Paula repeated.

"Paula, you can come and talk to me anytime," Stella assured her. "You can bring the baby. Anytime."

Paula never came. She called periodically and sent a photo of Randy, but she never volunteered her unlisted phone number. Stella considered asking for it, but a lingering unease about the events of the awful June night two years earlier held her back. She remembered the empty bassinet and the questions still unanswered.

Business as usual at the Sims house meant Paula hurried to the door when she heard Rob's Jeep. "I always met him at the door. I did that even when I had Randy. But then I got jumped on 'cause Randy could catch a cold with the door open.

"If Rob was working swing shift, comin' home at eleven, Randy was already in bed. I'd wait up, or sometimes I'd set the alarm. I'd put Randy to bed at nine o'clock, and I'd set the alarm for ten till eleven, so I would be there to greet Rob when he came home. 'Hello, how was your evening?' All that small talk."

Whatever time Rob arrived, even if it was at the midafternoon conclusion of a day shift, he expected Paula's attention. Randy's need to be fed and changed did not excuse her. "Are you about finished?" Rob asked as she fussed with the baby.

"Yeah," she replied, "in just a minute. I'm gonna get a clean diaper on him."

"Well, I'll be downstairs," he said, nodding toward his basement workshop. He stopped at the doorway. "Paula," he reminded her, *"I was here first."*

The workshop held his tools, laid out in drawers or hung on walls. His "toys" were there, too. "He bought remote control cars that cost over $300. He was always buyin' stuff like that. He must have had over a hundred Hot Wheels, those little cars. He'd say, 'When Randy gets big enough they'll be for him.' But he was doin' that even before we had Randy."

The basement also contained his *Playboy* magazines and a TV set on which he watched his favorite reruns, "Leave It to Beaver" and "Perry Mason." If he couldn't find a program on the regular channels, he viewed something from his collection of porno tapes.

"I tried talkin' to him," Paula said, "but he wouldn't talk.

Sometimes at night, when it got late enough, I'd go downstairs and say, 'Are you comin' up?'

"And he'd say, 'After this is over.' Ninety percent of the time I'd be asleep when he got there."

If Paula went to the grocery store, Rob watched Randy. Otherwise the boy was always with his mother. "Randy didn't have much of a social life," Paula said. "He was afraid of people. Me and Rob took him to church that one time, his first Easter. And then I took him a few other times that Rob didn't know about. Randy would just look around, a little scared, 'cause he wasn't used to people. Rob would always call about one o'clock, if he was workin' days, but by then I'd be home. I'd pick up my mom, and we'd go to church. Then I'd take her home, and I'd make it back just in time for his phone call."

Despite the danger of being found out, Paula became more venturesome as summer arrived and Randy began to show an interest in his surroundings. She planned her day around Rob's phone call from Jefferson Smurfit. "As soon as he'd call, I was gone. Or sometimes I would even leave early and try to make it back before the phone rang. Usually he would call at the same time each day. Sometimes I wouldn't make it in time, and then he'd want to know, 'Where were you?' and I'd say, 'Oh, I was in the shower,' or 'Givin' the baby a bath,' or somethin'. He'd keep callin' till he got me."

Her excursions were simple ones, usually to visit her parents or June, occasionally to stop at a yard sale. She carried the one blank check Rob had given her, but she never used it.

"Sometimes if I was goin' to my parents, I would just *tell* him, if it was a day when I was allowed to go over there. He didn't say I could go very often, not more than twice a week. He wanted me to stay at home, do things around the house, be there for his phone call. That was his rules, and I tried to abide by them.

"But Randy needed to get out. He needed sunshine. He needed to be around other people as much as I did. I didn't like livin' that kind of life, having the shades drawn all the time.

"My mom would come over after Rob had gone to work, or June would, sometimes. But they wouldn't come when he was there, because they had tried that, and they didn't like it. June was ill at ease if he even phoned when she was around, 'cause he'd be sayin', 'What's she doin' there?'

"Of course, I always had to be waitin' when he come from work. If I went anywhere, I had to be sure I got back before he got home. Sometimes he'd check the hood of the car to see how warm it was."

It was an uncomfortable regimen, one that required either obedience or lies, but it might have endured. Randy was healthy and thriving. Paula had passed the crisis point in the obsessions that plagued her after his birth. She felt calmer; her black visions were fading; she was managing motherhood. "Everything *is* gonna be all right," she told herself.

Then, in midsummer, when Randy was less than six months old, she discovered she was pregnant again.

III

Heather

=== 15 ===

Her morning queasiness alerted her. She hadn't yet returned to birth control pills, for she had just had her first
menstrual period since Randy's birth. She thought she was
still "safe."

"Maybe I'm pregnant again," she told Rob.

"You better not be," he said.

He stood waiting at the door as she returned from the
doctor's office. "Well?" he asked.

"We're going to have a baby." She managed a smile,
although she knew what his reaction would be.

"No!!" He didn't speak again for two days.

"He wasn't happy at all," Paula remembered. "Nobody
was. I was the only one that was glad. And my dad.
Everybody else, when I called to tell them the news, they
said, 'What? You're expecting again? You've *got* a baby.'"

Nylene, who had struggled through the upbringing of her
own closely spaced children, could see nothing but trouble
in store for her daughter. "What are you going to do, Paula,
when they both cry at the same time? Which one are you
going to pick up?"

"Oh, Mom, I don't know," Paula sighed. "Whichever one needs me the most, I guess. Depends what they're cryin' about. I don't know what I'm gonna do."

She soon began to experience the same shaky nerves, racing thoughts, and violent morning sickness she'd had with her previous pregnancies. Sometimes she couldn't make it to the bathroom upstairs or to the one in the basement. She vomited in the kitchen sink, holding Randy in her arms.

Rob repeatedly let her know how unhappy he was. "Another kid," he said, shaking his head as he headed for his workshop retreat, where he secluded himself, watching TV, reading magazines, or puttering with his tools.

"Maybe you could finish up some of this stuff," she suggested. Several projects around the old house were incomplete. Some had languished for months, for once the chain-link fence and the one-way film on the windows had assured privacy, Rob lost interest in the home improvements. His fussiness with each detail added hours to any job, and now his annoyance precluded any attempt to finish the work that remained.

"Leave me alone," he said. "I'm tired."

His fault-finding escalated. Many things irked him: the dinners she cooked, the lunches she packed, even her personal hygiene. "He was always on me to wash my hands. And I was washin' 'em. I was washin' 'em so much they was gettin' sore."

Each time Randy fell down, or knocked something over, or cried, Rob found an excuse to resurrect his displeasure. "Listen to him," he said. "And we have to go through all that *again.*"

She waited for him to get used to the idea of another child. "I thought *kids.* They're part of *him.* He can't stay this way. But I should have known."

When Rob's attitude appeared implacable Paula considered divorce. "I remember the last time I mentioned it. He was on me about something. It was at the supper table. I told him, 'I should leave you. I've had it with you.'

"He said, 'Fine. You know where the door is. You take that baby you're carryin', and I'm keepin' Randy.'

"I said, 'Oh, no, you're not keepin' Randy.'

"He said, 'Yes, I am. You can leave anytime, but Randy's mine.'

"I said, 'I'm not goin' nowhere without Randy.'

"He said, 'If you take Randy, I'll find you. And you'll be sorry.'

"I said, 'Is that a threat?'

"And he said, 'No, that's a promise.'

"And fear set in on me. I even remember callin' my mom and cryin' about it, sayin', 'What am I gonna do? I need to get out of this. I can't take it no more.'

"And she said, 'We'd like to help you, Paula, but you know he'll look for you here.' "

With a baby in her arms and another growing inside her, Paula could think of no alternative; she decided to stay where she was.

She told her friends, June and Rhonda, nothing about her unhappiness, but in early fall June met Paula's mother at a neighborhood yard sale. "Hey congratulations!" June called. "Gonna be a grandma again, huh?"

"Yes, I guess so," said Nylene.

"How's Paula doin'?" asked June.

"Well, I don't know," Nylene confided. "I just don't know how long that's going to last. She's getting pretty tired of his ways."

Nylene offered no details, and June was not comfortable asking for any. Instead she phoned Paula and made the question as casual as possible. "How are things?"

"Okay," Paula said.

"How're you and Rob doin'?" June asked, more pointedly.

"Okay," Paula said again.

June was mystified. There was nothing to do but wait and see, she decided.

Rhonda heard her first hint of difficulty when Paula

phoned in December, midway through her pregnancy. "It's all his rules."

"What rules?" Rhonda asked.

"Rules," Paula sighed, *"rules,* rules about everything." Her voice trailed off as though she wasn't completely concentrating.

"What are you talking about?" Rhonda persisted. "What rules?"

"Oh, I dunno," Paula said. "I dunno."

"Paula, talk to me," Rhonda begged. "What's the matter?"

There was a pause. "He's having problems," Paula said. "Maybe it's from his time in the service."

Rhonda had long ago figured out that Rob made the decisions in the Sims family, "including the kind of peanut butter they ate." If she asked Paula about some new product, something that was advertised, Paula answered in terms of Rob: "Yes, Rob thinks that's good," or "No, Rob doesn't like it." Paula judged things through Rob's eyes, Rhonda knew, so if Rob was "having problems," then Paula would have to solve them. "That's what she did for a living," Rhonda concluded. "She made him happy."

Rhonda wondered what to do about Paula's strange call; she didn't want to cross the fine line between helping and intruding. Before she could choose a course of action Paula called again. "Never mind," she apologized. "Forget what I said. I'm pregnant. I'm tired. That's all. Everything's fine."

Paula's growing belly prompted Rob to show some interest in the pregnancy. He read a magazine article that advised an expectant mother to sleep on her left side. Any other position, the article suggested, put undue pressure on the fetus and diminished its oxygen supply.

Accordingly, Paula trained herself to fall asleep on her left side. If, during the night, she turned, Rob awakened her. "Roll over," he reminded her. "Roll over! You're on the wrong side."

Her sleep was further disturbed when Rob removed the upstairs toilet. It was old, it didn't work properly, and with another child to think of, they would certainly need a new one, he said. He promised a replacement, but the toilet was added to the list of unfinished projects. As the weeks went by and her bladder was squeezed by her expanding uterus, Paula, in typical pregnant fashion, had to visit the bathroom more and more frequently. When she woke at night she first had to hoist her bulk from the water bed. Then she had to climb down two steep flights of stairs to the basement, where the house's only other toilet was located.

The emotional schism in the marriage was reflected in the Simses' sex life. Intercourse became an act of physical relief rather than an expression of a bond. "Sex was always at his convenience," Paula said. "Sometimes in the evening I would go downstairs to his workshop and say, 'Well, I'm going to bed.'

"And he would say, 'You want to make love?'

"And I would say, 'Yeah, okay, let's go on up to bed.'

"And he would say, 'No, I'm going to be down here in the workshop for a while. Let's do it here.'

"I was gettin' to the point where I was pretty big. It was hard for me to get up and down. And there was no bed or couch or anything down there. So I just stood there. It lasted five minutes, and then I'd go on up the steps. I got no satisfaction out of it whatsoever. As long as he was satisfied, that's all that mattered. It's not that we didn't *do* it. He never could get enough. But it was always for him. And lots of times I dreaded it. I really did."

While the gulf between them grew, pregnancy forced Paula to face life without the pot and pills on which she usually depended. There was nothing to take the edge off a sharp remark, nothing to make the winter days feel softer or warmer.

She clung to hope spawned by small niceties: Rob remembered Valentine's Day; he brought home a dozen doughnuts and a heart-shaped card that played a tinkling tune when she pressed it. She hung the crimson token on a wall, but its sight and sound were insufficient to counter the deepening bleakness of the relationship.

"Things kept on gettin' worse," she recalled. "I always thought they was gonna get better, but I was just foolin' myself. Finally I thought, I gotta get some help here. Maybe he'll come with me. I was ready to *admit* I needed help."

A month before she was scheduled to deliver, Paula phoned June, who worked part-time as a receptionist in a psychiatrist's office. She sounded nervous as she asked questions about June's job and the doctor for whom she worked. "Is it confidential?" she asked.

"Sure it is," said June.

"All the records and the patients and everything?"

"Yeah, all of it. Why?" Paula didn't answer. "Why?" asked June again.

"It's Rob," Paula said. "He's been havin' these bad nightmares about Vietnam."

The nightmares were real; at least, she thought they were. She felt him tossing and heard him talking, mumbling into his pillow. "What are you dreaming about?" she whispered when she nudged him.

"Vietnam," he answered.

"Vietnam?" June asked Paula. "You mean like flashbacks?"

"Yeah," Paula said, "I guess so. Flashbacks." It wasn't the whole story, but she thought it might be enough to get things started.

June suggested that Paula make an appointment. "If Rob doesn't want to come alone, then you come with him," she encouraged. It was what Paula wanted to hear. Maybe after she met the psychiatrist, after she was actually in his office, she could hint at something else, something that festered in a dark, secret place in her head.

June recited the fee schedule and explained the percentage of the charge that would be covered by Jefferson Smurfit's insurance. "You want me to make an appointment?" she offered.

"I better talk to Rob first," Paula said hesitantly.

The Sims property near Brighton, Illinois. Part of the long driveway down which Paula said the kidnapper ran is at the left; the pond that was searched is at the lower right. [*The Telegraph* (Alton, IL), John Badman]

Paula and Rob facing the press in their Brighton driveway shortly after taking polygraph exams. They hold a poster asking for information about Loralei. [*The Telegraph* (Alton, IL), John Badman]

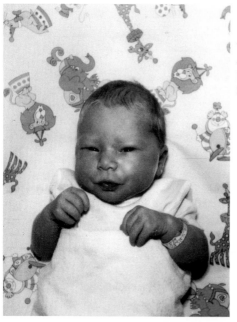

Loralei Marie, two days old, June 7, 1986. [Courtesy of Paula Sims]

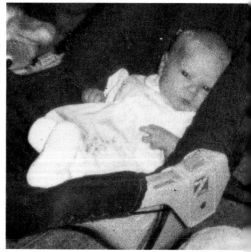

Heather Lee at eight days of age, Easter 1989. [Courtesy of June Gibson]

Paula (upper right) as a freshman with her junior high school basketball team, which had a record of 13 wins and 1 loss. [From the 1974 *Atalpal*, La Plata's yearbook]

Randy Blew as center on La Plata's varsity basketball team, which had a 16—8 record. [From the 1974 *Atalpal*]

Paula's high school graduation picture, which she did not submit to Civic Memorial's yearbook. [Courtesy of June Gibson]

Paula and June in a Wood River, Illinois, bar on New Year's Eve 1977. [Courtesy of June Gibson]

Paula and her father, Orville Blew, at his birthday party in January 1978. [Courtesy of June Gibson]

Paula after spending a day at the farm owned by June's grandparents, April 1978. [Courtesy of June Gibson]

Rob by the chain-link fence of the Simses' Alton home on April 30, 1989, the day after Heather's disappearance was reported. He watched police officers who stopped cars on Washington Avenue to ask drivers for information. [*The Telegraph* (Alton, IL), John Badman]

Curious townspeople outside the Sims home in Alton on May 4, the day after Heather's body was found. [*The Telegraph* (Alton, IL), John Badman]

Jersey County Sheriff Frank Yocom (left) joining Detective Rick McCain of the Alton Police Department in a press conference on May 7, 1989. [*The Telegraph* (Alton, IL), John Badman]

Herb Condray, Paula, Rob, and Rob's sister, Linda
Condray, at Heather's funeral on May 10, 1989.
Casket is at left. [*The Telegraph* (Alton, IL), John Badman]

Family tombstone at the grave sites of Loralei and
Heather in Wood River, Illinois. Banner proclaims
"Together Eternally in Love." Hearts say "Mom" and
"Dad." [Photo by Audrey Becker]

Paula at the Madison County Courthouse for a grand jury hearing, May 11, 1989. She holds hands with her parents, Orville and Nylene Blew. [*The Telegraph* (Alton, IL), John Badman]

Paula waiting in the courthouse coffee shop during grand jury hearings. [*The Telegraph* (Alton, IL), John Badman]

Paula's arrest at the home of her parents on July 11, 1989. At left is Diana Sievers of the Department of Criminal Investigation; at right, Jody O'Guinn of the Alton Police Department. [*The Telegraph* (Alton, IL), John Badman]

Defense attorney Donald Groshong conferring with prosecutor Don Weber during grand jury hearings on March 20, 1990. The grand jury was expected to consider Rob's complicity in the crime. [*The Telegraph* (Alton, IL), John Badman]

Rob in the hallway of the Peoria County Courthouse immediately after the verdict. [*The Peoria Journal Star*]

Paula escorted by court officer Angie Doehlert on the final day of the trial. In answer to press requests for a "photo opportunity," Paula was removed from the jail van in public view rather than in the sally port. [*The Peoria Journal Star*]

When they saw each other after the phone conversation June waited for Paula to approach the subject, but the reach for psychiatric help had been abandoned. Paula didn't mention Rob's nightmares again.

"He wouldn't have nothin' to do with it," Paula explained. He said, 'I'm not gonna talk to nobody. It's the past. It's buried.'

"I said, 'Yeah, you won't even talk to your own wife, so why should I think you'd talk to a stranger?'

"He said, 'That's right. Shut up about it. Nobody's goin' to no psychiatrist.' So that ended that plan."

If June and Rhonda had compared notes on Paula's phone calls, if they had realized that Paula, who seldom complained, had tried to tell both of them that something was wrong, they might have recognized, as Paula herself did, a situation growing critical. There was more stirring than the pushing and squirming of a new life, and it was strong enough that she felt its presence, recognized its portent, and tried to forestall it.

But Rhonda and June were loyal friends, and they did as they believed Paula wanted them to do. Each kept Paula's confidence to herself.

"Randy pulled up on couch to his knees and stood." Paula noted the achievement on her kitchen calendar, where she wrote everything she considered important.

The little boy wasn't walking, although he was thirteen months old. Neither Rob nor Paula gave him much encouragement. They were afraid he might fall. "He was crawlin' all around," Paula said. "Whenever Rob come home Randy would crawl over to him and pull up on his pant leg, but Rob would say, 'Just a minute. I gotta wash my hands before I pick you up.' Even though he always took a shower before he left the plant. He had this thing about germs. When he was home he took three baths a day. We went through I don't know how many hand towels, 'cause he'd wash his hands once and then throw the towel into the dirty clothes. By the time he got his hands washed Randy was cryin' because he wanted to be held and loved by his dad."

As Paula neared her delivery date Randy scooted around the floor in a walker, a rolling metal and plastic cart that he pushed with his feet. He propelled himself into Paula one day, when she was too pregnant and too clumsy to get out of the way. Her foot turned red and swollen. She was barely able to step on it, but she refused to see a doctor. He'd want to x-ray it, she said, and she wasn't about to have an X ray when she was in her ninth month of pregnancy. She wrapped the swollen foot in an Ace bandage and wore a slipper.

A list of prospective names for the new baby hung on the refrigerator. They were suggestions from Paula, crossed off by Rob if he didn't approve. As the middle of March arrived the boy's name was still in question; maybe Daniel Thomas, maybe Thomas Gene.

A girl would be Heather Lee.

The cesarean was scheduled for March 20, the first day of spring, but Paula carried a child eager for life. Labor began early, and Heather Lee Sims entered the world on March 18. After the delivery Paula had a tubal ligation.

Rob had taken Randy home for a nap when Paula emerged from the recovery room. She asked to be taken to the nursery, where she found her mother peering into the big window. A nurse handed the newborn to Paula, who kissed her and passed the tiny bundle to her mother.

"I got to hold her for just a minute," Nylene announced proudly when the family gathered in the evening. Rob's face turned red. "Your mother got to hold her before *I* did?" he asked Paula when the Blews had gone. *"I'*m her father!"

"So soon?" Rhonda asked when she received Paula's phone call.

Paula assured her that everything was fine, that the baby was healthy and beautiful. "I've counted all her little fingers and all her little toes, and she's just perfect!"

June visited the hospital the next day and found that coincidence had placed Paula in Room 285, the same room she had occupied when Loralei and Randy were born. Rules of the maternity floor stipulated that only immediate family members could be present during infants' room visits, but Paula called a nurse, introduced June as her sister "visiting from out of town," and asked for Heather. As they took turns holding the baby both of them cried. "I just thank God I had a chance to have another little girl," Paula said. She cradled the child and whispered an assurance. "Don't worry. Mommy's not gonna let nothin' bad happen to you. Mommy didn't let nothin' happen to Randy, and nothin' is gonna happen to you, either."

"You gotta relax," June counseled. "You gotta let yourself enjoy this baby."

"I've got a gun, and I know how to use it," Paula vowed.

"Take it easy, Paula," June soothed. "Nothin' bad is gonna happen." It was the same conversation they had had when Randy was born.

June watched as Paula kissed the tiny girl. "Nobody can take the place of Loralei," she cooed to her, "but you're gonna do a pretty good job."

"Bonding well," one nurse entered in the progress report.

"Mother seems to bond well," wrote a second.

"Mom bonding well," echoed a third.

A hospital X ray of Paula's injured foot revealed a broken bone, and she was advised to see a specialist as soon as she was discharged. As they had with Randy, the Simses behaved like wary victims. They declined to allow Alton Memorial's "stork lady" to provide a complimentary picture of their newborn; they requested that the baby be placed far from the nursery window; they put no announcement of the birth in the local paper. Photos taken in the hospital by Rob's sister Linda captured the family: an attractive, smiling young mother cradling her infant daughter while a sober, bearded father holds his toddler son.

"I got some new ideas about what I'm gonna do with this house," Rob announced when he phoned Paula in the evening. He talked of cutting holes in the floor, of building a new staircase, of adding a bathroom to the ground floor.

She thought about the projects still undone: the bottom of the steel door that wasn't in place, the upstairs toilet that had been missing for three months. "When are you gonna do it?" she asked.

"Oh, in a while," he said. "You and the kids will have to live upstairs so the dust won't get to you."

"Okay," she sighed, "whatever."

When he arrived at the hospital the next morning he was disgruntled. "God, I'm gettin' tired," he said, although he had arranged to take three weeks off work. "I gotta be watchin' Randy every minute. Do you know how long it took me to dress him? I yell at him, and he just squirms more."

Paula decided to go home even though she had been in the hospital only three of the recommended four days. Her mother tried to dissuade her, insisting that she use the extra day to rest and stay off her injured foot.

"I can't. Randy needs me," Paula said.

"I wish you'd listen to me," her mother scolded. "You need to relax. You're all wound up again."

Heather Lee Sims was carried to the house on Washington Avenue, where chain link, dead bolts, and loaded guns waited to protect her from outside peril. There was no such shield from the danger within.

16

"WE CAME HOME," PAULA WROTE IN THE MARCH 21 SQUARE ON her calendar, underlining the words twice. A silver and pink helium balloon came home with them, proclaiming "It's a Girl!" The balloon, a gift from Rob, was installed in a room next to the kitchen at the back of the house. Intended as a dining room, it served as something less formal for the Simses. There was a couch, an oak table, a chest, a bookshelf, and a picture of the Crucifixion. It was more a family room than anything else. Heather slept there, either in the bassinet that had held Loralei and Randy or in an adjustable padded plastic device known to young parents as a "pumpkin seat." The balloon floated above an array of baby supplies, its buoyancy contradicting the weight of family history.

Heather traveled to Washington Avenue in the company of a father whose past actions showed an attitude toward females that was at best ambivalent and often hostile, and a mother, unhappy and dependent, who had obliquely predicted after the births of all her children that something might happen to them.

One of Heather's first visitors was Rob's father, Troy, a man whose "immorality" had once cost him his teaching certificate and for a time his livelihood. The death of his wife Bernie three years earlier had left him publicly bemoaning his loneliness, and at the time he called on his newest grandchild he appeared to be living the quiet life of a retired widower, following a schedule highlighted by television viewing and bingo games. But even as he knocked on the door he harbored a secret that would soon pass in whispers through the ranks of police and press.

"Tell him we're leaving in a half hour," Rob told Paula.

"Where are we going?" she asked.

"Nowhere," he said. "I just don't want him to stay any longer than that."

Troy brought a tiny pair of baby shoes. "I Love Mommy" was embroidered across their toes. They were the shoes in which Heather would be buried.

Rob stayed home to help, for there was plenty to do with two children in diapers, Randy trying to walk, and Paula still limping on her injured foot. The doctor advised her to lift nothing heavier than ten pounds; since Randy weighed fifteen pounds more than that, Rob assumed responsibility for changing his diaper and carrying him upstairs to the nursery.

"But Rob had a hard time," Paula said. "I was downstairs listenin' on the intercom, and I heard him up there yellin' at Randy 'cause he wouldn't hold still. 'You're gonna listen to me when you grow up, boy!' And he cussed at him and slapped him on his little leg.

"I couldn't take it. I had to go upstairs. I brought the baby with me, and I laid her on the water bed, and I went into Randy's nursery. I said, 'Here, let me do it.'

"Rob said, 'You're not even supposed to be up here. Where's the baby?'

"And I said, 'She's in on the water bed.'

"And he said, 'Is she okay?'

"And I said, 'Yeah.'

"And then she cried or somethin', and he said, 'Go get her and take her downstairs. I'll get this diaper on him if it kills me.'

"And then Randy bit him, and Rob came complainin' to me with these bite marks on his shoulder."

A downstairs couch served as Paula's bed. It allowed her to avoid struggling in and out of the water bed, and it was closer to the one working bathroom. Except for climbing up the stairs to help Rob or down the stairs to use the only toilet, her life was concentrated on the ground floor of the little white house. Within days she sent birth announcements to family and friends, and she told those who phoned that everything was fine. Across Wednesday's and Thursday's calendar squares she inscribed the sentiment that one would expect to find in a young mother's heart: "We love you Randy and sweet Heather."

On Saturday, March 25, she turned to the calendar again and, in what would be a strange weekly ritual, marked the first milestone in her daughter's life:

1 week old

Two of Orville's sisters traveled to the Blew home for Easter. Their husbands came also, and a few grown children, Paula's cousins. None of them had seen Heather; some had never seen Randy. Paula asked them all to come for an afternoon visit.

"I was all excited about it, and so was my mom. Well, it got to be—Rob kept bringing up these rules. No one could come over if they had any kind of sniffles or anything. And they had to take their shoes off, and they had to wash their hands. And then he said none of the young people could come over, my cousins. And then he said, 'Their husbands don't need to come over. Your uncles don't need to come. Just your two aunts and your mom. And I don't really want your mom. I'd rather your dad bring 'em.'

"It just got too much for me, so I said, 'I'm gonna tell 'em to forget it.' I surprised him, 'cause I did it. I got on the phone and I told my mom, 'Forget it. He's addin' more rules, and I don't want to put them through that. Just tell 'em forget it, and I'm sorry. I truly am sorry.'

"My mom said, 'I knew he was going to do something like this.'

"I got off the phone, and he said, 'I can't believe you. Why did you call them?'

"I said, 'Because there's too many rules. I can't handle this, and I don't want them to be put through it. You leave me alone.' And I went and laid down on the couch, and I was cryin'.

"And he come over, and he got on his knees, and he said, 'Paula, call 'em back. Tell 'em to come over. All of 'em can come.'

"And I said, 'But still all the rules, right?'

"And he said, 'Yeah. You don't want your kids sick, do you?'

"And I said, 'No, of course, I don't want 'em sick.'

"And he said, 'I don't want 'em passed around. I don't want that baby passed around.'

"And I said, 'They don't even have to hold her. They just want to see her, Rob.'

"He said, 'Well, they can come over. I know they got gifts.' First he said everybody could come, but then he said, 'No, no, that would be a dozen people. Just your aunts. They're the ones that really want to see the baby. Them others don't need to come.'

"And I said, 'Forget it. Just forget it.'"

Paula phoned her parents early the next morning, as soon as Rob went out to buy a newspaper. "I called 'em quick and told 'em how sorry I was. My aunt Donna from Kansas City, she's the one I'm closest to, she said, 'I'd take you home with me, but I'm sure he'd just come looking for you at my house.'

"My aunt Joann from up by Peoria, she said, 'You can come and live with us. He'll never look for you with us.'

"I said, 'Well, thank you, but do you know what you're saying? I've got two small children, two babies. I have no way to get any money.'

"They were tryin' to help, but I passed that by. I passed it by 'cause I remembered what he said the last time I talked about divorce. He said, 'I'll find you, and you'll be sorry.' I figured he'd kill us or somethin'. There's no tellin' what he might do, 'cause he gets a little wild. His temper gets away from him sometimes. He puts holes in the wall, cusses, acts like a maniac."

When the relatives had left town Rob apologized. On a magnetic board attached to the side of the kitchen refrigerator he wrote: "Thank you, Paula, for giving us a beautiful daughter."

She accepted the apology and wrote a reply: "Don't thank me, thank God. I love you, Paula."

Paula's first journey from home took her back to the hospital, where she had twenty-two staples removed from her incision. The second took her to an orthopedic specialist. Her father drove her there while Rob tended Randy and Heather. She had to stop first at the office of her regular doctor to pick up her medical record, then at the hospital to pick up her X rays. When the specialist kept her waiting nearly an hour she asked to use a phone to call Rob. "You better hurry," he said. "Both kids started crying as soon as you pulled out of the driveway."

As she hung up the phone and sat down beside her father she began to weep. Orville patted her hand. "What's the matter, Paula?" he asked.

"I don't know," she said. "I don't know." She couldn't stop crying.

The specialist determined that the bone in her foot was healing properly; there was no need to apply a cast. "Just stay off your feet," he said.

"I can't," she replied. "I've got two small children."

She left his office in such a hurry that her father had trouble keeping pace. "Wait a minute," he called. "Not so fast. What's the matter?"

"I've got to get home," she said. "Rob's upset."

That was all Orville needed to hear. "Okay," he said as he

hurried behind her. He dropped her off in the driveway. "I better not come in with you," he decided.

When June called later to learn the doctor's diagnosis Paula was more interested in telling her about Randy. The boy was seldom allowed to play outside, but the spring sun was shining, and Rob had taken him to the backyard. "Paula said Randy was smilin' so big you couldn't even see his eyes, that's how big a smile, just touchin' the grass and stuff."

Paula's calendar noted the double significance of Saturday, April 1:

Randy's 14 months
Heather's 2 weeks old

Heather had already lived one day longer than Loralei.

Rob's sister Linda came to take more pictures, and Orville and Nylene visited, one at a time, so that Dennis wouldn't be left alone. The Blews had become a stronger presence in their daughter's life, partly because the Washington Avenue house was closer than the Brighton bungalow and partly because they were drawn by little Randy, their grandson. Heather's arrival suggested that the bond might grow even stronger.

Rob returned to Jefferson Smurfit; "back to dump," Paula noted on the calendar. It was work he described as "dirty" and "stinky," a job he detested but could not transcend. In the highly industrialized waterfront area there was little chance he would find a position more profitable or suitable, and with another dependent in the household he could look forward to a lifetime of carrying his work clothes and his Igloo lunch box into the gray confines of the paper plant.

His return to work left Paula, still walking gingerly on her broken foot, to assume full responsibility for keeping the house immaculate and caring for the children. Heather took a bottle every four hours; Randy, beginning to walk, was on a routine of naps, snacks, and playtimes. Diapers accumulated in a pail near the back door. Paula took them out regularly; Rob complained of the smell if she didn't.

She kept an eye on the clock, trying to keep both children on their schedules, remembering that she should be prepared to greet Rob when he arrived at the door. "I thought I could handle it. And most of the time I did. I *did* handle it. But I remember once Heather was cryin', so I picked her up, and then Randy started cryin' hard, and I bent down and picked him up. And he started pokin' her. And I thought, this ain't gonna work. He was trying to get her bottle. I had broken him of the bottle, and then he'd see hers, and he wanted it. I tried to explain to him, 'This is hers. This is Heather's.' I put him down, and he took the Kleenex and tore all the pieces out. He liked to do that, so that kept him busy for a while. And then he pulled himself up, and he wanted her bottle, and a couple times he smacked her in the back, just a little bit. He didn't know what he was doin'. He just wanted her bottle. They both started cryin' again. And I just—I remembered what my mom said to me: 'What are you gonna do when both of them are crying? How are you gonna handle it?' And I thought to myself, I *can't* handle it."

Yet when Rhonda or June called, Paula said everything was fine. She told them that life with two small children wasn't as hectic as she had expected it to be. She reported that Heather was a good baby.

She said nothing about the dark thought that burrowed through her head, even on the calm days, the thought that became stronger each time she tried to make it disappear.

"How could I tell them that? Rhonda and June, they were *good* mothers. They'd never understand something like that, like what I was thinkin'. *I* didn't understand it. They wouldn't know what to say to me. They wouldn't know what to think. How could I tell them? I just said everything was okay. And sometimes it was."

In the middle of the week Paula used the calendar to announce "We love Randy and Heather!!" The declaration crossed the squares of five days, as though the size of the letters could fortify her resolve to defeat the growing danger.

On Saturday, April 8, she turned to the calendar and

noted the photo she had taken to mark Heather's third week of existence. The line she wrote was prophetically simple:

1 picture Heather sleeping

She fought the black idea as she had always fought her fears, with pot and pills and a shot of whiskey in her Pepsi. There were ten-milligram Valium pills that June had given her, and more Valium that she had taken from Linda Condray's cupboard. There was Xanax from the bottle on her mother's kitchen windowsill.

"My pills!" Nylene said. "Do I need another refill? I just got one. Do you know anything about this, Paula?"

"No," she said.

There was marijuana in the basement, always. That's where she and Rob had decided they would smoke, away from the children.

Sometimes she failed to wake up when Rob came in at 11 P.M., after the swing shift. "I didn't hear you," she apologized in the morning.

"I covered you up," he said. "You were knocked out. You're smokin' too much pot."

"No, I'm not," she insisted.

She slept on the downstairs couch, near Heather's bassinet. Sometimes Randy fell asleep downstairs, too; Rob carried him up to his crib when he got home from work.

"Look at this!" he said to Paula as he pulled his shirt off his shoulder. "Randy's always bitin' me. Why does he do that?"

"I don't know," she said. "He'll outgrow it."

"He don't bite nobody else," he pointed out. "Why does he bite me?"

"I don't know," she said. "He's just a baby."

"Well," Rob said as he headed toward his workshop, "he's gonna listen to me when he grows up!"

She thought about leaving, about taking both babies, about finding a job somewhere, anywhere. "But then I thought of the kids bein' raised without a father, and I decided, no, this will be okay, I can handle it. But then I thought, this isn't goin' to be any life for them. They're gonna grow up like I'm havin' to live, like leading two different lives. 'When your father's not home you can run through the house, you can jump on the bed, maybe. But when he's home you can't make a noise.' How are you gonna explain this to little kids? I thought, that's no life. Am I gonna subject them to that kind of life? What kind of mother would do that? I just had so many things goin' through my mind."

And always there was the bad thought, the black thought, lurking at the edges of her consciousness. Sometimes it was a flash. Sometimes it was a feeling. Sometimes it was just there.

"How're things going?" June asked when she phoned.

"Not so good," Paula replied. She sounded weary; her voice was tight.

"What's the matter?" asked June. "Paula? What's the matter?"

"Just everything," Paula said. "I don't know how much longer I can take it."

"Take what?" asked June. "What are you talking about?" Paula didn't answer. "Come on, Paula. Tell me about it."

"No," said Paula, "I can't."

June promised to visit as soon as she could.

On Saturday, April 15, the calendar commemorated Heather's tenuous hold on life:

4 weeks old

June arranged to come at 10 A.M.; Rob would be at work, and both Randy and Heather would be awake.

The gathering seemed like a picnic, for June's two-year-old, Whitney, played with Randy on the floor, and June joined them there, holding tiny Heather while supervising the toddlers and their toys. "Oh, she's so beautiful," June said over and over as she cradled the baby.

She was. Everyone said so. She didn't have the bright red hair of Loralei and Randy. Hers was a softer color, a golden brown, like her mother's. When she grew restless Paula put her in the bassinet, where she slept soundly, bothered neither by the laughter of the older children nor the ringing of the phone when Rob called.

Whitney's chatter apparently caught Rob's ear. "Oh, it's just June," Paula explained to him. "Everything's okay. It's just June."

June had heard Paula give the same reassurance on other occasions. She was apologizing because she had company.

"How about a Pepsi?" said Paula when she hung up the phone. In the kitchen she took half a joint from the cupboard, lit it, inhaled, and passed it to June. June took a drag and offered it back, but Paula shook her head. "Go for it," she said.

June's gaze traveled to the refrigerator, where both the calendar and the message board overflowed with words of love: "Heather Lee Sims is beautiful . . . Thank you, Paula . . . I love you. . . ." Yet there was a hurt in Paula's eyes that June would swear she could actually see. She didn't know what to make of the situation.

She hugged Paula when she left. "Call me if you have any problems," she instructed. "Promise."

"I promise," Paula said with a nod.

"Call anytime. *Any*time. Day or night."

"I thought it would go away. It did with Randy. It passed. So I told myself, just take another drink, or pop another pill, or smoke another joint, and it'll be okay. I promised myself it would be okay."

Rob noticed that she didn't look well. She was hot and sweaty. She felt like she was going to throw up all the time. "I feel almost like I'm pregnant again," she said.

"What?" he exploded. "Didn't that doctor tie your tubes?"

"Yeah," she said, "he tied 'em."

On March 20, Rob's birthday, his uncle Bill picked him up to take him to a birthday dinner. They were meeting other relatives at the Golden Corral. "I wish you were coming along," Bob's uncle said to Paula.

"Me, too," she said. "But I'd have to take the kids, and Rob says they're not old enough to go out."

On about the same date Heather showed signs of an upset stomach. She drank her regular twenty-four ounces of formula, but she burped more than she usually did, and her bowels were loose.

"I got blamed for it," Paula said. "Rob said someone had come in with a cold or something, and she had a viral infection. Or my hands wasn't clean when I fed her."

Randy, at the same time, developed constipation. "I was on the phone to his pediatrician, trying to find out what to do. I was readin' all my baby books, gettin' whatever information I could. Randy's doctor said, 'Give him more prune juice.' "

Both children were irritable and miserable. Both were crying. "I kept hearing my mother's question: 'What are you gonna do, Paula?' And I thought, I know what I'll do. But I didn't. I didn't do it. I kept control of it, just like I promised I would."

Randy recovered, but Heather continued to fuss. On Saturday, April 22, Paula phoned her pediatrician, who was unavailable; the answering service referred her to another doctor. She made an appointment to bring the baby in on the same day. It was the first time Heather had left the house.

Paula told Dr. Janis Robinson that Heather was burping but not vomiting and that although her stools were loose, she did not have diarrhea. Dr. Robinson noted that the baby was active, alert, and well hydrated. She found no scratches, bruises, or fever. Her diagnosis was mild gastroenteritis, and she recommended that Heather be switched temporarily from Similac with Iron to a soybean formula.

After the examination Paula was able to include Heather's exact weight in her Saturday ritual:

9 pounds 2 ounces
Heather's 5 weeks old

* * *

On Sunday afternoon Paula took Randy to visit her parents. Heather, improved but not totally recovered, stayed home with Rob.

Nylene glanced at her daughter and, with a mother's eye, judged something wrong. "You don't look good," she said. "You look tired."

"I am," Paula said.

"Do you want something to eat?" she asked. "Let me fix you something. What do you want?"

"Oh, no, Mom, I can't eat," Paula protested. "I feel queasy. I feel like I'm pregnant again."

"That's not possible, is it?" asked Nylene.

"No," Paula said. "It must be something else."

Heather's symptoms subsided, and Paula's midweek calendar declaration covered the space of three days:

> Randy loves to walk!!
> Heather loves to smile!!

By Thursday, April 27, when the Blews came for an afternoon visit, Heather was completely recovered. It would be several days before her grandparents could see her again, for they had arranged to spend the weekend with relatives in Peculiar, Missouri, near Kansas City. Dennis, of course, would go along.

Paula called her mother in the evening. "I wish you weren't going," she wept. "I'll miss you."

"Well, we'll miss you, too," said her mother, surprised at the display of emotion. "But you know Aunt Donna and Uncle Tom are expecting us. They already got tickets for that country-western show."

"I know, but I'll *miss* you."

"We'll be back in a couple days," Nylene assured her.

"I know." Paula's voice sounded shaky. "Drive careful."

The following day, Friday, April 28, Rob's friend Acie Miles brought his ten-year-old daughter with him to see the new baby. They agreed with everyone else: She was beautiful.

"Call any time," June had said. "Day or night." Paula phoned on Friday afternoon, but June wasn't home. Her husband asked if Paula wanted to leave any message.

"Just tell her I called," she said.

On Saturday Rob slept late, for he was working swing shift. By the time Paula fixed his breakfast it was nearly noon. "Aren't you going to eat?" he asked.

"No, I can't eat," she said. "I don't feel right."

"Do you want me to stay home?" he offered.

"No," she said, "I'll be okay."

"You need to eat something," he advised.

The thought of food made her sicker. "I'll try to eat later," she said, "after Randy gets up from his nap."

Rob left for work shortly before 2 P.M. When he reached his locker he discovered that he had no clean workshirt. Paula had forgotten to send one. Annoyed, he climbed into his overalls, still wearing his "street shirt," the one in which he had traveled from home. That meant that he would have no shirt to put on when his shift ended.

At home Paula made her regular Saturday calendar note:

Heather's 6 weeks old

It was the last entry.

= 17 =

"SEE MR. SIMS AT 1053 WASHINGTON." THE NAME IN THE radio call meant nothing to Bob Eichen, who had worked with the Alton Police Department for less than a year. On Saturday, April 29, he had just come on duty when the message crackled through his radio at 11:24 P.M. "Possible kidnapping." A misunderstanding was more likely, Eichen figured. Some kid who had forgotten what time to come home.

Three minutes later the patrol car's headlights picked out a bearded man in bib overalls, his bare arms waving. Eichen rolled down the window as his car ground to a stop. "Set up some roadblocks!" the man called. "Our child's been kidnapped again!"

"What hap—" Eichen couldn't get out any more of the question before the man repeated his message.

"We've got to get some roadblocks up! They've taken my daughter!"

"Who? Who took her?" Eichen asked.

"A guy in a mask. We gotta get some roadblocks up!"

"Can you describe his car?"

"No." The bearded man shook his head. "I didn't see it."

"What did he look like?"

"I don't know. He hit my wife!" The man pointed toward the back of the little house.

Eichen rolled the patrol car down the driveway. He saw the young woman, in slacks and blouse, leaning against the back porch. She ran toward him, making the same suggestion her husband had. "We need to put up some roadblocks," she cried. "He took my baby!"

She held one hand to the back of her neck and gasped out her story between sobs: ". . . taking out the trash . . . a guy in a mask . . . 'Get in the house' . . . and something hit me. . . ." She rubbed her neck. "Heather's gone," she wept. "We've gotta do something!"

Her husband was insistent. "You better get some more cops here. We need roadblocks!"

Other officers were on the way, Eichen knew. Response was automatic in anything like a "possible kidnapping." In the meantime he tried to make notes, to ask the right questions, to follow procedures, but the woman's information came at him in bursts, in bits. A word, a phrase, then more sobs. "Where were you when this happened?" he persisted. She pointed to the small trash bag that sat upright at the bottom of the back porch steps. "And where was he?"

"Over there." She indicated a spot several feet away. "Look!" she said suddenly. A lighted window glowed in the back wall of the nearby apartment building, a building that stood only yards from the edge of her lawn. "Maybe they saw him. Maybe they heard something."

The patrolman nodded, considering the possibility. The area where he and the young couple stood was brightly lit. A dusk-to-dawn lamp beamed down from the roofline, and light spilled out of the house's ground-floor windows. "I'll check it out," Eichen said.

He knocked on the apartment window and gestured to the startled resident to meet him at the building's front door, but within minutes he was back to report that the man had seen nothing, heard nothing. "I'll need some more information," Eichen said, glancing at his fragmentary notes. "The intruder was definitely a man?"

The woman sobbed but calmed herself enough to take another stab at the questions. "Yes."

"His height?"

"I don't know."

"Was he as tall as me?"

"Yes." Eichen was six feet.

"His build?"

"What do you mean?"

"Light? Medium? Heavyset?"

"I don't know."

"Was he heavier than I am?"

"No, he was like you."

"Medium," Eichen said as he wrote. He realized that his questions were offering alternatives, but that was policy. Description by multiple choice. "His race?"

She shrugged. "He had long sleeves. And gloves. His face was covered. There was a mask."

"What kind of mask?"

"Black. A black mask."

"A kids' mask? Or a ski mask?"

"Yes." She nodded. "Yes, a ski mask."

"You don't know his race?"

She shook her head. "He sounded white."

"Did he have a gun?"

"Yes." The weeping threatened to surface.

"What kind of gun?"

"I don't know."

"A handgun?" She nodded. "What did it look like? Was it dark? Or shiny?"

"Dark. It was dark colored."

The usual procedure: "Was it like mine?" Eichen's was a blue steel 9mm automatic.

"Yes." The sobs recurred whenever the patrolman took time to write down her answers.

"And he hit you?" She nodded, her hand still clamping the back of her neck. "What did he hit you with?"

"I don't know."

"Was it something sharp? Or blunt?"

"I don't know."

"Well, what did it feel like?"

"It felt like a karate chop."

A six-foot assailant of medium build with a black ski mask and a blue steel automatic, someone who knew how to deliver a karate chop. But Eichen knew that the questions had offered the answers. "I better take a look around inside," he suggested. He followed the couple past the trash bag, across the back porch where a blue wind sock hung limply, and into the tidy kitchen. The man pointed out the location where he had discovered his wife unconscious on the floor.

Eichen looked at the woman in the light of the kitchen, but he could discern no marks of the fall on her face or forearms. "Could I take a look at your neck?" he asked. She turned her back to him, and he studied the pale skin beneath her hair. There was redness where her hand had pressed, but no swelling, no scrape, no bruise.

The man's suggestions were becoming more intense. "We need some roadblocks!"

The woman wandered to the empty bassinet in the next room as other officers began to arrive. Her sobs started again. "Please find my baby!"

"We gotta get things moving," her husband insisted. "This happened to us once before!"

Suddenly Eichen's memory kicked in. Sims. Paula and Robert Sims. It had been years earlier, long before he joined the department. In Jersey County, he thought.

The woman laid her head on her husband's shoulder. "At least our son's okay," she said.

Her husband patted her arm.

From the beginning, the investigation had an incredible sense of déjà vu. The names of the officers were changed, the uniforms and squad cars were different, but the procedures were standard.

"Track!" Richard Gillispie ordered Rex. The officer and the German shepherd began in the backyard, looking for the "hot" scent.

Detective David Hayes knelt by the porch steps to photograph the white plastic bag with a Venture logo. It encased another bag, a brown paper one, containing soiled diapers.

Inside the house Sgt. Terry Lane tried to piece together the story that Paula had told Officer Eichen.

Rob Sims repeatedly urged action, citing the unsolved disappearance of his first daughter. "Trails can get cold mighty quick on something like this," he warned.

There was little need for Rob to say much about Loralei. The members of the Alton Police Department—at least those who had been around for any length of time—were well aware of the case that had bedeviled Frank Yocom and Jim Bivens three years earlier. Although chief of detectives Rick McCain had been installed in his position just two days earlier, he had been on the force for a decade and had recently taken a crime-scene class from Jim Bivens. In the informal hours after classes Bivens often shared his frustrations with the crime-scene coverage in Brighton in 1986, explaining how the thoroughness of the dog searches had been compromised, how his request for Donovan's return had been denied by "some asshole in Springfield." The memory did not cease to upset him. Nevertheless, he was able to speak with some philosophical distance about the failure to indict anyone in Loralei's disappearance. "There's some you can't pop, and that's all there is to it."

It was an equanimity that sheriff Frank Yocom had never achieved. For three years the case file on Loralei Sims had sat on a table in his office, and he had promised himself that someday something would happen. Yocom had worked with McCain, Alton's new chief of detectives, on drug task forces; during late-night vigils the sheriff had shared some of his suspicions about Loralei's disappearance.

So on April 29, 1989, when a phone call from headquarters informed Rick McCain that Rob Sims had reported another kidnapping, the situation was immediately apparent. It was three years later, but they had the same family, the same empty bassinet, *the same story*.

The composure Paula displayed as officers arrived had been coaxed into place with tranquilizers, a final two gulped before she flushed the remainder of her precious supply down the toilet. She knew she couldn't have pills in the house; the house would be searched.

She resisted Detective Mick Dooley's proposal that she have her head injury checked by a doctor. "I want to stay here," she said.

It was not her need for treatment that motivated Dooley's suggestion; the only thing he saw when he looked at her neck was the imprint her fingers had made as she pressed them against her skin. Rather it was a desire to substantiate a *lack* of injury, for Dooley didn't believe her story, and it was obvious from the looks that passed among officers that no one else was buying it either. Nevertheless, Dooley spoke as solicitously as he could. "You really should be checked by a doctor, Mrs. Sims. There's nothing you can do here."

Paula looked to Rob for a cue. "Yeah, maybe you better get checked out," he concurred. Her gaze traveled from her husband to the other men who watched her, and she nodded reluctantly. Dooley led her outside before she had a chance to change her mind.

She walked to his car still holding her neck, her step steady. It was only as the car neared the end of the journey to the hospital that her condition seemed to worsen. Dooley watched, unimpressed, as she moaned, brought her head to her knees, and rocked back and forth in the seat. By the time he pulled up at the emergency room she appeared incapable of walking unassisted. He steadied her as they headed for the sliding glass doors.

While nurse Janet Harkey took her history and vital signs Paula cried. She had been struck on the head, she said; she had a headache, she was dizzy, and her neck hurt. Harkey noted that her neck was red but saw no hematoma, contusion, or abrasion.

It was an hour before Dr. Duk Kim performed a neurological exam, checking for paralysis, blindness, sensory awareness, and range of motion. Paula's reactions were normal. So were her blood pressure, respiration, and pulse. Dr. Kim found nothing symptomatic but some redness on her neck. His diagnosis was entered as "head injury," and he was ready to send her home with Tylenol and an ice bag. It was only because Detective Dooley insisted that the doctor drew blood and ordered an X ray.

Two hours after she entered the hospital Paula was discharged. She walked unaided to Dooley's car and held the ice bag to her neck as they drove to the police station. "Miraculously cured" was how Dooley would phrase it at the trial.

Sheriff Frank Yocom was on a drug stakeout when he received a cryptic radio call. Get to a phone for some important information, the dispatcher ordered. By the time Dooley brought Paula to the police station Yocom was there, too. He hovered in the background, staying out of Paula's sight; he didn't want to "kink up" any chance that she might talk to the Alton police.

In the squad room Detective McCain prepared to record Paula's statement. He pulled a tape recorder from a storage cabinet, plugged it in, and checked to be sure the reels were spinning. Then he and Dooley started the questions.

Randy had been in his crib, Paula told them. Heather, freshly diapered and dressed in a sleeper, had been downstairs in her bassinet. She herself had watched the 10 P.M. news before walking outside with the garbage sack containing soiled diapers. At the bottom of the porch steps she was confronted by a man in dark clothes and a ski mask. She couldn't tell if he was white or black.

The detectives worked on the description. Did the ski mask have square holes or round holes, they asked.

"Round," Paula replied.

McCain formed his thumb and forefinger into a circle. "Like this?"

"Yes."

"Then you must have seen the color of the skin around his eyes."

"The holes weren't that big," she said quickly, "and his T-shirt had long sleeves." McCain and Dooley exchanged a look that acknowledged the vagueness of the description.

Her story continued: The man was about fifteen feet away when he said, "Get back in the house." She set the trash bag down and did as she was told. When she entered the kitchen she felt a blow, something like a karate chop. She demonstrated a chopping motion of one hand on the other. After that she remembered nothing until Rob came home, roused her, and asked where the baby was. Together they checked on Randy and searched for Heather; then they called the police.

Detectives' inquiries went beyond the immediate event: Did she ever abuse her children? "Never!"

Why did she think something like this had happened to two of her daughters? "I don't know."

The questions continued for an hour, bouncing from the general to the specific. When the answers offered no new information McCain stopped the tape.

Paula waited for Dooley to take her home while McCain rewound the reels and prepared to play the recording for other officers. He turned the dial to "Forward" and listened in growing alarm as the tape slid by silently. No questions, no answers. He stared at the recorder in anguish, realizing that it didn't have the built-in microphone he thought it did. It required a plug-in microphone, and he had not attached one. He was facing the biggest case of his career, a case that was sure to garner attention from every corner, and he had just blown the recorded statement. He didn't even have interview notes, because he was planning to transcribe the tape.

With sinking heart he considered the possibilities. He could ask Paula to repeat the process, although any spontaneity would assuredly be lost. Or he could try to write a report later, from memory.

He looked at his watch. It was 4 A.M., and he still needed to get a statement from Rob. "Take her home," he told Dooley.

The tape recorder was properly assembled by the time Rob sat down to relate a story that outstripped Paula's in its simplicity: He returned home at 11:15 P.M. after working the swing shift, found Paula unconscious on the kitchen floor, and roused her; together they ran through the house, looking for their missing daughter and checking on the safety of their son.

He said nothing about the marijuana he had disposed of before he called the police, but the officers who listened to him would have had minimal interest in marijuana. They were trying to connect him to a crime they expected would go down on the books as murder.

Waiting for Rob to return, Paula sat in the dining room, silently smoking as Detective Hayes photographed everything around her. Colorful plastic trucks in straight rows on the floor; stuffed toys sitting upright and proper on the bookshelf. A table full of baby toiletries topped by a shiny balloon announcing "It's a Girl!" A neatly folded blanket over the side of an empty bassinet.

Officer Richard Wells processed the room for fingerprints. He used side lighting, which revealed a film of fine dust or baby powder on the surface of the table where the bassinet sat. There was no sign of disturbance in the dust.

Beyond Paula's gaze, outdoor areas were receiving equal attention. Officer Gillispie took Rex through a wooded region behind the yard, across the grounds of the junior high school next door, up to the school's roof. Conditions were ideal for tracking: temperature in the upper forties, humidity at seventy percent, wind below three miles per hour. Rex found nothing.

Sgt. Bob Paul Goldasich brought Yogi, a bloodhound, to pick up a scent off the baby's blanket and follow wherever it led. "Find," Goldasich said at the back door. Yogi stood still.

Inside, officers covered every floor. In the basement they found Rob's tools, arranged and aligned, each one carefully placed on wall or in drawer. Upstairs they saw the water bed and the red Janis Joplin poster that looked down upon it. In the kitchen, for no reason except that it was procedure, they opened the refrigerator.

As the activity swirled about her Paula puffed her Marlboro and listened to snatches of conversations from the second floor, words carried to her via Randy's cribside intercom. She asked the officers to be quieter. "My son is sleeping," she reminded them.

She ground out the cigarette and sat silently until a detective walked toward the back door with evidence bags and a mop that might have been used to clean up a crime scene. "My mop?" she asked. "Why are you taking my mop?"

It was the question of a woman accustomed to keeping things neat and clean.

18

"THE SAME STORY! THE SAME DAMN STORY!" THE EXCLA-
mation passed from officer to officer, tinged with amazement and disdain, for it was not only unbelievable but
insulting. Any explanation that Paula Sims might have
given for the disappearance of a child would have been
heard with suspicion, but *the same story* was a real slap in
the face.

"Damned if I know," Sheriff Yocom told those who
asked. "I guess if it worked once, why change it? Why argue
with success?"

Before 8 A.M. the next day Rick McCain and detective
Tony Ventimiglia were back at the Sims house.

Now in only his third day as chief of detectives, thirty-
three-year-old McCain was a man who looked hard and
tightly coiled. He wore his light brown hair clipped close
to his head, and his face had a lean, skeletal quality. He
tended to talk in a staccato monotone, even in private; his
public statements had a touch of nervousness thrown
in. Ventimiglia, forty-one, who had been assigned as case

officer in Heather Sims's disappearance, was slower, heavier, softer. His thick glasses and graying hair emphasized his age. Although they were physical opposites, the two men were united by their determination to break this case.

When they arrived on Sunday morning they found Rob and Paula in the kitchen, where fifteen-month-old Randy sat in a high chair, eating his breakfast. McCain and Ventimiglia, both fathers themselves, could see nothing abnormal in the way the boy's parents treated him. It was, in fact, the very normalcy of the scene that the detectives found unsettling.

Glancing at his watch, Ventimiglia explained that K-9 teams would soon return and that Randy's "scent" might confuse the dogs. His hope was that the Simses would voluntarily remove themselves from the property, for officers wanted to resume the search for evidence without Rob looking over their shoulders. The ruse was only partly successful; Rob agreed that Paula and Randy should leave, but he himself elected to stay.

Since her parents had not yet returned from their visit to relatives in Missouri, Paula said she would go to the home of Rob's sister and brother-in-law, Linda and Herb Condray. She packed a bag of toys, diapers, and baby food and drove away in Simses' station wagon.

At almost the same time Linda Condray arrived at the Sims home, where police denied her entry. She spent the morning in front of the house, pacing the sidewalk, arguing with officers, and sitting in her car.

A contingent of lawmen was at work by 8:30 A.M. Some spread to the neighborhood, asking residents what they might have seen or heard. K-9 handlers scoured the areas they had already covered, the lawn, the school grounds, the trees behind the house. A video camera scanned the home's interior. The bassinet, bearing residue of gray fingerprint powder, went to the crime lab. Doors and drawers were opened, their contents noted. One drawer offered an envelope marked "Loralei Marie, Abducted on June 17, 1986." Inside were negatives and photos of a red-haired baby.

Another drawer yielded the Polaroid pictures of Paula, naked and pregnant, the same pictures that Yocom and Bivens had seen three years earlier.

Officers marveled at the neatness, the order of the house. Cartons and cans were aligned in the cupboards; waxed packets inside cereal boxes were folded and secured with twist-ties; package openings were covered with foil. In the basement the tool drawers were laid out in near precision. Magazines were stacked squarely, alphabetized by title and arranged by date of issue. The place looked, one detective decided, "as though it had been prepared for company."

At noon chief of detectives Rick McCain held a news conference. His announcement verified what most reporters had already deduced: Heather Lee's disappearance mirrored that of her sister, Loralei Marie. McCain would not say that the little girls' parents were suspects, only that he could not "rule out any possibility."

After a middle-of-the-night phone call from Rob informed him that his second granddaughter, like the first, had been snatched from her bassinet, Orville Blew decided to wait until morning to begin the trip home. There were several things to consider. Everyone was tired; he, Nylene, and Dennis had made a six-hour journey across Missouri on Friday. They had attended a dinner for Amoco retirees and, on Saturday, had spent the evening at the Kansas City Opry. Dennis was asleep. Nylene, if not hysterical, was understandably and predictably upset. It seemed better for everyone to try to rest and then travel in daylight.

The Blews arrived on Sunday, just after 3 P.M. The relatives they had been visiting, Donna and Tom Ewigman, came with them. Another of Orville's sisters, Mary Lou, along with her husband, drove up shortly afterward, ready to offer consolation. The relatives stayed with Dennis at the Blew home while Orville and Nylene drove three blocks to the Condrays to pick up Paula.

As they waited, Orville's sisters decided to fix a stew for the gathering family, and Donna Ewigman descended to the Blews' basement freezer to find round steak. Returning to the kitchen, she discovered that she had mistakenly picked out sirloin, which she judged to be "too good" for stew. She put the sirloin in the freezer compartment of the kitchen refrigerator and went to the basement again, where she found there was not much meat to consider. She saw a ham, along with some bread and rolls, and concluded that it was time for her brother to restock. Locating a package of round steak, she went upstairs to start the stew, unaware that her observations would soon become crucial to investigators' theories.

There was a heavy silence at the Condray home as the Blews walked into the room where their daughter sat. Nylene studied Paula's face, and her question was hesitant, its slowness conveying its terrible import. "Paula, what has happened here?"

Paula understood the implication but deflected it. "I got hit in the back of my head," she said, lowering her eyes and rubbing her neck and shoulder.

Nylene waited for something more, something that would allow her to accept the impossible, something that would keep a lid on the hysteria that welled inside her. But Paula, head down and face covered, offered nothing.

She returned with her parents to their home and told of her injury before relatives had a chance to ask. Aunts and uncles nodded and sympathized. In the silent and self-protective style that characterized the family, they refrained from posing the troublesome questions that hovered in the air.

By early evening the press was camped out on Washington Avenue. Neighbors who had never before noticed the Simses stood in knots on the sidewalk, pointing at the house or peering down the driveway.

The first newspaper headlines appeared on Monday, May 1. "Family Reports 2nd Kidnapping" said the *St. Louis Post-Dispatch*. The region's smaller papers reflected the same careful skepticism. Their stories reviewed the similarities in the disappearances of Loralei and Heather and reminded readers of the Simses' failed lie detector tests and

Fifth Amendment—based refusals to testify before a grand jury.

At eight-thirty Monday morning Rob took the Jeep to the police station, stopping on the way to buy a newspaper. He waited twenty minutes for McCain, who told him that the police were doing everything possible.

McCain might have said that "everything possible," in addition to roadblocks and dog searches and neighborhood canvasses, included an effort to prove that the Simses, one or both, had murdered their second daughter just as they had killed their first. The skepticism displayed in the press was magnified in the squad room, where investigators huddled with Frank Yocom and Jim Bivens.

Yocom was insistent on staying out of sight. He didn't want either Rob or Paula to see him. "I knew that if I were present, they would just clam up." For some reason the Simses had never felt the same antipathy toward Jim Bivens, even though it was he who had delivered the grand jury subpoenas to them. Bivens had since retired from the Department of Criminal Investigation to pursue a private investigative practice, but he joined officers at the Alton Police Department, ready to go through the old case file.

Much of what Yocom and Bivens had to share, however, wasn't in any case file. It was feeling, opinion, instinct, not cut-and-dried facts. It came from the hours they had spent remembering, conjecturing, theorizing. Now they had another chapter, another episode to consider.

The community, too, had another chapter to consider. Three years earlier, when Loralei disappeared, there had been posters and pink bows; there had been people who believed, even after the incriminating polygraphs were announced, that the young couple could be, must be, victims of some nameless, faceless night-prowling stranger. This time it was difficult to find anyone who believed the story of the masked abductor. McCain told the press that Heather might be alive, that the Alton Police Department was treating the crime as a kidnapping; but the public was not convinced. Phone calls to authorities did not report sightings or sounds of a living baby, as several had in 1986.

One of the first calls reported a fresh grave in a wooded area. As a tip, it proved worthless; as a barometer of community speculation, it was on the mark.

After his morning visit to the police department Rob went to the home of his friend, Acie Miles, and to the office of the family doctor, where he requested something to calm his nerves. He had the prescription filled at Venture, stopped briefly at the Condrays, and then joined Paula and Randy at the Blews.

It was safe there. A high hedge offered some protection from prying eyes, and the Blews chose to ask no questions. Their way of coping with disaster was to not deal with it, at least not directly, not with words. Whatever visions of horror stirred in their brains, whatever questions tormented them, the Blews kept to themselves. They didn't ask Paula for answers, explanations, or assurances. They learned the details of Heather's disappearance from television newscasts.

To satisfy media curiosity and, he said, to free the department's telephone lines, Detective McCain scheduled regular news conferences. Refusing to believe police assurances that there were no new developments in the case, reporters from the small Illinois communities surrounding Alton, as well as from newspapers and television stations across the river in St. Louis, made sure that most of the police moves were covered.

On Tuesday McCain announced that he had been in contact with the Behavioral Science Division of the National Center for Violent Crime. The center, located in Quantico, Virginia, employed thirty researchers to gather data on arsonists, rapists, terrorists, and murderers. It also employed eleven profilers to study the data and develop predictions of the behavior patterns of each criminal type. The profilers, said McCain, forecast that the person or persons responsible for the disappearance of Heather Sims would experience "severe anxiety which will manifest itself in behavior the subject is unable to control."

Reporters questioned what he meant by "severe anxiety" and "uncontrollable behavior." McCain was not willing to say much more. He wanted the meaning of the statement to be determined by the person who had committed the crime.

At home on Washington Avenue Rob whispered insistently to Paula. The police had almost certainly bugged the house, he said. He passed a note each time he wanted to convey a message, however innocuous.

Paula had to use a rag to clean up the residue of gray fingerprint powder that covered doors and floors, for as she had noted, her mop was gone. As she worked she glanced at her kitchen calendar. It was Tuesday, May 2, their eighth anniversary.

With only Randy's babble to break the silence the Sims family spent a quiet day. "Come on up to bed," Rob said to Paula when the sky had turned dark.

"I'll be up in a while," she said.

"No," he replied. "Come on. You need to rest."

As they lay on the water bed he reached for her. "I thought you said this place was bugged," she whispered.

"I don't care if they hear," he said. "At least they'll know we're sleeping together."

=== 19 ===

LOCK AND DAM 26, LOCATED AT ALTON, WHERE THE MISSISSIPPI
River separates Madison County, Illinois, and St. Charles
County, Missouri, was part of the system built in the late
1930's by the Army Corps of Engineers to allow large boats
to travel the length of the Mississippi River. On the Missouri side of the dam was a narrow beach with a sloping
stone wall that surrounded an inlet known locally as Alton
Lake. Fishing was popular, and in good weather people of
all ages lined the beach and the wall, hoping to catch cat-
fish, crappie, buffalo, bluegill, or carp. A boat ramp was
available, and a large parking lot was adjacent. The facility
was just a few feet from the highway, the first right turn off
the bridge as one traveled from Illinois to Missouri.
Known officially as the West Alton Access Area of Lock
and Dam 26, it was an unlikely site for the notoriety about
to befall it.

On Wednesday, May 3, one of the lock and dam's frequent
visitors, Ernest Springer, checked the trash barrels for
aluminum cans. There were forty barrels, large, silver
fifty-five–gallon drums spaced throughout the parking lot,

the picnic tables, the beach, and the boat ramp area. Springer was at the lock and dam early, for he expected it to be a good day to sit on the wall and try for some striped bass or bluegill. He had become something of an expert on fishing conditions at Alton Lake since his retirement. In nice weather he fished four days out of five.

There was another reason for Springer to arrive early. He made a bit of extra money by collecting aluminum cans, and the best pickings were early, before anyone else had a chance to rummage through the barrels that caught the most garbage. Those beside well-traveled walkways were the place to begin, and he checked a few when he arrived at the access area just after 6:30 A.M. He didn't spend much time at the aluminum-can pursuit; the fishing looked too promising.

On the same morning cars slowed as they passed the Sims home on Washington Avenue. Occasionally a driver stopped to ask a reporter if anything was happening. Reporters asked one another the same question as they prepared to spend another day tracking the Simses, the police, or both.

At the police station McCain faced the press once more. He spoke of an "all-out" search, of twenty officers from the Alton Police Department, the Illinois Department of Criminal Investigation, and the FBI hard at work on the case. Again he repeated the prediction of the FBI's Behavioral Science profilers: "severe anxiety which will manifest itself in behavior the subject is unable to control."

Announcement of the FBI prediction was designed to pressure the perpetrators to rid themselves of the infant's body; if the body had already been dumped, perhaps they would feel a need to check on it. The violent crime experts assured McCain that the person or persons responsible for Heather's disappearance would indeed act in such a predictable manner. But how soon would that happen? How long before the severe anxiety and uncontrollable behavior took over? That was harder to prophesy.

Paula heard a TV newscaster repeat the prediction and wondered what it meant. Were they trying to tell her that she would kill everybody else in her family? No, she told herself, that was crazy; she could never do such a thing. Then she remembered what she had already done.

The Alton police asked the state's Department of Criminal Investigation to set up surveillance on Rob and Paula. Viewing would not be difficult, for the Sims house had a junior high school on one side, an apartment building on the other, and trees in the rear. Considering the need for secrecy and the cost of the surveillance, officials decided it would be wise to delay the stakeout until nightfall.

At 10:30 A.M. Ernest Springer put down his fishing pole and ambled toward the restroom. The path led through the parking lot and up a gentle slope to the two bright green lavatories. Springer automatically took a peek into each trash barrel he passed, vigilant for the glint of aluminum. From the debris at the bottom of one he picked out a Miller High Life can.

By 1 P.M. the sun shone brightly on the forty trash barrels as Springer once again walked the well-traveled path to the restrooms at the top of the slope. His fishing was over for the day. It was the third of the month, and the postman would deliver his social security check sometime between 1:30 and 2 P.M. Springer didn't like to leave the check in the mailbox.

He took a last look into the trash barrels as he went. Pickings were slim. In a barrel near the parking lot—the same barrel that had yielded the Miller beer can—was a black plastic trash bag he hadn't noticed before, but Springer wasn't interested. He went home to wait for the mail.

It was nearly 7 P.M. on Wednesday evening when Charles Saunders arrived at Lock and Dam 26. A regular visitor since 1947, he wore a sweatshirt to ward off the evening chill, for the temperature regularly dropped into the forties. There would be hardly any time to fish, since the Corps of Engineers closed the area at 8 P.M., but with a true fisherman's dedication Saunders wanted "to see what the fish were doing." Spoonbill would be starting to run, he expected, and white bass, too, and there was always tomorrow. He watched the activity of the thirty anglers at the lake long enough to determine that the fishing was "slow."

His Chrysler's engine had been guzzling oil, so before starting home Saunders added a quart from the supply he carried in his trunk. With the empty oil can in his hand he headed to the nearest trash barrel, the one by the sidewalk that led to the lavatories. He dropped the can into the barrel's rusty interior, where it settled among soda bottles, a Taco Bell soft drink cup, an empty Benson and Hedges cigarette pack, a ham-and-cheese sandwich wrapper, and a black plastic bag.

Saunders contemplated the crumpled bag, its opening swirled into a knot. Probably food, he figured. The round shape in the bag's corner looked like a head of lettuce. When he picked up the plastic package he was less sure; the round object seemed too heavy to be lettuce.

Although many people would ask, Saunders would never be able to explain why the bag caught his attention, or why he pulled out his pocketknife and cut a slit across the black film. He was a reasonably curious man, he admitted, but not a man who regularly poked around in trash cans. On this chilly May evening, however, the black plastic bag captured his interest, and for some reason he wanted to know what it contained.

He saw the feet first, then the tiny head.

Halfway to his car Saunders stopped. Maybe it's a doll, he told himself. He went back to the barrel and looked again at the small figure, one hand near its mouth, as though it had just fallen asleep after sucking its thumb. It was human, Saunders saw, and it was a girl. The pinkness of her skin gave him a second's hope that she was alive, but she was too still, too cold. Saunders approached a man and woman in a pickup truck and asked them to guard the barrel while he drove to a phone. He realized he was shaking.

Ten minutes later the first officer arrived. Saunders led him to the barrel, and the two men stared down at the bag. There was condensation inside it, and a long, narrow pocket of water along its bottom seam. A few drops of moisture beaded on the baby's face, but her expression was serene, angelic. How could she look so beautiful, so peaceful, in such awful surroundings, Saunders wondered. He fought back a sudden urge to cry.

It was nearly 9 P.M. when Rhonda Scott returned from her mother's birthday celebration. The phone was ringing as she and her family walked in the door; a friend informed her that television stations were carrying news of a body found at the lock and dam. As Rhonda and her husband flipped through the channels to find more information the phone rang again. "I'm havin' a quiet moment," Paula said. "I thought I'd give you a call."

Rhonda was flooded with relief. The body can't be Heather's, she assured herself. If it were Heather, Paula would have been told. "I'm so glad to hear your voice," Rhonda said. "How are you doing?"

"I'm hangin' in there," Paula replied. "But I can't talk about any of it."

"Okay," Rhonda said. She didn't know if Paula meant that she was emotionally unable to speak of the kidnapping, or if she had been advised by the police not to discuss it. Either way, the restriction put a strain on the conversation; the most urgent occurrence in their lives was off-limits. There were gaps between sentences as they talked of inconsequential things—the activities of Rhonda's children, her mother's birthday party. In pauses, as Rhonda searched for safe things to say, she became aware of the silence in the Sims house, a silence so total that "it was eerie." Randy was in his crib, Paula said. She did not mention Rob.

Rhonda stood at her kitchen phone, peeking at the TV screen that was visible through the living room doorway. News bulletins began to offer live coverage from the lock and dam, but the information was sketchy, and Rhonda couldn't hear whether the body discovered was that of an adult or a child. She thought of telling Paula about the bulletins, but the longer they talked, the surer she became that the news wasn't about Heather. The body couldn't be a baby's, or the police would be knocking on Paula's door, asking her to make an identification.

When she hung up the phone Rhonda felt calm. As she walked into her living room a TV newsman interrupted the regular program to report that the body found at the lock and dam was indeed that of a female infant.

By the time Orville Blew arrived an hour later to pick up Paula and little Randy, television vans lined Washington Avenue. Neighbors mingled with reporters on the sidewalks; photographers hovered at the Simses' chain-link fence.

Although Orville pulled his car well into the driveway, he could not protect his daughter from the lenses and the lights. Paula had to pass within inches of the cameras as she fled, clutching Randy against her chest.

She was gone so quickly that the crowd was left pointing and murmuring. Even reporters, ready to call out their questions, could only watch and wonder as Orville's car sped away.

St. Charles County sheriff's deputies scoured the lock and dam area. Officers from other jurisdictions—the Alton police, the Jersey County sheriff, state DCI investigators, and the FBI—hovered on the edge of the activity, waiting for their chance to inspect the pathway, to peer inside the barrel.

The location of the discovery presented jurisdictional problems for investigators and prosecutors. If this infant proved to be the baby they believed her to be, they were faced with a victim found in Missouri and a crime committed, probably, in Illinois. That the victim was found just *barely* across the state line—less than a quarter mile—did nothing to alleviate their difficulty.

Investigators comforted themselves by noting that the body's location meant that the autopsy would be performed by Missouri's Mary Case. Chief medical examiner of both St. Louis County and St. Charles County, Dr. Case was recognized for the expertise of her examinations and the effectiveness of her courtroom testimony.

On Thursday morning, May 4, at the St. Louis University Decomposition Facility, Case began her study. The subject, she noted, was an unknown white female infant, well nourished, clean, 22½ inches long, just under ten pounds, probably six to eight weeks of age. The baby had blue eyes and a sparse growth of light brown hair. Her nose contained a few drops of liquid blood.

The infant's only visible injury was on her upper lip. Its inner surface had lacerations in three areas; the largest was five millimeters; the smallest two millimeters. The tiny cuts indicated application of pressure, Dr. Case concluded— pressure in which the lip was held in contact with the maxillary ridge, or upper gum. "Asphyxia by Suffocation."

The body was well preserved externally; there was no skin slippage or discoloration. The child's chest and abdomen, however, contained fluids of decomposition; her lung tissue was beginning to decay. The process of autolysis, the breakdown of internal organs by the enzymes they contained, was further advanced than the outside of the body would lead an examiner to expect. And three deep pink spots, indicative of exposure to cold temperature, marked the baby's left forehead, cheek, and neck.

A difference in internal and external decomposition, and three rosy spots. "Probable Freezing of Body Postmortem."

At 6 P.M. the FBI office in Springfield, Illinois, announced what everybody already knew. A comparison of footprints proved that the baby in the barrel was Heather Lee Sims.

IV

The Police, the Press, and the Public

20

FISHERMAN ERNEST SPRINGER PHONED AUTHORITIES WHEN HE saw television footage of the metal trash barrel beside the lock and dam walkway. He recognized it as the one he had checked at least twice on Wednesday. He didn't notice a black plastic bag when he looked in the trash can at midmorning, he told police, but he saw the bag when he passed by on his way home in the early afternoon.

With little else to go on, police accepted Springer's recollection as an official timetable: The body was dumped between 10:30 A.M. and 1 P.M. Unfortunately, even such precise parameters were of little use in the case against the Simses, for authorities had no idea where Rob and Paula had been during those two and one half hours.

Despite the fact that Rick McCain had been in contact with the FBI's profilers for three days, despite repeated announcements that the guilty person or persons would experience "severe anxiety" and would exhibit "behavior the subject is unable to control," authorities had not begun their surveillance. The cost involved in a round-the-clock watch of as many as three locations (the Sims home, the

211

Condray home, and the Blew home) had led decision makers to delay the operation until nightfall. But by then the black plastic bag had been discovered.

Unable to say with certainty where the Simses had been, authorities turned the question around: Where had Heather been? "Probable freezing of body postmorten," the medical examiner speculated. Police knew the little body wasn't in the Simses' refrigerator on Saturday night when they searched the house. Paula's aunt Donna Ewigman would say she saw no body at the Blews' home when she hunted for stew meat. Was Heather kept in more than one refrigerator, authorities wondered; was she moved from place to place? At ten pounds and 22½ inches, she could have been stored almost anywhere.

The assumption of deliberate preservation of the tiny body added particular horror to the plot, for in addition to displaying an unfathomable lack of feeling, it suggested that the murder might have been carefully planned and an effort made to disguise the time of death. Heather was kept "on ice," some authorities speculated, and then dumped in a highly visible trash can, where she was likely to be found. The condition of the corpse would suggest that she had been dead only a day or two; that would mean she was alive *after* the Simses reported her missing. Not only did her parents kill her, but they were trying to use her well-preserved body to prove their innocence.

Not all authorities accepted this complex theory. They argued that the corpse was dumped in panic, a reaction to the FBI's much-publicized prediction, and that the trash can was chosen because its proximity to the parking lot enabled a driver to toss the plastic bag while leaving the cover of his vehicle for no more than a second or two.

Wondering how things had become so crazy, Paula watched newscasts in which reporters explained one theory or another. She should have expected it, she reminded herself; it had happened before. Once it had been a strange tale from a woman in a Jerseyville card shop, a tale about a baby with half-open eyes. Now it was theories about freezers and refrigerators and the pronouncement that someone had clamped a hand over Heather's mouth. Why was it all coming out so wrong?

There was no one she could ask, for she had launched the craziness. "I started the ball rollin', and it just went completely out of control."

On Thursday, May 4, the day after Heather's body was found, Rick McCain phoned Rob and Paula at the home of Paula's parents, where they had taken refuge from the press, and requested that they come to the police station for interviews. When Linda Condray picked them up that evening she yelled at photographers to get out of the way and threw something at one who didn't. Followed by reporters' vehicles, she drove three blocks to her own home and turned the car over to her husband Herb, who continued on to the station with Rob and Paula.

They were greeted by McCain as others watched from the wings. Alton officers were planning a full evening's agenda; the FBI was ready for Rob, and women detectives stood by to question Paula.

"They wanted to know if Heather had cried a lot. I said, 'That's not what happened.'

"And they said, 'Well, did she cry a lot?'

"And I said, 'No, she didn't.' They started accusin' me, these women did, and I instantly copped an attitude, and I got up. I told 'em, 'I don't have to listen to this.'

"So I went lookin' for Rob, and there was a couple guys in the hall, and they said, 'Who you lookin' for?'

"And I said, 'Robert Sims.'

"And they said, 'He's not here. We don't know any Robert Sims.'

"And I walked on down the hall, but all the doors were shut. He was behind one of them doors, I guess. I went and found Herb and said, 'They're accusin' me.'

"Herb said, 'Well, let's get outa here. Where's Rob?'

"I said, 'I can't find him.' I started to go back in to look for him again, but one of those guys I had talked to said I couldn't. I said, 'I want my husband.'

"He said, 'You can't have him. We've got him.'

"I said, 'You just told me he wasn't in there.' And he just smiled at me. So I went ahead and had Herb take me home."

Herb and Paula left by the back door, avoiding the pack of cameramen and reporters staked out at the front entrance.

Behind one of the closed doors that had deterred Paula Rob spoke briefly with McCain and then with Tony Ventimiglia, the detective assigned as case officer; but neither McCain nor Ventimiglia was the big gun. That was FBI Special Agent Carl Schulz, assigned to the bureau's St. Louis office. Schulz showed his credentials and explained that Rob was not under arrest and could leave at any time. Rob chose to stay, as DCI agent Jim Bivens and Sheriff Frank Yocom had predicted he would. They remembered his 1986 requests for FBI participation and his pile of detective magazines; they were betting that an interview with someone like Schulz was a challenge Sims would not forgo.

Schulz began by telling Rob that Paula's tales of masked abductors were "totally preposterous" and that he and Paula themselves were prime suspects. He ridiculed the idea of anyone singling out a family and coming back for a second baby girl three years after taking the first. "No jury in their right minds would believe these stories," Schulz challenged. He asked if Rob might have said some things that were untrue. Rob said that he had not.

The interview was a balancing act that both men were prepared to play to the full extent of their abilities. From time to time Schulz emerged to share with hovering lawmen the status of the encounter. Then he returned to the interview room, where Sims sat stoically.

Just prior to 9 P.M. Schulz upped the ante. Even as they spoke, he told Rob, search warrants were being executed at the Sims house on Washington Avenue and at the Blew home on Virginia Avenue. "That's fine," said Rob. "We have nothing to hide."

Detectives displayed their warrant to Orville Blew. High among their priorities were trash bags and freezers. Orville directed them to the upright freezer in the basement and asked if he could accompany them. They suggested that he remain upstairs.

Minutes later other detectives entered the Simses' vacant Washington Avenue home, breaking a window in the attempt. A gathering crowd cheered the splintering of the glass. Inside the house officers photographed things that had not been of major interest to them four days earlier, when they were last at the scene: the freezer; the meticulously arranged shelves of supplies that lined the basement stairwell. From the topmost shelf they confiscated a roll of "Curb Side" black plastic trash bags.

When they moved their exploration to the Jeep, the station wagon, and the camper in the driveway, their efforts were exposed to the bright lights of television crews. Onlookers surged forward, offering opinions to one another and encouragement to the searchers. The crowd's mood was upbeat, and several reporters filed stories that likened the scene to a circus or carnival. One of the Simses' neighbors invited the press to her kitchen for coffee and doughnuts.

Shortly after 11 P.M. detectives who had executed the search warrants at the Sims and Blew homes returned to the station, which was still surrounded by antenna-topped minivans that had beamed live coverage to TV viewers. Rob remained inside the building, in session with agent Carl Schulz.

Just before midnight attorney Donald E. Groshong, who years earlier had represented Rob in his divorce from Terri, appeared in the station lobby. He had been retained to represent Robert Sims, he told officers, and he wanted to see his client. The police declined; Sims was not under arrest, they said, and had not requested the presence of an attorney. Groshong was caught in the glare of television lights as he used the lobby's pay phone to call two judges, urging them to order police to interrupt the FBI interrogation and allow him access to his client. Both judges refused.

With Groshong's intervention thwarted, Rob sparred for more than seven hours with Carl Schulz, who surfaced periodically to recount his progress for waiting lawmen. In the early morning hours he came out shaking his head in disbelief. The information that so amazed him was Rob's declaration that on May 2, their eighth anniversary, only three days after Heather's disappearance, he and Paula had enjoyed "better and longer-lasting sex" than they had had in "a long, long time."

Shortly after 3 A.M., eight hours after he had reported to the station, Rob was driven back to the Blew home by police. The interrogation had produced talk of "tire tracks" at the lock and dam; there had been mention of a "hair" found in the Blews' freezer. Attorneys would later argue about who had said what, and under what circumstances, but Schulz's expertise and the long hours of probing had eroded Rob's composure. Before leaving the station he conceded that Paula might have "done something" to her daughters. He volunteered to go home and pressure her for more information.

"I was layin' down, and he come in the wee hours of the morning, and he confronted me and said, 'You gotta change your story, Paula, or they're gonna take Randy.'"

The Simses began an argument that roused Paula's father and then her mother, bringing everyone to the Blews' kitchen. "Now even Rob is accusin' me," Paula wept. "I told him to get out. I don't want him here."

Rob apologized. "I don't know what to think anymore," he said. "But they want you to make another statement, Paula. If you don't, they're gonna take Randy away."

"Oh, bull," Paula replied. "They'd never do that."

The following day William Haine, the Madison County state's attorney, was informed that Rob had told Agent Schulz that Paula had a key to the Blews' house and might have been able to hide Heather's body in their freezer while he himself was asleep at home. Rob expressed concern for young Randy's safety, Haine was told, and said that his brother in Texas might be able to care for the child. Haine decided that Randy's safety was in question and petitioned the court to make the child a ward of the state.

DYING DREAMS

Late that afternoon Rob and Paula visited the office of their newly retained attorney. Paula took time out from the meeting to phone her mother. "How's Randy doin'?" she asked.

"He just woke up from his nap," her mother said. "I'm getting ready to feed him."

At 4:45 P.M., as he was eating his snack, fifteen-month-old Randy Sims, who had never had a baby-sitter, was taken from his grandparents' home by the Illinois Department of Children and Family Services. A court order citing "imminent danger and risk" sanctioned the action. Nylene and Orville watched helplessly as a social worker picked up their frantic, wailing grandson and carried him away.

=== 21 ===

THE ARRIVAL OF THE WEEKEND DID NOT CURTAIL THE NEWS
conferences. Sheriff Yocom came out of hiding to join the
Alton police in the briefings; he answered questions about
Loralei's disappearance three years earlier in Jersey County.
Information was doled out in portions large enough to keep
the case in the news. On Saturday Detective McCain met the
press to say that Randy had been taken because the child's
own father feared for his safety. On Sunday he told reporters
that Rob had expressed doubts about Paula's "masked
gunman" stories.

The effort to drive a wedge between Paula and Rob was
obvious, and some members of the press grumbled about
being used to manipulate the suspects. They reported
McCain's statements nevertheless. This was not a story that
anyone dared miss. By the weekend it had made the *New
York Times,* and Alton detectives were fielding calls from the
likes of ABC, CNN, "Inside Edition," "A Current Affair,"
"America's Most Wanted," *Time, People, USA Today,* the
Chicago Tribune, the Associated Press, and UPI. The many

requests for information were used to justify the daily or twice-daily news conferences. The police said they were just saving time.

Sunday newspapers, including the area's largest, the *St. Louis Post-Dispatch,* featured the Sims story on their front pages, accompanied by photos. Several papers had more than one story, breaking events down in terms of time, location, or child. A kind of journalistic abbreviation developed as the press spoke of "the Loralei case" or "the Heather case." It was the only identification necessary.

The bizarre nature of the incident—*two* baby girls, *two* masked gunmen—made the story a natural for television stations, which, during early May, were in the midst of the periodic ratings game known as "sweeps," traditionally a time of journalistic excess and promotional hyperbole, a time when sex, violence, and scandal masquerade as the evening news. The Sims story was made to order for "sweeps." Not only did it have sex, violence, and scandal, it actually *was* news. Since all the channels were featuring it, the contest became a question not of *what,* but of *how much.* Which station could give the story the most air time, the most intriguing spin?

Whatever the focus of the story, the pictures included Paula. Paula carrying Randy to her father's car. Paula on her way to the police station. Paula at her attorney's office. Wherever and whenever she was photographed, her face was blank. Her eyes reflected nothing.

As Paula's expressionless face became familiar to anyone who picked up a newspaper or turned on a TV set, the public began to assume her guilt. They talked not about *whether* she had done it, but about *why* she had done it. Maybe the Simses were devil worshipers. Maybe the babies were sacrificed. Maybe Paula was hypnotized, guessed some who wondered about her lack of response. Maybe she was a victim of postpartum depression, guessed others who had heard on "Oprah" and "Donahue" about seemingly loving mothers who killed their babies with bullets, rocks, or bathwater.

People called and wrote, offering opinions and suggestions to authorities in both Jersey and Madison counties. An operator of a funeral home in a community close to Alton contacted police to say that his nineteen-year-old daughter had been Paula's maternity-ward roommate in the days after Heather was born. Detectives should hear her story, he suggested.

The young woman, Stephanie Werner, wrote up a three-page document and brought it to the police department. At first Paula had been irate to learn there was no private room available, but she became friendlier after a rest, Stephanie reported. They discussed the births of their babies, and Paula explained that Heather's delivery was her second cesarean. Stephanie complained about the agonies of labor; Paula sympathized and said she knew what that was like. Stephanie asked how Paula could know the pain of labor if she had had cesarean deliveries. It was then that Paula explained about Loralei and told Stephanie that three years earlier, while her husband was at work, a masked gunman had hit her on the head when she was taking out the trash, or perhaps burning the trash. Stephanie could not remember which it was, but she was certain that Paula had mentioned the trash.

This was the section of the story that interested police. Had Paula inadvertently told Stephanie Werner of her plans to murder Heather?

Chief of detectives Rick McCain related Stephanie's story to the Madison County Juvenile Court. He maintained that Paula had forecast the circumstances of Heather's abduction six weeks before she told police of the karate-chopping kidnapper. She tried out the story on Stephanie, saying it had happened three years earlier, with Loralei. When Stephanie accepted the account, Paula figured it was a tale convincing enough to use when she murdered Heather.

In an attempt to persuade Judge Ellar Duff to keep young Randy in protective custody McCain also cited Rob's statements to FBI agent Carl Schulz, statements that seemed to indicate that he feared the boy might come to some harm at the hands of his mother.

Although attorney Groshong argued that Rob's statements had been misconstrued, Judge Duff ruled that Randy would be kept in a foster home until a later hearing could sort things out.

On the same day, police searched three shower-room lockers and a tool locker that Rob maintained at Jefferson Smurfit. They filed a list of confiscated items, which included bib overalls, work boots, a hair brush containing hair samples, a photograph of Randy, and fifteen paperback books. The books' titles were specified. A few (*One More Time, Secrets, The Watcher*) were romance novels. Most (*Abnormal Ones, Education of Lydia, Girl High, Girls in the Office, Love Too Soon, Mistress of Morwood Manor, Nina, Sex Shuffle, The Shame of Jenny, Traded Wives,* and *The Abnormal Wife*) were pornographic. One, *The House of Seven Gables* by Nathaniel Hawthorne, was a classic nineteenth-century American novel whose plot, in a twist curiously appropriate to the case at hand, traced the effect of human actions on later generations.

There was also "a picture on a cloth showing a naked woman sitting on a large skull."

The explicit list marked the official end of police candor. After nine days of accessibility, Madison County State's Attorney William Haine declared that there would be no more news conferences. He worried that further publicity might interfere with justice. "I hope to try this case somewhere in the Western Hemisphere," he said.

With Randy gone and murder charges looming, Paula found herself painted into a lonely corner. "I was scared to death. I didn't know what to do. I've always had trouble makin' decisions. I've had other people makin' them for me all my life." At least once each day she decided to tell the truth, to sit down with somebody and explain, but she couldn't. She didn't have the answers everyone wanted. She could have told *what* happened; it was the *why* she couldn't supply. Each time she came near confession her own lack of comprehension confounded her.

She thought of telling only the *what* and letting her

motives be deciphered by others, but each time she approached the decision a friend or relative would smile kindly or squeeze her hand. Sometimes they actually said the words: "We believe in you." Other times they let her know by their silence, by the questions they didn't ask, that they were *trying* to believe. "They knew me. They knew how much I wanted my children and loved them. They'd never understand how I could do such a thing. My dad told me he believed in me, he *knew* me. My mom, on the other hand, she remembered a few things. She remembered the night they left [to visit relatives near Kansas City], that I was cryin' on the phone to her. I didn't want them to go. I think my mom all along kinda thought something. She didn't want to believe it, of course. My mom would have been crushed if she thought I had done something to my babies. My family that has always loved me and has always gave me everything, they would have been absolutely crushed. And I had many other people that knew me, and they believed I wouldn't be capable of something like that. But then again, they didn't know. They didn't know how things were."

As the police version of the murder solidified, her confession became more and more unthinkable. Authorities propounded a scenario that had her planning the murder six weeks in advance, holding her hand over Heather's mouth, freezing the body, and transferring it from one refrigerator to another. "I couldn't have done that, you know, how she was supposedly—you know, how it supposedly happened, the way they said. And how [medical examiner] Mary Case said. I couldn't have done that. No way. No way."

The distorted official version of the murder became Paula's justification for not confessing. She told herself that she really wasn't guilty of the crime they described. "I hadn't done that. Truly, I hadn't done that."

On May 10 a thirty-minute private funeral service was held for Heather Lee at the Bethalto First Baptist Church. News vans trailed the hearse and family cars to the Woodland Cemetery, where a ten-minute graveside service followed.

The cemetery association feared problems and requested that the press refrain from speaking with those in attendance and remain at least fifty feet from graveside. The press complied, but zoom lenses caught Paula's heaving shoulders. The sound of her sobs—deep sobs, not the dry gasps of the Brighton videotapes—carried across the gentle hill. Rob turned for a last look at the coffin as he and Paula walked away with the Condrays. Then photographers rushed forward, and cameras peered into the grave as the small white casket of Heather Lee Sims was placed beside that of her sister, Loralei Marie.

On May 11 Paula, the Blews, and the Condrays answered subpoenas to appear before the Madison County grand jury. Word of their presence spread quickly through the courthouse, and bailiffs had to use long wooden benches to keep away the curious.

Interest was not so easy to turn off as the state's attorney might have wished. The public had been given a day-by-day accounting of developments in the investigation. They had been reminded of the details surrounding the death of Loralei. They expected an ending; they wanted a charge and an arrest. No one was content to let the story drop.

Paula and her parents stayed only a few minutes behind the closed door of the secret proceedings, leading to speculation that they had cited their Fifth Amendment rights and refused to testify. The Condrays did not stay much longer. Afterward the family ignored reporters' questions and walked silently and quickly to their cars.

The next day phones began to ring in the news vans parked around the Alton Police Department. Paula was about to surrender in Jersey County, where Loralei had died, confided an "anonymous" police department source.

The hurried influx of television minivans and reporters' cars startled Jerseyville residents going about their business on a sunny morning. The vehicles quickly filled up every available parking space near the courthouse. By the time one of Groshong's associates drove up with Paula, the only parking spot left was in the municipal lot two blocks away.

"There she is!" someone called as Paula emerged from the car. She walked, in pink sweater, navy slacks, and beige pumps, past the staring crowd, some of whom ate their lunch as they watched her pass. TV cameramen trailed her or walked backwards ahead of her in order to photograph her face. Reporters held out microphones, hoping for some word from her or from Groshong. There was no comment from either of them, but onlookers were not as restrained. They applauded when Paula entered the old-fashioned stone building. Inside, workers left their desks and clustered in the hallways to get a look at her.

Before the bench of Circuit Judge Claude J. Davis Paula was charged with concealment of Loralei's "homicidal death" and three counts of obstruction of justice. In simple terms, the county was accusing her of lying to investigators. There was some urgency to file the Jersey County charges because the three-year statute of limitations on obstruction and concealment in that case would expire in a month, on June 17, 1989, the third anniversary of Loralei's disappearance. The county could add a murder charge at any time; there was no statute of limitations on murder.

Paula spoke only one word, a "yes" when asked if she understood the charges. Her bail was set at $100,000. The ten percent bond was paid by a cashier's check remitted by her father.

Later that afternoon Paula and Rob stopped at the home of Rhonda Scott. Paula was calm, but it was apparent that she had been crying. Rob was the one who was nervous. Would there be more charges? Would the next ones come from Jersey County or Madison County? Would charges be filed against *him?* He paced. His hands shook. He was, in Rhonda's opinion, "scared shitless."

Rhonda turned on the TV to see if newscasts might have any more information. She put Paula on the couch and sat with an arm around her as they watched the footage from Jerseyville: Paula and attorney Groshong, Paula and the crowd, Paula taking quick glances at the reporters who thrust microphones in her face. "This is unreal," Rhonda thought as she looked at the television screen. She didn't know what to say.

Paula never returned to the Washington Avenue house. She asked her friend June Gibson to clean up the glass from the broken window and to gather Heather's things. The house was placed on the market for $39,900 and sold in a few weeks for slightly less. Rob rented a storage locker and, with the help of his friend Acie Miles, moved the Simses' belongings. Miles told detectives that when he and Rob entered the house Rob laid a finger across his lips and whispered that the place was bugged.

When detectives Mick Dooley and David Hayes knocked on June Gibson's door she was, in typical fashion, ready to tell them everything she knew. There were problems in the Sims marriage, she said, citing Paula's unhappiness with Rob's "rules." She told the officers of her hesitation to visit the Sims house when Rob was at home and of Nylene's comment that Paula was "tired of his ways." June even told the detectives of the pot that she and Paula smoked.

After the officers had gone June remembered Paula's concern about Rob's Vietnam nightmares, so she phoned the police station to add the information. She had learned from newspaper profiles on Rob and Paula that Rob had never served in Vietnam. Now, in retrospect, Paula's comment seemed peculiar.

Although June told the police that Paula had mentioned Vietnam to justify an inquiry about psychiatric help, that fact was lost along the way. Police chose to emphasize the fact that Paula, or Rob, or both, had lied about his service record.

Thus the most telling piece of evidence about Paula's emotional condition went unexamined. Whether Paula's quest for psychiatric help was based on the dark impulse she felt taking root in herself or on her growing unhappiness at trying to survive in a household governed by rules and repression (a distinction she herself did not attempt to make), the need for assistance was something she clearly felt. But her effort to seek help was lost, as she herself would soon be lost, in the adversarial system of justice.

June's candor, a trait for which she was recognized, should not have surprised Paula, for the two women had been close for more than a decade. Yet when Paula learned that June had spoken freely to the police, that she had told everything she could think to tell, their relationship was abruptly and dramatically curtailed. It would be years before Paula communicated with June again.

Rhonda was naturally more reserved and cautious, but when the police arrived it was not just her innate restraint that kept her answers short. She had observed what had happened to the relationship between June and Paula after June told "everything." With that lesson in mind, Rhonda took the opposite tack. She answered officers' questions, but she didn't elaborate; she didn't volunteer opinions; she didn't talk about the difficulties in the Sims marriage. She said nothing about Paula's despondent phone call six months earlier, midway through her pregnancy— the phone call in which she spoke of Rob's "rules" and of his "problems." Rhonda said as little as she could, because she assumed that was what Paula would want her to do.

Another woman who might have shed some light on Paula's post-delivery emotional reactions was Stella Hyatt. She vividly remembered Paula's phone call after Randy's birth, and she would have explained that Paula had been lonely, crying, and depressed. But no one thought to ask her.

The outline of the story lay hidden in the statements of Paula's friends, women who had witnessed her isolation, heard her sobs, and surmised her unhappiness. A careful, unbiased inspection might have connected the stories and comprehended the design, but that was not to be. Battle lines had been drawn.

On May 21 a subdued family observed Paula's thirtieth birthday. Her brother Dennis gave her his usual gift, a bottle of perfume. This year it was Ciara. Nylene baked a cake. Rob signed a birthday card.

On Memorial Day many people who visited Woodland Cemetery stopped for a moment at the graves of Loralei and Heather. Some left flowers. The grave site was identifiable only by a temporary marker, and area residents decried the lack of a permanent plaque or stone. There was talk of donations to purchase something suitable, but the cemetery association forewarned that only "family markers" were allowed.

Thereafter the Blews did install a gravestone. On it were two sleeping cherubs. A narrow banner swirled from the little angels, curling around the "Sims" name and heralding "Together Eternally In Love." The banner message was interrupted by two hearts containing the words "Mom" and "Dad." At the bottom of the gray stone were the names, "Loralei M.," "Heather L.," "Paula M.," and "Robert E." The birth date of each was given. There were no dates of death for Loralei or Heather.

The fact that Loralei and Heather were in the ground while Paula was free on bond aggravated many in the community, most of all the Alton police, who looked at pictures of the tiny, helpless girls and compared them to photos of Paula, tall and athletic, cold and withdrawn. Officers who had spoken with her found her to be at best introverted and aloof, at worst antagonistic and combative.

Although a motive would have strengthened their case, the urgency lay not in understanding why the murders occurred but simply in proving that Paula had committed them. If necessary, lawmen could live with the puzzle; they could accept the idea of a killer who came without reason and claimed her victims. A sign in block letters over the desks of Detectives McCain and Ventimiglia said all they needed to know:

S̲udden I̲nfant M̲urder S̲yndrome

<h1 style="text-align:center">22</h1>

ALREADY INDICTED IN JERSEY COUNTY, PAULA AWAITED MADI-son County's legal action. "I knew it was comin'. I knew things were gonna get bad, real bad. But they turned out to be more awful than I coulda imagined."

She and Rob were allowed to see Randy once each week for twenty-five minutes; a social worker, accompanied by two armed guards, delivered the child to the nursery of the Bethalto Baptist Church. At each visit the reports of Randy's condition worsened. He had been taken to an emergency room for a high fever, the social worker said. He refused to eat. He didn't relate well to his foster mother. He had inadvertently been exposed to chicken pox.

With another arrest imminent and her little boy crying each time she handed him back to the social worker, Paula made a decision. Nylene no longer kept her Xanax on the kitchen windowsill, but Paula had managed to find the hidden bottle. She had been gulping a pill every day, hoping her mother wouldn't notice. "It's not like I was strung out all the time. Just enough to ease the pain, or ease my hurt, or

228

keep me calm, or somethin'.'" It would only require a few extra Xanax, plus some Valium from the cupboard of Rob's sister Linda. Pills and booze, that was the combination she had heard about. There was liquor, long forgotten, in her parents' basement cabinet—a few ounces in one bottle, a few ounces in another, five or six bottles in all.

She took the pills—at least a dozen of them, maybe more—not bothering to count, and washed them down with the alcohol, methodically draining the remains in each container. Habit made her replace the cap on every bottle. There would be no mess. When her head was spinning enough that she could drink no more she lay down on the basement couch, asked God for forgiveness, and closed her eyes.

More than twelve hours later she woke and stared, disappointed, at the ceiling. Her eyes burned; her mouth was dry; her head throbbed as she slowly climbed the stairs. When she opened the basement door her mother looked up. "You slept a long time," she said. "That's good. You needed some rest."

Rob's sister Linda Condray told interviewing officers she was "pretty well convinced" that Jersey County Sheriff Frank Yocom was responsible for Heather's death. He had been unable to pin Loralei's murder on Rob and Paula, she theorized, and his frustration led him to retaliate. Officers duly recorded Linda's opinion; then they called Yocom to tell him the news.

One objective of the interviewers who talked to Linda was to probe the mystery of Heather's well-preserved body. Investigators wondered if Paula had gone directly to her sister-in-law's house when she was asked to leave Washington Avenue the morning after Heather disappeared, or if she had gone somewhere else first, perhaps to the Blews' empty house, where Heather lay in the basement freezer.

As far as she knew, Linda told officers, Paula had spent "almost the entire day" at the Condray home. She was unable to be more specific because she herself had been at

Washington Avenue, angry that police would not allow her to enter her brother's house.

Investigators turned their questions to May 3, the date that Heather's body was found in the trash barrel. Linda said she could not remember how she had spent her time on that day. Her husband Herb had had a photography session from 10 to 10:30 A.M.; she could not recall what he had done after that. Neither could Herb, when he was asked. As far as they knew, the Condrays said, the Simses had spent that day at home.

Throughout June officials continued to say that charges in the death of Heather were forthcoming. Or imminent. Or impending. Attorney Groshong offered to deliver Paula to the police station whenever Madison County wanted her. Police ignored his offer and instead arrested her at her parents' home on Saturday, July 1. She was charged, as she had been in Jersey County, with obstructing justice and concealing a homicidal death.

State's Attorney Haine told the press that the arrest was made on Saturday afternoon because Saturday was a day that "wouldn't encourage excessive media coverage." Paula's attorney, Donald Groshong, stated what most people figured out for themselves: The arrest was made on Saturday because the banks were closed and bail arrangements could not be made until Monday. He pointed out that Paula had offered to turn herself in, a procedure which would have engendered even less media coverage.

At Monday's court hearing Paula appeared in handcuffs, shackles, and orange jail garb. Groshong complained to Judge Edward Ferguson about the $250,000 bond that had been set: "If her name was anything other than Paula Sims, you would never, ever see a bond this high." Detective McCain testified that he believed Paula might flee, and the prosecutor assigned to the case, Don Weber, told the judge that she would soon be charged with murder. Ferguson refused to lower the bond. Orville Blew posted $25,000 for his daughter's release.

The following night a large chunk of concrete smashed through the back window of the Simses' station wagon, which was parked in front of the Blews' house. Police were unable to determine who had vandalized the vehicle.

Keeping Paula in jail over the weekend was the first of three pressure strategies attempted by authorities. The second was a letter from prosecutor Weber to defense attorney Groshong suggesting that the Simses' son Randy, who had been in protective custody for almost two months, might be returned. The condition tied to Randy's return was that Rob must agree to testify against Paula. Word of the letter was leaked to Alton's *Telegraph* by Herb Condray, who labeled the move "KGB tactics."

The third pressure point was aimed at Herb himself. More than a decade earlier Terri, Rob's first wife, had observed a camaraderie between Herb and his father-in-law, Troy Sims, and had ascribed it to their maturity and their common experience as schoolteachers. Investigators discovered the two men shared something beyond age and occupation.

Herb and Linda Condray were summoned a second time to appear before the grand jury. When they reported to the courthouse a thirtyish black woman in a bright red dress stood with police in the marble hallway. The woman's identity, at least in terms of her connection to the case, was soon shared with favored newsmen by "sources within the investigation." She was a "special friend" of Herb Condray, a friend he visited weekly, a friend he reportedly escorted to bingo games, a friend to whom he gave money. The story became even juicier as the press learned that Herb was not the only member of the Sims clan to be thus entertained. His father-in-law, Troy, was also among the black woman's visitors.

The woman, of course, never entered the grand jury room, and the ploy was obvious once her identity had been leaked. The crux was Paula's arrival time at Herb's house on Sunday, April 30. Police were convinced that she had gone not directly to the Condrays, as she said she had, but to her parents' home to keep watch on a well-chilled baby, ready to move the evidence whenever it became necessary. Herb could bolster the police theory, by saying she had arrived at noon or later, or he could come down on the side of the defense, by saying she had arrived at 8 A.M. Police hoped he might think carefully about his answer if he realized they were aware of his extramarital activities.

Herb was given plenty of time to think as he waited to be questioned. After he and Linda were given a good look at the woman in red they were left to cool their heels in separate waiting rooms. Neither of them was called to the grand jury room; they left the courthouse without testifying.

The black woman's relationship with Herb and Troy was generally viewed as an indication of the peculiarity of the entire Sims clan. Had authorities been so inclined, they might have looked upon it as an indication of the misogyny in the family. The information did little more than raise eyebrows and occasion smirks, but a serious consideration of the "bingo" games might have included some thought of the position in which Linda was placed. The news that her father and her husband were partners in an effort to deceive her would surely prove traumatic.

For both Troy and Herb the alliance suggested a capacity for intrigue that far outdistanced their capacity for intimacy. With his wife, Bernie, dead for more than three years, Troy certainly might have desired female companionship. That he sought it in a woman whose favors he shared furtively with his son-in-law rather than in a suitably available woman—a woman with whom he might have had an emotional as well as a physical experience—defined his limitations.

The quest for a motive, or at least an explanation of the crime, led authorities to explore relationships in the Blew family as well. Specifically, they wondered if Paula might have been sexually abused. Questioning of the Blews' former La Plata neighbors revealed her link to her brother Randy. The two had been close, everyone agreed; very close.

In La Plata a whisper of incest circulated after the official questions ceased. Since Randy was not around to deny it, the rumor grew. Talk became so persistent that people who had never before considered the possibility began to wonder.

In official circles, Randy was not the only member of the Blew family under suspicion. Police wondered, too, about Orville, but they were more circumspect in their inquiries.

Although they were on the right track, investigators never delved deep enough into the family history to discover the unsavory habits of Grandpa Blew. To search out that information would have been nearly impossible, for the old man had died, and Paula had never told anyone of the terrors he had inflicted upon her during her summer visits.

Paula's parents, Orville and Nylene, were subpoenaed to appear before the grand jury on the same day that Herb and Linda Condray waited to appear. Police had hinted, and on occasion actually stated, that the Blews were "possible suspects," but no one said exactly what they were suspected of. Unable to determine what charges, if any, might be filed against them, and unable to predict how their testimony might affect Paula's case, attorney Don Groshong advised them not to testify.

On July 10 Nylene, represented by Groshong, cited her Fifth Amendment rights and declined to offer testimony. Prosecutor Weber took her immediately before a judge who granted her immunity. When everyone returned to the grand jury room Weber surprised Groshong by objecting to his presence. Because Groshong represented Paula, Weber insisted, it was inappropriate for him to hear the testimony of a witness who might give evidence against her. Groshong, fuming, took Nylene back to the judge. The judge agreed with Weber and ordered Nylene to return with separate legal counsel. Orville went through the same process.

The order for the Blews to retain separate counsel received wide publicity and furthered public speculation that the grandparents must indeed have had something to do with the baby's death. (Although State's Attorney Haine would later say that they were *not* suspects, his exonerating statement received less coverage, and the Blews were left tainted.) With a new attorney Orville and Nylene spent nearly four hours on July 11 answering the grand jury's questions. At their home a police car was parked, standing guard on their daughter.

Inside, Paula waited with Rob, wishing the police would knock on the door and get it over with. Her parents returned from the grand jury hearing, Orville angry that the prosecutor had asked him if he had ever procured birth control pills for his daughter. The implication was clear.

"How are you doing, Mom?" Paula asked Nylene.

"I can't talk about it, Paula," Nylene answered. She used a legal excuse to cover her turmoil. "It's confidential. I just can't talk about it."

"I don't wanna know what they asked you, Mom," Paula said. "I just wanna know how you are."

"I have to lie down," Nylene protested. She stopped at the bedroom door. "Paula, I want you to know, whatever has happened here, I love you. And I will always love you." She closed the door behind her.

At 5:45 P.M. a Madison County murder indictment was issued. The charge was two counts of first-degree murder, both of which related to Heather. The filing of double charges, allowing a choice of murder theories, was common legal practice in Illinois. In this case, one choice stated that Paula *intended* to murder Heather; the second, that she knew her actions *could* cause Heather's death. However a jury might choose to see it.

There was another twist to the indictment; its phrasing included the possibility that Paula could be convicted of murder even if she personally hadn't done the deed. Paula Sims "or one for whose conduct she is legally accountable," the document read. Illinois' doctrine of accountability allowed that anyone who aided in a crime, or failed to attempt to stop a crime, could be convicted as though he (or in this case *she*) were the perpetrator of the crime. Although it was not directly stated, it was obvious that the "one for whose conduct she is legally accountable" was Rob. He was the only other person mentioned in the report of the grand jury.

At 6:25 P.M. officers knocked on the Blews' door. Rob clung to Paula, declaring that he didn't know what he would do without her. Her manacled walk to a police car was recorded by television and newspaper photographers. Orville yelled at them to get off the lawn.

Two days later Paula made a silent appearance in handcuffs and shackles while Groshong filed her plea of innocent. This time there was no bond; she stayed in jail.

The next months were a round of hearings on one charge or another, in one county or another, in one court or another. Donald Groshong, Paula's attorney, and Don Weber, the assistant state's attorney assigned to prosecute the case, argued through them. The most startling news to emerge concerned the trash bags. The FBI determined that the black plastic bag in which Heather was discovered had been manufactured at the same plant, during the same twelve-hour period, as bags the Simses had purchased at K-mart and stored in their home.

Ten days after Paula's arrest Linda and Herb Condray were called yet again to appear before the grand jury. A day after that Troy Sims, Rob's father, answered a subpoena. The proceedings being secret, there was no way reporters could know how the presence of the woman in red had affected the witnesses. Herb testified for less than twenty minutes. His only remark to the press was "It's a charade."

Troy Sims said nothing to reporters. (Two months earlier, shortly after telling the *Post-Dispatch* that Rob had enjoyed "a normal boyhood, just like any other boy," Troy had begun to distance himself from the case. He told Alton's *Telegraph* that he was not in close contact with Rob. "I've only talked to him one time since this started. I don't want to get involved any further. I don't know anything. I'm just trying not to become involved.")

Paula remained in the Madison County jail in Edwardsville. Reporter Tom Herrmann of the *Telegraph* interviewed a woman released from the jail who told him that when Paula had first arrived other prisoners had taunted her with comments and innuendos about trash bags. But things had settled down, the woman said: "All she does at night is cry and smoke a lot of cigarettes."

The Alton police, too, were interviewing released prisoners about Paula. A notice was posted in the booking area of the jail advising personnel that no female prisoner who had been in the facility longer than a few days was to be released without prior notice to the Sims case agent, Tony Ventimiglia. Defense attorney Groshong, who had tried to circumvent such tactics by requesting separate incarceration for Paula, complained to a judge: "The State has, in effect, made all female prisoners in the jail their agent-informants. . . ."

In actuality, Paula's cellmates were not providing much useful data. From one woman police learned that Paula slept most of the time and that Rob had found an apartment. Another said that Paula cried often and was "heartbroken" that authorities had taken Randy. A third said that Rob had been recently baptized and that Paula herself prayed every day.

Before Paula's third and final arrest on July 11 she and Rob had stopped several times at the home of Rhonda Scott. Rhonda had urged them to come. They needed somewhere as a refuge, she believed. They needed a moment away from lawyers, a moment away from Paula's family, with whom they had continued to live as their legal difficulties mounted. Rhonda offered warmth, acceptance, and a determined belief in the innocence of her friend.

After Paula was jailed Rhonda insisted that she phone regularly. Paula called on Tuesdays; Rhonda knew when the phone would ring and was always home to accept the charges. Frequently Paula asked for news about the latest court proceedings. "I don't understand it all," she said when Rhonda wondered why she had questions about her own case. "What does the newspaper say about it?"

Rob, too, kept in touch with Rhonda, stopping as he

drove by the Scotts' home. Invariably he asked Rhonda if Paula had called, and if they had talked about the case. If Rhonda said yes, he was always upset. "I told her not to talk about it," he complained.

Rhonda encouraged Rob's visits. "He seemed so lost," she judged. "So scared." At Halloween he brought candy for the Scott children. At other times he brought photographs.

"Look at these pictures," he said to Rhonda. "Can't you see how happy we were?"

23

GROSHONG CHALLENGED THE FIRST TWO MADISON COUNTY judges assigned and tried to disqualify the third as well. When that effort proved unsuccessful, the Sims case landed on the docket of A. Andreas Mateosian. In early November prosecutors announced they intended to seek the death penalty, which, under Illinois statutes, was allowed "if the murdered individual was under twelve years of age, and the death resulted from exceptionally brutal or heinous behavior indicative of wanton cruelty."

It was generally agreed that the Madison County case against Paula—the Heather case—was stronger than the Jersey County—or Loralei—case. Jersey County had never filed its murder charges and might not need to, if the Madison County prosecution was successful. If one jury found Paula guilty of murdering Heather, they could sentence her to death. There would be little point in another jury finding her guilty of murdering Loralei and, perhaps, sentencing her to death again.

Groshong argued that Paula could not get a fair trial in

Madison County. The trial there had already taken place, he said, in the press; there was no resident unaware of the case, and few who had not made up their minds about its proper outcome. The judge concurred. He moved the trial to Peoria County and scheduled it for January 8, 1990.

On another matter Groshong lost, and the loss was a major setback. The contention began when prosecutor Weber let it be known that he wanted to introduce testimony about *Loralei's* disappearance in Paula's trial for *Heather's* murder.

Everyone in Madison County knew that there had been *two* little girls, *two* tales of masked gunmen. It was the duplication that made the case so bizarre, so compelling. Paula Sims would not be the first woman to kill her children and place the blame on someone else; women before her had told tales of phantom figures who stalked the night. But none had tried it *twice*. None had told the same suspicious story a second time, knowing full well that it had been heard with incredulity the first.

The transfer of the trial to Peoria County gave the defense a chance at a populace that didn't automatically couple the names of the little girls. Paula would be tried for the murder of only one of her daughters, and a tale of one masked gunman was not as improbable as a tale of two. If Weber were allowed to introduce Loralei's name into the trial for Heather's murder, however, the advantage of a new locale would be diminished. It would be impossible for a jury to forget the first little girl when ascribing blame for the death of the second.

And yet, legally, the trial was supposed to be a judgment of only one killing. Paula had not been charged with killing Loralei three years earlier. She was *still* not charged with the murder of Loralei. Officially, Loralei's death was not classified as murder; its cause was "undetermined." Groshong was impassioned as he argued against introducing testimony about Loralei.

Weber was just as emotional as he argued in favor of it. It was, after all, the repetition, the duality, that made the case unique. How could jurors properly judge the truth of Paula's story about the black-garbed intruder's kidnapping of Heather if they didn't know that she had told the story before, about Loralei? The two incidents could not be separated, Weber insisted; Paula had linked them by telling the same story.

The judge ruled in favor of the prosecution. Testimony on Loralei's death could be introduced at the trial; a jury would determine if the evidence indicated a "pattern of crime."

The outcome was cause for joy in Haine's office. Late summer and autumn had seen case after high-profile case in which Madison County defendants were acquitted. The state's attorney was losing cases, open-and-shut cases, cases in which victories had been confidently predicted. The public was beginning to wonder what was wrong with William Haine, or his staff, or both. The Sims case was one the prosecution needed to win. It wasn't just Paula Sims' future that was on the line, it was the political future of some prominent Madison County officials.

As 1989 drew to a close Randy Sims had been in protective custody for more than six months. Paula had not seen him since she went to jail; Rob had continued to visit him each week for twenty-five minutes, as had the Blews.

When a full-blown hearing on the custody issue failed to materialize until six weeks before the criminal trial, it was widely regarded as a preview of the coming attraction. The prosecution would have to reveal at least some of the cards it held, for the state's object was to convince a judge that Randy would be in danger if he were returned to the Simses, and that meant using the same evidence, and some of the same witnesses, that would be offered in the criminal trial. Although it was Randy's future that was to be decided, not Paula's, the hearing was nevertheless seen as a kind of "dress rehearsal" for the main event.

It began at the end of November and then, because of the unavailability of witnesses, looped over to mid-December. Word circulated quickly the first time Paula was brought from the jail to the courtroom. A sheriff's deputy escorted her from the elevator, her hands cuffed to a wide leather belt buckled around her waist, her feet in chains. Cameramen lined the hallway; their lights turned on as the elevator doors opened. Paula emerged, pale and blinking. Her hair was limp and drab, but the most remarkable change in her appearance was her loss of weight. She appeared almost frail, and her unseeing stare through the crowd added a note of otherworldliness.

In the small courtroom of Judge Ellar Duff three rows of reporters filled the benches. This being family court, no "civilian" observers were allowed. The Simses sat next to each other at a table only a few feet from the press, occasionally whispering while trying to keep their faces turned away from observers. Rob, too, was thinner. His hair and beard were closely trimmed. His shoulders had grown more stooped, making him look older than thirty-seven. He carried a Bible, and during recesses, when Paula was handcuffed and taken to a holding cell, he studied the book of Job, the story of a man who had borne great affliction with fortitude and faith.

As they sat at the table during respites in the legal action a few moments of intimacy passed between the two: He stroked her arm; she straightened his collar; he squeezed her hand when she wept. More than physical contact, it was eye contact that united them. She studied his face; he stared at hers, nodding almost imperceptibly; then, as though by silent, mutual consent, both focused on the tabletop before them.

Rob wiped his eyes as he viewed a videotape of the scene at the lock and dam access area, a tape that showed Heather's naked body in the trash can. Paula chose not to watch.

FBI agent Carl Schulz testified that Rob had said Randy might be "in clear and imminent danger" because Paula "could wring his neck in just a few seconds," but under Groshong's cross-examination Schulz admitted that Rob had made the statements only after he was supplied with information designed to convince him that his wife was guilty. Schulz described the sleeping arrangements at the

Sims house and quoted Rob's "best and longest-lasting sex" statement, an item that had surfaced at an earlier hearing but that, mingled with other information from the case, had received comparatively little attention.

Three more FBI agents took the stand to explain the mysteries of trash bag manufacture and to tell of their efforts to link the bag in which Heather was found to those in the Sims house. Their previous estimate that all the bags in question were made within twelve hours had been considerably refined. "Within ten seconds" was the new judgment. Heather's bag had been manufactured within ten seconds of those on the open roll on Paula's shelves. It was an estimation so surprisingly precise that Groshong asked the agent to repeat it.

But no, the agents said, they hadn't been able to match the perforations on Heather's bag to those on any other bag, and they didn't find the Simses' fingerprints on the plastic.

Stephanie Werner, Paula's hospital roommate, made her first public appearance. She had married in the time since she had shared a room with Paula; she was now Stephanie Cook. The press didn't know what to make of her. She was young and pretty, and she sounded reasonable as she explained how Paula had connected the trash removal to *Loralei's* kidnapping, but reporters looked at one another with raised eyebrows when she said she hadn't read newspaper articles or listened to television reports on Heather's disappearance.

Waiting for a decision on their son's future, the Simses sat side by side, staring at nothing.

It didn't take Judge Duff long to rule that Paula presented a risk to the child, but she declared that the state had not met its burden of proof in regard to Rob. She ordered the boy returned to his father "instantly." It was only a temporary ruling, but it brought Randy home for Christmas. Rob and Paula wept and embraced. When reporters asked him for a comment, Rob said, after a pause, "I praise the Lord."

Tidbits from the hearing brought the Sims case back to page one. The "ten-second" determination on the trash bags made all the papers, as did the Simses' "best and longest-lasting sex" three days after their daughter was supposedly kidnapped. People reacted to Rob's remark in predictably different ways. Some were unable to imagine how any couple could have thought of sex at such a time. Others admitted that some of their most intimate moments had come at critical times when they were looking less for sexual gratification than for closeness and comfort.

Everyone agreed that telling an FBI agent about the experience was stupid.

V

The Trial

24

IN PEORIA, 160 MILES FROM MADISON COUNTY, THE COURT-house was under renovation. A new sally port wouldn't be ready until the second day of the Sims trial, so on January 8, 1990, the jail van deposited Paula on the curb, much to the satisfaction of photographers and TV cameramen, who scrambled to document the moment.

The first morning's audience was composed of reporters, some of whom had traveled to Peoria in the antenna-topped minivans that lined the streets. A ban on cameras in the courtroom resulted in the presence of a half dozen sketch artists who staked out the front rows, spread their equipment, and waited.

Judge A. Andreas Matoesian entered, zipping up his robe, and motioned for the hastily rising press corps to be seated. "Okay," he called to the attorneys, "come on in." Matoesian's informal, easygoing style was contradicted by his stern features. A prominent nose and sagging cheeks highlighted a face that lent itself to quick capture in the work of the sketch artists.

Harder to portray were the opposing lawyers, assistant

247

state's attorney Don Weber and defense attorney Donald Groshong. Both in their early forties, both with mustaches, the two men shared sloping chin lines that made them appear vaguely similar in artists' drawings. In dress and demeanor, however, they differed. Groshong wore dark suits and colorful ties. His straight silver hair was too short to mask a tiny hearing aid in his left ear. Weber favored sports coats, sometimes wore cowboy boots, and always combed his dark hair carefully over an incipient bald spot.

Groshong avoided reporters and, when cornered, responded with a terse "no comment." Weber courted the press, ready to volunteer an opinion or reaction. ("She was murdered because she had diarrhea," he said of Heather as he circulated in the hotel the evening before the trial. To listeners who appeared startled, he repeated the alleged motive. "Diarrhea," he said, nodding knowingly.)

Groshong was joined at the defense table by one of his law partners, Jim Williamson, a genial, portly figure with "southern-gentleman" manners who limped slightly and carried a cane. Assisting Weber was Kit Morrissey, a young, dark-haired, serious-looking assistant prosecutor. Ms. Morrissey's presence, suggested a reporter from southern Illinois, was designed to circumvent any suggestion that the case was a contest between powerful male officials and a weak female defendant.

A slow, almost dreamlike quality marked Paula's entrance. Even thinner than she had been at the custody hearing, she wore a striped sweater and slacks with flared legs, a style from some long-ago season. A skirt was out of the question, for no hosiery would survive the shackles she donned when she traveled from jail to courthouse, but the slacks accentuated her gauntness. Her hipbones protruded; her legs were lost in the fabric of the pants.

Her light brown hair fell below her shoulders and hung limply, close to her head. Her eyes were dark and hollow, her gaze lingering only briefly on those who watched from the spectators' benches. Moving silently on crepe-soled brown oxfords, she took her place in an armchair at the end of the defense table, close to onlookers but turned away. She crossed her legs and folded her hands in her lap. She appeared haggard, startled, frightened, and much older than thirty, a combination of qualities that artists struggled to capture.

Both prosecution and defense began with bravado. Groshong, arguing a preliminary motion, added, ". . . assuming there's a conviction, which in this case there won't be." Weber responded with a forced, exaggerated chuckle. When his opportunity came for prediction, Weber countered with, ". . . this murder of Heather for which Paula Sims will be convicted in a couple weeks." Another Weber remark ended up in most reporters' stories: "Murder was percolating in her malignant heart," he intoned as he pointed at Paula.

The chief business of the trial's first days was the selection of twelve jurors and three alternates. A dozen at a time, the candidates climbed into the jury box. Almost without exception they acknowledged their exposure to the extensive news coverage of the case. Some admitted they had already formed opinions and would be unable to judge the evidence fairly. Those who claimed an ability to ignore the stories they had heard or read faced interrogation from Weber and Groshong. Weber questioned their willingness to judge a woman and, if they found her guilty, sentence her to die. Each time he said "if you find that Paula Sims murdered her daughter . . ." he pointed at the defendant.

To assist Weber the state's attorney's office had hired a Des Moines, Iowa, jury consulting firm. Two women from Starr & Associates sat in the front row, scoring prospective jurors on age, attire, occupation, and responses, attempting to predict those who were prosecution-minded.

As questions ground on, Paula's stillness did not waver. She faced panel members, but her focus was on the wall above their heads. Even when one of them acknowledged he would be comfortable sentencing her to death she showed no reaction.

Groshong tried to determine which prospective jurors might harbor some intentional or unintentional empathy. Did they have any children? What were the children's ages and sexes? Did they have any knowledge of Sudden Infant Death Syndrome?

The SIDS question brought exchanges of startled glances among the press. Was this a hint of defense strategy? Would Groshong suggest Heather was found lifeless in her crib? And Loralei also? Two little girls fallen victim to some mysterious but natural cause? The SIDS query was persistent, and reporters struggled to imagine a scenario to fit it.

The subject that did not come up in Groshong's interrogation was postpartum psychosis, a condition other attorneys had suggested privately might be a logical defense. There was no suggestion that Paula's mental condition was relevant.

Groshong's approach confused the press, who couldn't forecast what direction his defense would take. Apparently postpartum was out; it was to be either SIDS or the masked man.

At the end of the second day Groshong made a plea for toiletries for Paula. The Peoria jail had offered her no soap, toothpaste, or shampoo since she arrived, he complained. Matoesian ordered a court officer to remedy the oversight. On the third morning Paula's hair appeared fresher, although her dour expression and colorless clothes overshadowed any improvement. Still, Groshong renewed his request. The judge, impatient, asked why his order had been ignored. Because the prisoner brought her own supplies from Madison County, someone answered. Groshong again stepped forward; she did bring her own supplies, he acknowledged, but they were taken from her and locked up as personal property. The judge glowered; his tone was sharp as he spoke once more to a court officer.

Paula sat through the hours, silent but sadly attentive. Weber asked a woman from the jury panel if she felt any sympathy for the defendant. "She looks so unhappy," the woman replied hesitantly. Weber quickly excused her.

Finally, at the end of the third day, after the questioning of eighty-eight candidates, a jury was seated: eight men and four women, two of them black, with three male alternates. They were blue collar and white collar, ranging in age from the twenties to the sixties. Some were unmarried; several had children; a few had grandchildren.

The trial's first three days produced a variety of legal motions, most from the defense and most denied by the judge. Groshong moved repeatedly for an order sequestering the jury. He cited the flood of stories in the Peoria press and displayed headlines to prove his point. Matoesian declined, instead warning jurors to avoid the publicity.

Groshong asked the judge to order prosecutors and law enforcement officers to refrain from comment to the press. The judge deemed it unnecessary.

The defense's only success was a request to suppress a toxicological scan that had detected marijuana in Paula's blood. (No mention was ever made of the alcohol and tranquilizers she had consumed). Marijuana might be prejudicial, the judge agreed; he granted the motion.

Opening arguments brought a larger crowd to the courtroom, more reporters, more spectators. A growing group of sketch artists jockeyed for space. The judge requested that the press squeeze into the wooden benches on one side of the room, freeing the other half for "civilians."

Paula, clad in slacks as usual, entered quietly to face the increased audience. As she walked to her chair at the defense table she focused steadfastly on a point high on the back wall. So intent was her apparent interest that several spectators turned to see what had caught her attention.

Shortly after 9 A.M. Weber began. He was calm as he gave the dates that began and ended the lives of Loralei Marie and Heather Lee. "The last person to see Heather and Loralei alive was the defendant." He pointed at her. "Paula Sims." She killed them, he said, "mercilessly and in cold blood."

Paula's story was "as close to a fairy tale as you can get in a murder case," Weber said, a tale involving a "roving Rumpelstiltskin" who showed up on her doorstep twice. "Nobody sees or hears or smells this Rumpelstiltskin, this fairy-tale figure," he mocked. Reporters liked the Rumpelstiltskin image; pencils were busy.

Weber hinted at motive: "Paula doesn't hate baby girls. She just doesn't like them. Robert doesn't like them. . . . There have been three children born to the Simses. The boy survives. The girls are dead."

Paula's crucial mistakes, he claimed, were the trash bag and her alleged injury; she didn't realize the bag could be traced so accurately, and she complained of a wound that left no trace.

It was her "cold-blooded, murderous face," Weber concluded as he pointed at her once more, "that was the last face Baby Heather and Baby Loralei saw."

Eager to know the direction of his defense, reporters were attentive as Groshong stood. Paula was a victim, he began, not a perpetrator. Her explanation was discounted just because it was out of the ordinary. The police never looked for the real criminal; they heard Paula's story, decided it couldn't possibly have happened, and focused on the Simses as the only suspects. "The facts of this case may be unusual, but they are true," Groshong insisted.

That was it, then. The masked man.

Groshong dealt immediately with the issue of the trash bag, offering his theory before the jury had a chance to hear the FBI's careful data. The trash bag probably did come from the Sims home, he conceded; the abductor picked it up in the kitchen to carry Heather, just as a thief picks up a pillow case to contain the valuables he steals.

Weber smiled and shook his head.

Testimony would bring more questions than answers, Groshong warned, but it would clearly show that Paula was a good mother. And the defendant herself, he promised in conclusion, would testify.

Paula watched her attorney sit down. It was impossible to

tell how she felt about his presentation. There were no supporters in the room to whom she could look for an opinion; her friends and family members—those whose names appeared on the witness list—were barred from court until after their testimony.

She would face judgment alone.

=== 25 ===

EACH WITNESS SWORE TO TELL THE TRUTH, THE WHOLE TRUTH; but truth could be offered only in response to questions asked, and the questions were structured to bolster opposing theories. Opening statements had drawn the outlines. The prosecution looked at Paula Sims as a "malignant heart," a mother who didn't want daughters and casually killed them. The defense saw a star-crossed victim stalked by a dark stranger. Any "truth" that didn't add color to one portrait or the other was left on the palette. No realistic portrait would emerge; it was to be a choice between caricatures.

Marvin Hyatt, the neighbor to whose home Paula had run for help on that summer night three and a half years earlier, told his story simply and directly. She had been "very excited, crying," he said, "like you would expect a person to be in that situation." He told of the police, the sheriff, the search, the confusion. His words were factual rather than judgmental, as though he was still absorbing what had happened. The Simses had been so happy to learn they were having a child, he remembered, "thrilled."

Before Marvin left the stand Groshong asked him to look at Paula and evaluate her physical appearance. Marvin shrugged; he didn't seem to know what to say. At Groshong's request Paula rose slowly from her chair, her hands clasped self-consciously in front of her. Still Marvin hesitated. Groshong put the question directly: Had she lost weight? It was no use. Marvin shook his head. He was unable to judge.

His wife showed no hesitation when she was asked. Paula had definitely lost weight, Stella Hyatt observed, "a lot of weight." Stella was anxious as the questioning began, but she recalled her own words, Marvin's words, Paula's words. Time had not dimmed her memory.

Paula said she was never afraid back by the woods because she had her dog Shadow, Stella explained. Weber asked if Stella had heard any barking from Shadow before Paula pounded on her door. "No," she said quietly. Weber raised an eyebrow and cast a knowing smile at jurors and spectators.

Sheriff Frank Yocom began the parade of lawmen who told what they had done and seen and heard on June 17, 1986. Yocom was obviously accustomed to testifying. He had a presence that filled the witness chair as completely as his portly body. He spoke directly to the jurors and phrased his answers in concrete terms: The slit in the screen door was "slightly longer than my hand"; a "gut feeling" told him "something wasn't right"; the undergrowth on the hillside was "knee-high."

Yocom was difficult to pin down on the subject of the dog searches. Apparently the lawmen had decided that a little equivocation was better than admitting they weren't sure where the dogs had been, that someone from Springfield had refused to send Donovan and Jud back to the scene, and that no one was certain what had been searched, or when, or by whom.

Bear, Sergeant, Tracker, Rocky, and Jud were introduced through the statements of their masters. The dogs' efforts were described, and their lack of success. When questions turned to the wooded area where Loralei's body was found the K-9 handlers were vague. The problem of *who* had been *where*, and *when*, was buried in other detail. The point stressed was that Loralei's remains were eventually found by one of the dogs, a hundred feet from her parents' back door.

Rainy weather increased the number of people hoping for a seat at the trial, but once in the courtroom, spectators frequently found more tedium than tension. Circumstantial evidence depended upon accumulation of detail, relentless recitation from the investigating officers. Each man told of his activities, his observations. Weber's allusions to the abductor were repetitiously sarcastic: "if this *phantom* . . . so this *bandito* . . ." Groshong's cross-examination was meandering and often lasted longer than the direct examination. Witnesses' stories began to flow together.

The routine was broken as two television monitors were hauled into the courtroom. Through a series of legal missteps and maneuvers, a DCI videotape purporting to "reenact" Loralei's abduction—a tape that had been previously rejected by both the custody hearing judge and the trial judge—was declared admissable. Groshong's objections continued even as the equipment was set up to play it. The tape was "not accurate," he charged, and was "never intended to be accurate." He was repeatedly overruled.

DCI lieutenant Wayne Watson explained that six versions had been recorded. In each, Sheriff Yocom did a countdown ("Three, two, one, go"). Watson, as the kidnapper, ran up the stairs from the basement family room. DCI officer Debra Morgan, playing Paula, lay on the family room floor until she heard the screen door slam, then followed him. When they exited the house the cameras picked them up.

In some versions Watson was empty-handed; in some he carried a gun and a doll. Twice he headed directly down the driveway. Twice he headed around the house and down the wooded hillside, then back up and on to the driveway. Once he ran just to the edge of the woods, where he pretended to throw an object. Once he actually threw the three-pound doll, sending it fifty-seven feet into the trees. No matter how he did it, Morgan was close behind him—close enough to get a clear look at him as he passed under the dusk-to-dawn lamp. Sometimes she reached the light before he did and stood waiting there as he passed.

All the versions made the same point: If a kidnapper had run down the lane, Paula's proximity would have produced a clearer description than a "shadowy figure" and "footsteps in gravel."

When Watson left the stand Groshong moved for a mistrial. Evidence on Loralei's death had no place in a trial in which the defendant was charged with murdering Heather, he insisted once more. His motion was denied.

The most dramatic link between the two abduction stories was Stephanie Werner Cook, Paula's hospital roommate. Stephanie entered the courtroom, demure and pretty in an aqua satin dress. Her curly brown hair cascaded onto a huge white collar. She was again pregnant, she said; her condition had not begun to show.

Groshong directed his questions to Stephanie with a force he had not used on other witnesses, but she remained calm and sweet in her answers, always addressing him as "sir." At his prompting she reiterated the beginning of her testimony: Paula had asked for a private room and was angry to find she would have a roommate; she complained to the nurse, who said nothing could be done.

Groshong picked up a paper, walked to the witness stand, and slapped it into Stephanie's hand. It was Defense Exhibit #1, a room-request form from Alton Memorial Hospital that began "I, _____, request a semi-private room. . . ." In the blank was Paula's signature. Spectators buzzed as Stephanie read the form. Yes, she agreed with no change in her tone, it was a request for a *semi*-private room.

Defense Exhibit #2 was Paula's hospital record. Stephanie acknowledged there was nothing in the nurses' written comments about a private-room contention. Groshong stated directly what the papers hinted: "This fight you had with Paula over a semi-private/private room, this never happened, did it?"

It happened, Stephanie insisted, but she quarreled with his characterization: "It wasn't a fight." She went over the crucial part of her testimony once again: It was *Loralei* whose kidnapping involved the trash. That's what Paula had said, and that's what Stephanie told her mother when she shared the news. And it was her mother, six weeks later, who called to tell her that another Sims baby had been kidnapped. Stephanie was adamant that she herself had not confused the details.

Groshong produced five copies of the *St. Louis Post-Dispatch,* editions that featured Heather's disappearance. Stephanie admitted that her parents subscribed to the paper but said she was "not a newspaper reader" and had not watched television more than "once or twice" before she visited the Alton Police Department to tell her story.

"You were her roommate," Groshong countered. "Weren't you curious?"

"It wasn't the biggest thing in my life," she insisted. Her answers remained soft and reasonable, but by the end of Groshong's cross-examination there was an edge to her voice. She played with her necklace and stared coldly at the defense attorney as she waited for his next question.

Stephanie's mother, Barbara Werner, followed her to the stand. She had visited Stephanie in the hospital, she said, and Stephanie told her that Paula had been taking out the trash when Loralei was kidnapped. And six weeks later, Mrs. Werner added, when she heard the news reports on Heather, her first thought was "Oh, no, that's Stephanie's roommate, and she was taking out the trash again!"

She spoke with no trace of irony. Weber grinned, letting the statement hang in the air until all the reporters had it down: ". . . that's Stephanie's roommate, and she was taking out the trash again!"

Before the jury assembled to hear June Gibson's testimony, Judge Matoesian ruled that Weber could ask no questions about marijuana; the entire issue was prejudicial, he decided. Weber concentrated instead on the phone call that took place three weeks after Heather came home. June confirmed that the Simses were sleeping on different floors at the time. Weber questioned her about Paula's mood, her attitude. "She didn't know how much longer she could handle it," June replied. June was unable to define "it" or to explain why Paula was unhappy, but the content and juxtaposition of Weber's questions linked Paula's dissatisfaction to the sleeping arrangements and, by implication, to sex.

No one asked June about the other phone call, the one in which Paula inquired about making an appointment with the psychiatrist. With the defense centering solely on the reality of the masked man, that inquiry had become irrelevant. Groshong wanted to paint Paula as a normal young mother whose tranquility was shattered by a kidnapper. Weber wanted to paint her as a cold-blooded killer. Indications that she was a *troubled* young· mother struggling against some growing danger didn't fit the picture presented by either side.

June's testimony helped the prosecution make the transition from 1986 to 1989. The parade of lawmen resumed, talking this time about Heather. The props became more tangible, more intimate. A spectator caught her breath when the bassinet appeared. White wicker with side handles, it was still coated with an uneven gray film of fingerprint powder. The mattress pad and blankets were there, too, silent testament to the babies who had slept on them.

Rex Warner, vice president of Polytech, the trash bag manufacturer, traced the steps in the production process. A Teflon–taped heat seal stamped a continuous plastic tube into separate bags and left distinguishing marks on them, he explained. The Teflon tape was changed every twelve to twenty-four hours, but in twenty-four hours a single manufacturing lane turned out more than 22,000 bags—thirteen bags every ten seconds. Five million pounds of those bags had been distributed among two-thousand K-mart stores just before Heather disappeared.

The material was technical, and the numbers were large. Several jurors copied the math and the sketches that Warner put on a chalkboard. Some looked confused.

Three special agents from the FBI's crime lab followed, presenting the strongest circumstantial evidence in the state's case. They explained the scientific equipment they used to study the trash bags; they passed around photos that enlarged tiny areas of the bags' heat seals; they showed how they traced lines and markings from one bag to the next. Even jurors who had looked confused nodded under the sheer weight of the technical information. This was the FBI talking.

Heather's bag had probably been the first bag off the roll, the experts concluded. The bag after that was missing. Then came one of the bags seized from a Sims garbage can. Next another missing bag. Then the second bag seized from the Sims garbage. Another missing bag. And then the remaining roll from Paula's shelf.

As the prosecution called medical examiner Mary Case to the stand Groshong escorted Paula from the courtroom. This was testimony she chose not to hear.

Dr. Case made a stylish entrance, wearing a white suit with mounds of pearls at her throat. Tucked under the pearls was a metallic gold scarf. Her shoes and handbag, too, glinted with gold. She and Paula passed at the courtroom doorway, two women drawn together by murder, but unlike in almost every other aspect. Mary Case, blond and sparkling, was attractive, accomplished, assured. Paula was blank and colorless, her face drawn, her clothing drab, her future dim.

Dr. Case had an impressive eight-page résumé, and Weber spent more than thirty minutes establishing her expertise: chief medical examiner of St. Louis County and St. Charles County; one of only four or five people in the entire country certified in both forensic pathology and neuropathology; expert also in anatomic pathology. Pathologists study disease and perform autopsies, Dr. Case explained; forensic pathologists specialize in dealing with the law.

Weber questioned her about articles she had written, presentations she had made, cases on which she had worked. Groshong lounged in his seat. Jurors listened dutifully. Spectators began to fidget.

Weber's queries veered from one of Case's specialties to another. Neuropathologists concentrate on diseases of, and injury to, the central nervous system, Dr. Case answered. Suddenly Groshong looked up. Before Weber could phrase another question Groshong was on his feet, his protests fervent. Those whose attention had drifted, who hadn't heard "diseases of and injury to the central nervous system," wondered what all the fuss was about. Even some who had been paying attention didn't make the leap of logic required to understand that Weber was qualifying Dr. Case to testify about something more than the condition of Heather's body. "Injury to the central nervous system." That wasn't Heather. That was Paula.

Groshong's objections were intense. He waved a pencil as he argued, but his attempt to forestall the coming testimony was futile. It would be allowed, declared the judge.

Weber grinned at Madison County authorities in the front row. Groshong sat slowly, leaned his head on his hand, and stared at the yellow legal pad in front of him.

The autopsy was first. A well-nourished, clean female infant, said Dr. Case, six to eight weeks of age. A sparse growth of light brown hair. Blue eyes. A few drops of blood in the nose. Three lacerations on the inner surface of the upper lip, indicating an application of pressure in which the lip was held in contact with the maxillary ridge, or upper gum. A case of asphyxia by suffocation.

To suffocate a child of Heather's size to the point of unconsciousness would require about two minutes, Dr. Case specified. The victim would feel a burning sensation in her chest. She would kick her legs, attempting to push away the obstruction. Death would take a minute or two more.

Case stated the facts simply, with no attempt to emotionalize them. Heather's death took three or four minutes. For two of those minutes she was in agony.

Red spots on the victim's left forehead, cheek, and neck indicated exposure to cold temperatures, perhaps below freezing, the doctor went on, as did a difference in the decomposition levels of the inside and outside of the body.

Photos were passed of Heather's lifeless form, pink and pretty, on the morgue table. Three red spots marred her skin. Three tiny cuts hid under her lip.

The testimony was graphic but not unexpected. Dr. Case's findings had been in the news months before, in the days after Heather's body was found. Weber turned to neuropathology. This was the surprise he had promised to the ever-inquisitive reporters, the payoff in a drawn-out cat-and-mouse game with the defense.

After the autopsy eight months earlier the prosecution had notified the defense that Dr. Mary Case would be a witness. Jim Williamson, Groshong's partner, had deposed her. He had learned what testimony she would offer about the condition of Heather's body and the clues it provided. But in the weeks before the trial Weber had been looking for a medical expert to refute Paula's claim of a blow to the head. The Alton police had relayed his inquiry to the FBI: Who might be able to testify about the effect of a head injury? The answer: Mary Case. Having already notified the defense that Dr. Case would testify, Weber contended he was under no further obligation to inform them that she would testify as an expert in more than one area. Groshong and Williamson had been provided with her résumé; it stated her multiple qualifications. If the defense attorneys didn't catch on, so much the better. Weber wanted them to be caught by surprise.

The defense had evidently never considered that Case might testify about neuropathology. Groshong seemed stunned. Once more he objected. Again overruled, he had no way to prevent Dr. Case's evaluation of Paula's story.

Weber sketched the details of that story in his question. What about a blow to the back of the head, unconsciousness from 10:30 to 11:15 P.M., then a frantic search for a missing baby?

The doctor replied that a blow resulting in forty-five minutes of unconsciousness would involve injury to the brain stem. The victim would be difficult to rouse and could tend to slip back into unconsciousness. Symptoms would be most evident immediately after the victim awakened; she would not develop them later, in a police car on the way to the emergency room.

Even a five-minute loss of consciousness was severe, Dr. Case explained; anything over thirty minutes would result in retrograde amnesia. Paula would have no memory of her injury and perhaps no memory of the five to ten minutes preceding it. "She may not remember any of that episode," said the witness firmly. "Certainly she wouldn't remember the blow."

Weber's face glowed in satisfaction.

The success of the surprise attack was verified when Groshong asked only three questions of Dr. Case, all of them concerning the autopsy. Unprepared to challenge her on the neuropathology testimony, he mentioned nothing about Paula's injury, hoping, no doubt, to diminish the importance of the doctor's conclusion.

But Mary Case's words hung in the air long after the doctor herself had walked confidently from the courtroom. A simple statement, she had spoken it with enough command and assurance that it cut out the heart of the defense case and laid it on Paula's vacant chair: "Certainly she wouldn't remember the blow."

After fifty-one witnesses the state rested.

=== 26 ===

By the trial's third week the first two rows in the "civilian" half of the room were regularly saved for VIPs: officials visiting from Madison County or Jersey County; employees of the state's attorney's office or Groshong's firm; relatives of court personnel. Waiting spectators grumbled as the number of available seats dwindled. Those who couldn't get into the courtroom sometimes stood with their ears pressed to the crack in the door.

Defense attorney Groshong became increasingly elusive, taking unexpected routes through the courthouse hallways. Television cameramen assigned to film him were stuck with fleeting shots of his back as he turned a corner. Reporters who got close enough to ask a question were answered with a testy "no comment."

The defense began its presentation to the jury with an effort to prove that Paula was a normal, loving mother. The first witness was Rhonda Henson Scott, her longtime friend, the matron of honor at her wedding.

Petite and slender, Rhonda raised her hand nervously to take the oath from the court clerk. As she finished she cast a quick glance at Paula. Before Groshong's first question she tried again, a tentative smile this time. There was no response.

Rhonda told the court that Paula had been pleased after each child's birth. When Loralei was delivered she was "thrilled to have a girl." When Randy was born she was "real happy." When Heather arrived she said, "I've counted all her fingers and I've counted all her toes, and she's just beautiful."

Rhonda's testimony was brief. As she left the stand she sent repeated glances and wan smiles in Paula's direction. Paula stared at the water pitcher.

Linda Condray, Rob's sister, sounded determined, even on the "I do" with which she responded to the witness's oath. She was blond and stout; her walk to the stand was aggressive, her answers to questions loud and clear.

She appeared confident as Weber began his cross-examination. He asked if the Condrays took their film to Missouri to be developed. Yes, Linda said, they drove to Missouri an average of three times a week. Did that route pass Lock and Dam 26, he asked, implying that she or her husband might have placed the body in the trash can. "So I have been told," she responded.

"Your husband does that, doesn't he? Herb?"

"We both do."

Weber skirted the question of Herb's relationship with the woman in the bright red dress by asking about family ties. "You're sort of a close-knit family, all of you, aren't you? I mean Robert and you and the Blews and Paula and Troy, Robert's dad?"

"Not particularly."

"Well, your husband, Herbert, and Troy, Robert's father, go out—"

"Not anymore."

"They used to, though?"

"They used to go to bingo. He started taking Daddy to bingo after Mom died."

"They told you they go to play *bingo* on those nights?" Weber's voice hinted at surprise and amusement.

"Yes," she replied curtly. The point was dropped.

Weber turned to Sunday morning, April 30, the time Paula insisted she had spent at the Condray home. Time had become peculiarly important as the prosecution attempted to refute Paula's story and the defense attempted to refute the conclusions of expert witnesses. Hours, and sometimes even minutes, were dissected as the possibilities were scrutinized: Was Paula knocked out for forty-five minutes, or thirty minutes, or fifteen minutes? Could she possibly have recalled a blow that sent her into unconsciousness? Did she arrive at the Condrays' house early on Sunday morning, as she said she did? If she wasn't at the Condray home, where was she? When did she find an opportunity to take the body to the trash can? If she didn't, who did?

Weber probed the timetable with Linda. "You went over to the Simses' house, didn't you, in the morning on Sunday?"

". . . It was early morning, for a very short while."

"Who was there?"

"Well, I saw my brother. I didn't go in the house that morning, if I remember right. I wasn't there very long."

"Paula was there," Weber said, "but she was getting ready to leave, right?"

"I don't remember anymore. It has been too long. I didn't take notes."

Linda's sarcasm failed to deter Weber. "Paula was there, getting ready to leave to go over to the Blews' house, wasn't she?"

"I said I don't remember. I didn't take notes," Linda repeated. "You probably know."

"Well, I know what you said to the grand jury."

"Then that must be right."

". . . Let me ask if you made this statement." Weber picked up the grand jury transcript. "Question: 'Now when you got there, who was there?' Answer: 'Lots of police, my brother Rob. I believe Paula was there, but she was preparing to leave with Randy to go to her parents' home because

Rob wanted her to.' Question: 'That's on Sunday?' Answer: 'Yes.' Now does that refresh your memory as to who was there?"

"Yes."

"And Paula was going to the Blews' house?"

"Yes."

"Was Paula upset?"

"I didn't see Paula. She was preparing to leave."

Weber was persistent. "When is the next time you saw Paula?"

"I saw her later that day."

"Okay. It was after three o'clock?"

"No. I think it was during the afternoon; it was earlier than that." The fact that Linda put the time earlier than three o'clock was lost for the rest of the trial. Weber continued to say she had set the hour at 3 P.M., and no one ever corrected him.

He asked about the reflective film on some windows in the Sims house, film that concealed the home's interior from outside eyes. "I don't know what kind of windows they had in their house," Linda replied, her impatience surfacing. "I haven't had a child kidnapped."

"Well"—Weber didn't resist the opening—"they haven't either." He turned to the startling comment she had made to Alton officers: Did she say that she believed Sheriff Yocom was responsible for Heather's death?

"I have suspicions," she replied loftily.

Jurors looked incredulous. Even the normally poker-faced judge lifted his eyebrows.

"You told the grand jury you thought Sheriff Yocom kidnapped Heather, didn't you?" Weber asked.

"I told the grand jury that I thought Sheriff Yocom had some knowledge of it," Linda corrected. "Obviously he didn't *do* it."

Groshong had no difficulty getting Alton officers Tony Ventimiglia and Rick McCain to acknowledge their early misgivings about the Simses' story. Neither would say, however, that Rob and Paula were the main focus of the police probe. "I didn't have enough facts to focus in on anybody," McCain explained.

Ventimiglia acknowledged that the repeated news conferences were intended to pressure the offenders to get rid of the infant or, if they had already done that, to ascertain that the body's hiding place remained undetected.

Then why, Groshong demanded of both detectives, *why* didn't you put the Simses under surveillance? If you were trying to force them into some precipitous action, some stupid move, why weren't you watching them?

McCain could offer no good answer. "It was discussed," he said lamely. He cited limited manpower, a lack of facts. Besides, he added, ". . . They already had plenty of time to do whatever they wanted with the body."

Groshong asked McCain to identify the calendar from the Sims kitchen, the calendar filled with declarations of affection for Randy and Heather. McCain admitted seeing it when he arrived at the house but said it was not an item seized by the police. It should have been, Groshong argued, for while it might not prove someone guilty, it could suggest someone's innocence. McCain disagreed. The statements of love on the calendar, he said, "could have been written five minutes before I walked in the door."

Paula surprised all those accustomed to her lack of response. She shook her head, smiled weakly, and rested her chin on her hand.

The momentary lapse in control, small as it was, became significant in the context of her utter stillness, which had caused comment among observers. "A cool customer," they had decided. But as a woman on display she found few alternatives. "What else could I do?" she sighed. "Don [Groshong] said they'd be watchin' me, every move I made. 'Just sit there,' he told me. 'No reaction, Paula. Don't hit your fist down on the table. Don't dare jump up. Just sit there. Don't move.' And I did that, didn't I? I did exactly what I was told."

Orville Blew walked to the stand with an uneven gait that suggested the weight of burdens life had delivered him: one son and two granddaughters in the grave, another son trapped by the seizures and symptoms of epilepsy, a daughter accused of murdering her beautiful, helpless infants. Orville had reached his sixty-first birthday during the trial, but his sad, weathered face and gray-white hair made him look much older.

He told of visiting Paula in the hospital after Loralei's birth, of watching her and the baby. "She loved her daughter . . . she loved her daughter."

He had visited the hospital after the birth of Heather, too, he said, and had listened to Paula's concern when a nurse burped the baby: "Looks to me, Dad, like she hit her a little hard."

He talked about the late-night phone calls that told him his granddaughters were gone. "I couldn't believe it," he said.

Weber's cross-examination was quiet. Did Paula have a key to the Blews' home? Yes. Did she know they would be away that weekend? Yes.

"What did she tell you about what happened?" Weber asked.

"She didn't tell me anything that happened," Orville answered. "What I learned was out of the newspaper . . . The only thing that she told me was, I was standing there with my arm around her, and I said, 'I thought you told me this would never happen again.' And she said, 'Dad, I was headed for the gun.'"

Reporters scribbling in notebooks looked at one another for confirmation. Was it "I thought you told me this would never happen again"? Yes, it was. Did Orville mean he knew, or at least suspected, that Paula had some control in the matter, that she might have prevented "this" from happening again? Or was he talking about chance, probability, likelihood? Weber let the statement pass, and Groshong never followed up on it.

The prosecutor asked Orville about his granddaughters: "You loved both of these little girls?"

"Yes, sir." Orville nodded, his voice suddenly hoarse.

"Like they were your own babies?"

"Yes, sir."

Weber refused to let go of the painful theme. "You were very upset to find out what happened?"

"Yes!" said Orville, with such fervor that Weber had to acknowledge his emotion.

"I understand," Weber murmured. "I believe you."

Paula maintained her composure throughout her father's testimony, but she angled her chair more determinedly away from the audience. Jurors could see her face; spectators could not.

When he was excused Orville unexpectedly walked toward the back of the room rather than around the judge's bench, as had every other departing witness. The path took him directly past his daughter. He smiled. She reached out quickly and clutched his hand. Their fingers met for a few seconds, held, and parted. Orville continued his exit.

Paula turned around in her chair, ignoring her attorney's admonition, braving stares from the packed benches, and watched until her father was out the door.

An ever-growing crowd forced the courthouse staff to lay down some rules. Security officers locked off the hallway usually crammed with hopeful spectators and ordered those waiting for a seat to form a line around the rotunda railing. The bailiff squeezed in an extra row of chairs before the day's star witness, Robert Eugene Sims, took the stand.

Rob's face was slightly flushed behind the gray-red of his beard. His sport shirt was unbuttoned at the collar, exposing a bit of white undershirt. He walked slowly, stoically to the witness chair.

"Paula is my wife," he said in answer to Groshong's question. His voice sounded sure and warm, and he looked directly at Paula as he spoke. It was a good answer. Some reporters concluded later that it was his best answer of the day.

"We wanted to have a boy and a girl," Rob replied when asked about children. His speech was low, controlled. He was present throughout Loralei's delivery, he said, and heard the doctor say the baby was a girl. "I was very pleased.

Ecstatic . . . proud." When Paula went to recovery he went home "so I could report our good news."

He admitted Paula had phoned to say she wished, for his sake, the baby had been a boy. "Just kind of a little apology" because she thought he wanted a son. Groshong's inquiry about the date of Loralei's birth caught him off-guard. It took him a few seconds to remember "the fifth of June."

As questions continued Rob's short, sure answers grew longer and longer. His deep voice became a relentless drone as he traced his activities on June 17, 1986: Toy Chest, Venture, Target; all the particulars that Sheriff Yocom and Agent Bivens had found so remarkable. The monotone faltered when Rob told of Paula's phone call to Jefferson Smurfit, the call that told him of the masked intruder: ". . . he'd stolen our daughter, Loralei."

He described his route from the paper plant to Brighton, specifying the locations of every stop sign and traffic light. "I ran the red light at Cut Street and Broadway, come up Main Street. I run the stop sign at Main Street and Brown Street. Still on Main Street, I run the stop sign at Main Street and College Avenue. . . . I was drivin' like a madman."

His hostility toward the police surfaced when he spoke of the scene he found at home. Officers were in the driveway, he said, "standing around there in all the glory of their big fancy police cruisers." Paula met him at the front door, shaking and crying. "She says, 'Rob, I'm so glad you're here. You can get these guys to doin' something.'" It was *his* idea to get a dog from the Wood River Police Department, he recalled; *his* idea to call the FBI.

He verified the solitary nature of daily existence, even after he and Paula left the isolated Brighton bungalow and moved to Alton: "People had generally left us alone. . . . We kept to ourselves. We left them alone; they left us alone. . . . We never had a whole lot of friends. We kept to ourselves." They were "paranoid" about anyone "other than necessary people" knowing that they were having a second child, he said. He had no trouble with Randy's birth date: "February first, 1988."

A question about Heather's birth date, however, gave him

pause. Groshong asked him twice before he said, "She was born the eighteenth [of March]. At home "everything was normal" until April 29. Rob plunged into explicit detail as he told about going to work. "I took off my street clothes, and there was something a little out of the ordinary. I did realize I didn't have a clean work shirt to put on. My overalls, I usually wear them about three days, and I put on a clean shirt every day. I didn't have any clean work shirt to wear, so I did have to end up wearing my street-clothes shirt underneath my overalls."

The failure of order and cleanliness bothered him enough that he brought it up again when Groshong asked him about the end of his shift. He couldn't change into a clean shirt, not when he had worn his "street-clothes shirt" for his work shift. He had to drive home with bare arms. "It was either take a shower and put on a dirty shirt or go without the shirt, and I chose to go without a shirt."

When he got home at 11:15 P.M. he found the back door unlocked, something "extremely out of the ordinary," and Paula lying on the kitchen floor. "She was lifeless, completely lifeless. . . . No movement. No groans. No anything." He checked the dining room, he said. "Heather wasn't in her bassinet. She wasn't in her pumpkin seat. Then I was really scared because if Heather isn't in her bassinet or her pumpkin seat, she's in one of our arms."

After he roused Paula and listened to her story he went "leaping the steps up the stairs. Paula was not too far behind me." They touched Randy to see if he was alive, then went downstairs, where they stood, "dumbfounded, you know." It was Paula who said they had to "call the cops."

Groshong's questions took him past the events of the night to the time when police returned the next morning and requested the Simses leave the house. "I told Paula she needs to, she ought to go over to my sister's house and take Randy and get Randy away from the press, and go over there and relax as much as she could, and I would stay there with the police until they got done, and I would be over to meet her."

"Did Paula leave?" Groshong asked.

"Yes."

"Do you know where she went?"

"She went over to Herb and Linda Condray's house.
. . . Paula left somewhere around seven-thirty, eight in the morning, as soon as we got Randy fed his breakfast, and she loaded him up and took off."

"When is the next time you saw Paula?"

"I saw Paula about somewhere around noon, very early afternoon."

"Where did you see her?"

"I saw her at Herb and Linda Condray's house."

In the evening, Rob said, he called Detective McCain and offered advice. "He made the remark he was doing the best he could, and if I had any complaints about what he was doing, let him know, any suggestions. And I told him just, you know, keep at it and put every man he's got possible on it. And I questioned him and asked him if he was using any of the DCI agents, you know, to not feel too proud to ask for help, and asked him about the FBI."

Rob's sense of self-importance erupted again as he spoke of visiting the police department the next morning. "I first talked to the desk sergeant, told him who I was looking for, and told him who I was. And he acted like he didn't know who Robert Sims was. I told him, 'My daughter was kidnapped.' And he said, 'Oh yeah. . . .'" Rob complained that he was kept waiting twenty minutes; then McCain apologized. "He says he knew he had somebody waiting for him, but he didn't realize it was me. If he had known it was me, he would have been out to talk to me immediately." Once more, Rob said, McCain asked for his input: ". . . If I had any suggestions, if I didn't think he was handling the investigation right, he told me again to tell him. He would do whatever I asked."

The strange boasting continued as Rob described his effort to get an appointment with the family doctor. A receptionist said no appointment was available, he explained, but after he instructed her, "Go tell the doctor it's

Robert Sims and I need to see him," she told him to come right over; the doctor agreed to see him "immediately" and gave him a prescription "to help calm my nerves a little bit."

Even on the witness stand, where it was crucial for him to be as sympathetic as possible, Rob couldn't hide his egotism: in the midst of tragedy he had found a way to feel important.

Groshong progressed to the day Heather's body was discovered in the trash can. "On May third, did you get up in the morning and go anywhere?"

"No."

"Go anywhere that day at all?"

"I never left the house that day. Paula never left the house. . . ."

He spoke of his visit to the police station the following evening, when Ventimiglia, McCain, and FBI agent Carl Schulz accused him of lying. "They accused Paula especially," Rob said. "They told me they had evidence against Paula, and under the circumstances I must be covering up for her. . . ."

Agent Schulz, he insisted, talked of tire tracks and hair: "They told me they had copies, impressions, something to that effect, of tire tracks from our 1979 Chevy station wagon that were found at the site where our daughter's body was found. They also told me they had hair samples out of Paula's parents' freezer that matched our daughter, Heather. And I asked them again, you know, 'Are you sure those are Heather's hair?' I didn't want any mistake about any of this. And he said, 'Yes.' I asked him at least three times, 'Are you positive?' He said, 'Yes, it is her hair.'"

"That made you doubt your wife, did it?" asked Groshong.

"A little bit, yes, it did, because I knew I hadn't driven the car over there." That was when he went to the Blew home, he said, and awakened Paula. "I started grillin' Paula and said, 'Paula, you're not being truthful with me.' . . . I talked to Paula like I had never talked to her in eight years of marriage."

Later, Rob said, he learned there was no tire track, no hair from Heather. ". . . I was the fool. I was the one that believed the lies that that FBI agent had told me."

"Do you believe her [Paula] now?"

"Yes, I do. Absolutely."

Would he cover up for Paula, Groshong asked, if she had killed Heather?

"I wouldn't cover for anyone that would harm a hair on any of my children, no matter how much I loved them."

Was he sure Paula was innocent?

"I am positive. No doubt in my mind. Paula is a good mother, an excellent mother. She's a wonderful wife."

Weber's cross-examination was loud and rapid-fire. Why did the Simses wait five years to have children, he asked. Because Paula was working, Rob answered, and because they wanted to buy a home first. Weber asked if it wasn't because Rob feared they might have "genetically defective children" like Paula's brother Dennis. Rob denied the charge. He said he and Paula had an agreement that, should anything happen to the Blews, they would care for Dennis a short while, but he "would never live with us full time."

Weber's questions led to a discussion of Paula's mental and physical condition after she got up from the floor. "Robert, what's the first thing you did when you found out that Paula had supposedly been knocked out? You ran upstairs to see Randy, didn't you?"

"That's right."

"And she followed you up that spiral staircase running right behind you, didn't she?"

"She followed me. . . . I don't know if she was walking fast, running, or whatever, but she was behind me."

"Well, *you* ran up there?"

"I ran up there, yes."

"And when you got up there, she was right in back of you?"

"Yes."

"Did she just *walk* up?" Sims didn't answer. "Did she crawl up the stairs?" Still no answer. "Did you help her up the stairs?"

"No. . . . No, I don't believe so."

"Okay. Now after she gets upstairs, what does she do then? Is she wobbling and staggering around like she has been knocked out for forty-five minutes?"

"She is not acting completely normal."

"Well"—Weber paused only a second before grabbing the opportunity—"what's normal for Paula Sims may be another matter. But I want you to describe how she's standing and walking and what she's doing. Is she swaying?"

"Slightly."

"Did you have to hold her up?"

"No."

"Did she want to sit down?"

"No."

"Did she say, 'I've just been knocked out for forty-five minutes. Maybe I better lay down'?"

"No."

"The next thing that happened is what?" Rob stared silently at the prosecutor. "You ran back downstairs, right?"

"That's right."

"And she followed you, right?"

"Right."

"Did you help her on that spiral staircase?"

"I don't believe so."

". . . Now, you were sort of delirious, running around. You were hysterical, very upset, weren't you?"

"Yes, I was."

"But Paula said, 'We have to call the police,' right?"

"Right."

"So she had the cool head of the bunch, right?"

"At that time, yes."

"She was oriented as to what had gone on and as to what you're supposed to do, right?"

A pause hung in the air before Rob agreed. "Right."

Rob acknowledged that Paula had driven off by herself the following morning. Weber lifted an eyebrow. "Robert, Paula is distressed. She's upset. She'd just had her second baby stolen. You let her get in the car and drive *by herself* over to the Condrays' house?"

"Yes, I did."

"Why didn't you have Linda take her over there?"

Paula said she would be all right, Rob responded.

And that was at 8 A.M.?

Yes.

"Robert, Linda Condray says she didn't get there until three. How do you explain that?" ("Three" was Weber's misstatement of Linda's testimony. Linda had actually said Paula arrived "earlier than that.")

There was another pause before Rob said, "I don't think she's remembering correctly."

Was Paula told that the Blews were returning?

Yes.

"So if she had anything over at the Blews' house that she didn't want found, she would have to go over there and move it, right?"

"What would she have over there?" Rob asked slowly.

"A dead baby in a freezer."

The pause was the longest yet. "No. I don't think so."

"When you talked to the FBI you told them that your wife had keys to the Blews' home, and she could have put Heather in the freezer while you were asleep, right?"

"I remember something like that, yes."

"And you told them you were real worried about Randy's safety?"

"After what they had told me, yes, I was concerned about Randy."

"And you told them that during the time that Heather was alive you slept in your bedroom, and Paula and Heather slept together in a different part of the house, right?" When Rob quarreled with the statement, Weber read aloud from the FBI report and asked him again.

"I don't remember my exact testimony," Rob answered. "You've got to remember at that time I had not had any sleep in almost forty-eight hours. I had not had a meal in almost twenty-four hours, and I was on a tranquilizer."

"You were really wrung out . . .?"

"I have been wrung out for over three years."

That gave Weber an opening for the question reporters

were anticipating. ". . . Then how come Tuesday before the body was found you and Paula had the best and longest-lasting sex you've ever had?"

Rob's face reddened as he stared at the prosecutor. His eyes did not waver, but seconds ticked by in silence. "Let me tell you something," he said at last. "Sex can be a stress reliever. We loved each other very much. I was trying to comfort her. She was trying to comfort me. I believe in my wife. We tried to comfort each other."

"And it was the best and longest-lasting sex you ever had?"

More silence. "It was good. It usually is."

"And that was right after your second baby, Heather, had been kidnapped and taken to parts unknown . . .?"

The pause was a short one. Rob's reply was angry. "What are we supposed to do twenty-four hours a day?"

27

"UPSTAIRS. FORM A LINE. YOU KNOW THE ROUTINE." IT was the litany of courthouse guards who had grown complacent about the throng. On Wednesday, January 25, the day Paula was scheduled to testify, they were startled to find hopeful spectators in line at 5:30 A.M.

Some people brought their lunches so they could immediately rejoin the line at the end of the morning session and perhaps squeeze in during the afternoon. One woman carried a Bible; another nibbled from a bag of popcorn tucked into her handbag. (The Bible was allowed in the courtroom; the popcorn wasn't.)

Paula moved slowly to the stand at 9:30 A.M., dressed in blue slacks, striped sweater, and the ever-present crepe-soled shoes. Women who had become "regulars" exchanged resigned looks. They thought that someone—a friend, a family member, maybe even the defense attorney—might get her something softer, prettier for this crucial day. She needed a touch of color, a little makeup, something to suggest femininity or, at least, humanity.

Her voice, tinged with a bit of midwestern twang, quavered in response to her attorney's initial questions. She admitted to being "a little" nervous, and she kept her eyes trained on Groshong, ignoring the rest of the room.

"We wanted one of each," she replied when asked about children. The first time she discovered she was pregnant both she and Rob were pleased, she said. ". . . We was ready to start a family."

Groshong showed her a small, delicate pink and white dress. It had been hers, she told him; the dress in which she was photographed at fifteen months of age. She had kept it for a daughter.

She identified a blond Barbie doll and tiny clothes her mother had sewn for it, and then another doll, softer and more cuddly. It was named Sally, she said. "I saved it for my daughter someday."

She sounded calm and reasonable, an ordinary woman talking about ordinary things: dresses and dolls, the reminiscences of girlhood, the dreams for womanhood. Yet she admitted to disappointment when she was told that her first child was a girl. "We would like to have had a boy first," she explained. "Every man wants a son."

Groshong's questions led to the night of Loralei's disappearance. "I was settin' in the chair, and the weather was on," Paula said. "I noticed a man comin' down the stairs. . . . I was scared. I was scared to death." The gun was hard for her to describe: "It was—it was a big—it was a big black gun." The kidnapper had a low voice, she said; there was "no question" that he was white.

"Is that what happened on the seventeenth of June?" asked her attorney. His voice was kind, fatherly.

"Yes, it is."

"Is that the truth?"

"Yes, it is." She was dry-eyed, definite. She spoke to Groshong, not the jurors.

He took her to 1987, when she and Rob bought the Washington Avenue house. How was life, he asked.

"We were makin' it." The answer was a sigh, tentative and shaky, but her volume and energy picked up when she discussed her succeeding pregnancies. After each delivery she was taken to the same hospital room, she said, Room 285.

She denied any argument with Stephanie Werner about a private room. "It wasn't even brought up." There was a "masked gunman" conversation, she admitted, but the subject didn't arise as Stephanie said it did, during a discussion of labor pain. It came up when Stephanie was considering the possibility of leaving her baby Jacob in the hospital a few extra days. "I told her I wouldn't leave my baby anywhere because babies get stolen."

The questions led to 1989. Paula said she had watched soap operas on the afternoon of April 29, the day Heather disappeared. (She didn't say how she managed to watch them on a Saturday, and neither attorney asked.)

In late evening, she said, she watched television news, straightened the house, and took out the trash. "I saw a masked gunman standing there with a gun." Again the gun was hazy: "It was a big black gun, and it scared me to death."

And then Paula did what she had always done when trouble closed in on her: She lied. But this time it was lie upon lie, and her story went careening out of control. "It looked like the same man who had taken Loralei in 1986."

It was an embellishment that might have slid by someone unfamiliar with earlier versions of the tale, but she was in a room full of people who had heard the original—who knew it, apparently, better than she did. Groshong managed to show no surprise, but reporters turned to one another in amazement. Had Paula forgotten that she said the first kidnapper was white? Had she forgotten that she claimed to be uncertain about the race of the second abductor? That his sleeves were long, and he wore gloves, and a mask covered his face? The "same man" identification was a new wrinkle. Groshong went quickly to other issues, sliding past the inconsistency.

The intruder told her to go into the house, and her plan was to head for the gun, she said. "I felt a blow to the back of my head, and that's all I remember."

Groshong progressed to the next morning, when the police returned with dogs. Paula said she left "about eight o'clock, somewhere around in there" and "went straight to Linda and Herb Condray's."

Groshong asked, "Who was there when you got there?"

"Herb and Sammy, his son."

"Was Linda there?"

"No, she wasn't. I passed her on the road. She was going to our house."

". . . When you got to Herb's house, did you stay there?"

"Yes, I did, the whole afternoon, whole morning and afternoon."

"Did you hear Linda testify a day or two ago?"

"Yes, I did."

"Did you hear her the same way I did, say you didn't get to her house until three o'clock, something like that?" (Even Groshong had accepted Weber's misstatement of Linda's testimony.)

"Yes, I believe that's what she said."

"What about that?"

"Well, she wouldn't know because she wasn't there."

The concern about time called attention to Herb Condray's absence from the trial. He was the only adult who might verify the hour she arrived at the Condray home, an hour that had become strangely important, and he had not taken the stand. The woman in red had evidently been as intimidating as police and prosecution had hoped.

Press vans were on the street when the Sims family went home to Washington Avenue on Sunday night, Paula said, and they trailed her again on Monday, when she spent the day with her parents. It wasn't until Tuesday that she had a chance to do something about her house. "I had to clean the kitchen because there was black powder all over from doing fingerprints. And, of course, Randy played on the floor. And, of course, we was getting it all over our socks. And it was a mess. It was all over the counters. And, sure, I had to clean that up. And I didn't have my mop, so I cleaned it up with a rag. The floor, I mopped the floor with a rag." The missing mop was stuck in her mind, as important to her as the missing work shirt was to Rob.

She heard of the trash-barrel discovery from a ten o'clock newscast on Wednesday night, she said. Shortly after that her father came to get her and Randy, "to keep us safe." After leaving with him she was not in the Washington Avenue house again: "I never went back."

She was careful in describing her contentions with Rob during their two and a half years in the little white house. "When you lived at Washington Street," Groshong asked, "did you or your husband . . . have any rules as far as people visiting at the house in relation to your children?"

"Yes, we did."

"What kind of rules did you have?"

"Well, we always had the rule to take your shoes off, even before we had children. My husband was raised like that."

"What other kinds of rules did you have?"

". . . No one to come over with a cold because we didn't want our children catching a cold when they were real little. And wash your hands before you held the baby and—"

"Was Rob real concerned about stuff like this?"

"Yes."

"You, too?"

She shrugged. "Yes, I agreed with most of the rules."

"Ever cause you any trouble?" She hesitated so long that he asked the question again. "Did you ever have any problems with these rules?"

"Yes," she said, "a little bit."

Groshong didn't pursue the subject.

A noon recess allowed everyone—no doubt the defense attorneys particularly—to consider Paula's identification of the two intruders as the same man. After lunch Groshong edged her back to the testimony. She reaffirmed the identification but sidestepped the black/white contradiction by basing her judgment on what she had heard rather than what she had seen. "Definitely, it was the same guy," she acknowledged. "I know that. Especially from his voice. I remember that voice. If I heard it today, I could recognize that voice."

Facial expressions indicated the press didn't buy the explanation; the jury was inscrutable.

Groshong's last questions were explicit. "On May third did you go over to West Alton and hide your daughter's body in a trash barrel?"

"No, I did not."

"Did Rob . . .?"

"No."

"Did you lie to the police about this?"

"No, I have not. . . . I told them the truth."

"Did you kill either one of your daughters?"

"No, I did not." Her response was strong. "I loved my daughters, and I still do."

"Did you have any plans for your daughters?"

Her voice wavered. Her gaze fell to her hands. "I had a lot of plans. They're all gone now."

Responses to Paula's direct examination were split. Her dolls, their tiny dresses, her baby photo, all painted a picture of a normal little girl, a girl who wanted to grow up and have a daughter of her own. But she sounded as concerned about her missing mop as her missing babies, and she had lied once too often. The "same man" was destined to be tomorrow's headline.

Weber began the cross-examination by asking why the Simses had waited so long to have children. It had nothing to do with Dennis, Paula said, and nothing to do with epilepsy. Before they were married Rob had asked if the condition was hereditary, and she had assured him that it wasn't. She was defensive about Dennis and, when Weber referred to him as "retarded," took time to set the record straight: ". . . My brother is not retarded!"

Weber asked if she had ever suffered from postpartum depression. "No . . . I maybe had the blues, if that's what you want to call it, right after I delivered Randy."

"But just after Randy? Not after Loralei?"

"No."

". . . You're telling the jury you were happy with Loralei?"

"Yes, I was very happy."

Did she run down the driveway calling Loralei's name, Weber asked. "Yes . . ." Then why didn't the Hyatts hear her through their open windows? "I do not know."

Did she tell Stella Hyatt that she felt safe because her dog Shadow heard everything? "I don't recall that."

"Stella Hyatt mistaken?"

"I don't know. You would have to ask her."

The phrasing of Weber's questions seemed designed to bring out the "I don't know" response. He turned to her earlier testimony about a shadowy figure. "What did the shadowy figure look like?"

". . . I really don't know. I can't really describe it. . . . It was a shadow."

"Was it a man?"

"I'm not sure."

"Well, shadows are on the ground. Did you see this on the ground, or did you see it up in the air?"

"I saw it on the ground, yes." She sounded relieved to have a definite answer.

"All you saw was a shadow on the ground?"

"Yes."

"What was casting the shadow?"

"I do not know."

"Was it moving?"

"I think it was, but I'm not sure. I don't recall."

She was equally indefinite about what she had heard. Weber picked a line from her written statement: "'I could hear what I thought was someone running on the driveway gravel.' Right?"

"Right."

"Now is that what you heard? Someone running on the driveway gravel?"

"I heard gravel. I don't know if it was the driveway gravel or not. . . . I *thought* I heard the driveway gravel."

"When did you decide that you weren't sure that it was down the driveway? After you heard the testimony about the police dogs?"

"No."

Weber insisted upon an answer. "When did you decide it wasn't the driveway gravel?"

"I'm not sure what gravel it was."

"When did you become 'not sure'?"

"I don't know."

Weber used an aerial photo of the scene. "When the police were out there, and they were conducting all of their search at this lake, and down this driveway, and in this field, and both sides of this road, and these fields over here, did you tell them to go around back? 'Maybe I'm mistaken. Maybe the guy went around back'?"

"No."

"You never told them that?"

"I never told them where to search. They searched where they—"

"If you were unsure which way the guy went, why didn't you redirect the police, because you knew they were relying on your statement?"

"It wasn't my position to tell them where to take the dogs."

"Well, you wanted your baby found, didn't you?"

"Yes, I did."

"That would have helped, wouldn't it?"

Paula's left hand tightened around the fingers of her right. She sank into the chair. "I wasn't going to interfere with their investigation."

Weber turned to the statement that had startled reporters earlier in the day, the declaration that both babies had been taken by the same man. He started by asking about Loralei's abductor. "And it was a *white* man?"

"Yes."

"And you say it was the same guy that hit your house three years later . . .?"

"Yes, it was."

"Then why didn't you tell the police the second man was white?"

"Because I wasn't sure, except for the voice."

"When did you become sure? Was it during the trial? . . . After you heard the evidence? Is that when you became sure?"

"No."

"When did you become sure?"

She tightened her grip on her fingers. "I think I told the officer that night that I thought it was the same man that had taken Loralei."

"Now you never did find out the sex of Heather before she was born, did you?" Weber asked.

"It wasn't important," Paula replied. "Any of the times, it wasn't important."

"Well, I think that's for the jury to decide. But the question is, you never did find out, did you?"

"I could have went back for another sonogram, but I—The main thing was that the baby was going to be healthy."

"Well, the sonograms you were taking were in your third trimester," Weber pointed out, "and you couldn't have had an abortion anyway, could you?"

"I would never have an abortion," Paula said with sudden sharpness. "I am totally against abortion."

It was an opening for one of Weber's sarcastic rejoinders, but he let it slip by. Instead he probed for a motive. "Sleeping arrangements were different after Heather came home? . . . You were downstairs; Robert was upstairs?"

". . . The sleeping arrangements was mostly for convenience, so I wouldn't have to go up and down stairs."

"Did you make the statement to June Gibson that you didn't know how much longer you were going to be able to stand this?"

"No, I don't recall ever making a statement like that to June."

"She's a good friend of yours, isn't she?"

"She's a friend of mine." The missing adjective reflected the disintegration of Paula's bond with June.

Weber went back to *time*. Did she tell officers that she went outside at 10:30 with the trash?

No, she told them that she looked at the clock at 10:30, cleaned up the house, and *then* went outside. It might have been 10:45 or even 11 P.M.

If she and Rob were so security-conscious, Weber asked, why did she "just walk out the door that night"?

"I walked out the door to put the trash out."

"Were you worried about security?"

She paused. "Didn't enter my mind at that time."

When Weber questioned her actions and reactions after the blow, Paula sometimes hedged. "I don't recall," she said. Or "I don't remember."

"Is there some reason you're having trouble remembering things?" Weber asked.

"Yes."

"What is it?"

"I was hit on the back of my head."

Was she capable of driving the next morning, when she supposedly went to the Condrays?

"Yes."

"You felt emotionally stable enough to drive the car and go off by yourself, even though your baby had just been kidnapped ten hours before?"

"We were instructed to leave the house, so I did what they wanted me to."

"Rob could have driven you over there, couldn't he?"

"I guess he could have." Her answers turned combative. "Or the police could have driven me over there."

"Did you ask them?"

"No. And they didn't offer."

Did she sleep upstairs with Rob after Heather disappeared?

"Yes."

She had to know the question was coming: "That Tuesday night, did you and your husband have the best and longest-lasting sex you'd ever had?"

Groshong's objection was sustained, but Paula, her face flushing, had already answered. "No, we did not."

She was on the stand for almost four hours. When she stepped down she took her usual seat at the table. She sipped water from a paper cup, folded her hands in her lap, and directed her gaze to the safe spot at the front of the room. Groshong leaned over her chair.

"He came up to me and whispered in my ear, 'You did such a great job, if I could, I'd kiss you right here.' That's what he said to me. And I thought to myself, 'Yeah, right. Real good job, Paula.' 'Cause I knew what I had done. I knew my testimony wasn't true."

= 28 =

By THE END THERE HAD BEEN MORE THAN EIGHTY WITNESSES. Friends, neighbors, and relatives trying to maintain their belief in Paula's innocence, for the alternative was too awful to consider. Officers, deputies, and agents convinced she was an unnatural mother who had shoved her baby in one refrigerator or another so she could hurry upstairs to the night of best and longest sex awaiting her. It was one extreme or the other: Paula Sims, hapless, forlorn victim, or Paula Sims, scheming, cold-hearted killer.

Spectators looked forward to the final arguments. The jurors were totally attentive as Weber rose. It was their last chance to figure out the strange case that had unfolded before them. "She's the person who murdered Heather." Weber pointed at Paula, who shook her head slowly from side to side.

The choice Weber presented was a simple one: If you believe her story of the "imaginary *bandito,*" find her innocent. If you consider that story preposterous, convict her.

He turned to sarcasm: Futile efforts to find any trace of the abductor suggested the man must have stood with a gun in one hand and a communicator in the other, calling "Beam me up, Scotty." Some jurors suppressed smiles.

Weber took a stab at motive. "Ladies and gentlemen, I have to confess to you, I can't tell you why this happened. I can tell you a few things I know. Paula Sims didn't like little girls. Paula Sims didn't like the sleeping arrangements. Paula Sims, the neatnik, didn't like Heather making a mess in her house. I mean, someone who's going to worry about the police taking her mop is going to get upset about other minor things. Probably, if you took all the psychiatrists in the world and interviewed this woman, you would never figure out exactly why she did this."

He called her "wily," "cunning," "icy," "cold-blooded," "audacious," "brassy," "bold," and "daring." She wanted the jury to believe she had done the "Olympic high hurdles" running up and down the steps, although the blow she claimed would have made it unlikely, if not impossible.

The prosecution came up with a tally of Paula's *I don't know*s. She used the response sixty-four times in cross-examination, Weber said. The number broke through her self-imposed trance. She looked at him, startled. He repeated it: sixty-four times. She turned back to the safe spot at the front of the room.

Weber attacked the defense case, pointing out that Paula had driven herself and young Randy away from Washington Avenue on the morning after the alleged kidnapping. She headed to her parents' home, he insisted, and remained there until midafternoon, in a house where no one was available to offer sympathy or support. She had to remain there, he theorized, to guard baby Heather, stiff and cold in a refrigerator.

Once more Paula slowly shook her head.

Weber took full advantage of the confusion about the morning hours. On the railing of the jury box he placed three photos entered as exhibits, photos of freezers and refrigerators in the Sims and Blew houses. On each he centered half a walnut shell. He deftly inserted a pea under one of the shells and switched it from picture to picture as he talked, suggesting that the little corpse was likewise transferred from place to place. "It's the old shell game," he explained, "with a tragic and grim twist."

His next prop, a poster titled "Irrefutable Roll Call of Defendant's Guilt," was a list of twenty-five people who had testified. In order to believe Paula, he insisted, the jurors would need to disbelieve each of the twenty-five witnesses on his "Irrefutable Roll Call." A red rectangle bordered Dr. Case's name.

In order to acquit her, he told the jurors, they would have to believe that the *bandito* knew when Paula was home alone with her children, that he was interested in taking only little girls, and that he took them just to murder them. The tale the defense offered, Weber concluded, presented "an impossible story under implausible circumstances. And that's why you should convict Paula Sims of murder."

He sat down an hour and a half after he began. Paula slowly shook her head.

Donald Groshong labeled the state's case "just a theory." He suggested the words used to describe his client's story— "preposterous," "imaginary," "unbelievable"—should be used instead to describe the prosecution's version of events. The state wasn't dealing in evidence, he insisted; the state thought it didn't need evidence because everybody already believed Paula was guilty.

He broke the prosecution's case into six arguments. The supposed motive, that Paula didn't like little girls, stood refuted by loving looks on the young parents' faces in family photos, by the birth announcements sent to friends, by the observations of those who witnessed them with their children, by the abundant child-care items in the home, by notes of love and affection on the family calendar. Paula refused X rays for a broken foot until Heather was safely delivered; she named her daughters after herself and close relatives; she took Heather to a pediatrician for a mild case of diarrhea. None of this suggested a dislike of little girls.

Point two: the prosecution's claim that Paula's statements to Stephanie Werner proved premeditation. Groshong scoffed; the hypothesis suggested Paula made a decision to kill the baby within hours of her birth, chose the story she would offer after she committed the murder, and told the story to someone with whom she had just had a fight. "Stephanie Werner is a liar!" Groshong didn't bother to hide his antipathy for the young woman. "A lawyer doesn't call someone a liar unless he is sure."

The third point brought Groshong back to the Loralei evidence, the material he had fought to exclude from the trial. He cited reasons to believe the 1986 crime was exactly what Paula said it was, a kidnapping. The dual incidents were bizarre and unusual, he admitted, but not unbelievable. He pointed out the assassinations of John and Robert Kennedy.

Next, the trash bags. Groshong didn't try to contradict the FBI. Heather was found in a trash bag from her mother's kitchen, he conceded. He reiterated his "pillow case" hypothesis; the kidnapper needed a container for the "loot". The trash bags were right there, boxes of them in the nearby stairwell, a few kept handy behind the bread box in the kitchen.

The fifth point was the blow to the head: Paula's avowal that it happened versus Dr. Case's assurance that if it had, Paula would be unable to remember it. Dr. Case is a pathologist, Groshong argued, not a neurologist. She doesn't work on living people; she works on corpses. How can she be so positive Paula wouldn't be able to remember? What about a boxer who is knocked out and then gives an interview in which he accurately describes the preceding round? What about an accident victim who rouses from unconsciousness to remember whether the light was red or green? If they can remember, why wouldn't Paula remember?

His last point brought the jurors full circle, back to Weber's discussion of refrigerators. Why would Paula hide the body in her parents' house, knowing they would come home as soon as they heard the news? Why would she bring the body back to her own kitchen, knowing that she was a suspect and that the police might return to search at any moment? Why would she move the body in broad daylight, to an easily visible public trash can, knowing that the police could be watching? "This is one heck of a plan, boy!" Groshong's voice rose in sarcasm. "And we always use our own trash bags when we do that."

The state's case was "character assassination," he concluded; in the absence of evidence, "let's talk about your sex life." He pointed to the prosecution table. "The authorities have a big stake in this case. They're under a lot of pressure. They're under a lot of pressure from the public; they're under a lot of pressure from the press. When you lose major cases you're under a lot of pressure."

He turned to look at Paula, who sat motionless, zeroed in on some private point her watchers could never know. "I'll tell you what she is, ladies and gentlemen. She is a woman who's lost two children. That is a hard loss." He stood behind her, as though he needed to make some excuse for her lack of response. "It's hard to cry when you have suffered as much as this woman has."

Paula gave no indication she heard his words. Everyone in the room watched her. She did not move.

As prosecutor, Don Weber had one final chance to persuade the jury that the state's argument was valid. There was no "bandit," he insisted. "The guy is not out there. *That*'s the person who did it." He pointed at Paula, as he had so often during the preceding weeks. "Right there." He ridiculed the idea that the little girls' deaths might be recurrent kidnappings. "Lightning like this doesn't strike *once*. This isn't lightning. This is an imaginary story made to cover up murder."

The people of Illinois wept for Heather, he said, even if her mother did not. "When Paula Sims was smothering that baby and its chest was burning and it was flailing its arms and kicking its legs"—he spat out the words Paula had once used to describe her first loving look at her newborn daughter—"I wonder if Paula counted every 'precious little finger' and 'precious little toe'!"

Spectators were silent and still. Paula reached slowly for her paper cup and took a sip of water. Hers was the only movement in the room. She put the cup back on the defense table and once more folded her hands in her lap.

"A baby is a precious gift from God," Weber continued, "not a piece of garbage." On one side of him was the white wicker bassinet, smudged with fingerprint powder. In it rested Paula's Barbie doll, in its shoe box. On the other side was the silver trash barrel, covered with plastic and sealed with evidence tape. Weber picked the boxed Barbie doll from the bassinet and set it atop the plastic-covered barrel. "A baby belongs in a bassinet, not in a trash can." He kicked the barrel angrily, then turned and pointed at Paula. "She doesn't know the difference."

It was nearly 5:30 P.M. when the case was given to jurors. Some television crews remained on the scene, but most reporters left, assuring one another there could be no decision before morning. Everyone was back at 9 A.M.

Paula's fate had become a focal point for more than a hundred people: news teams, jurors, attorneys, law enforcers. A woman unremarkable in her achievements and unknown to most of her neighbors had occupied more minutes of airtime, more inches of newsprint, than any other female in the history of Missouri or Illinois.

As the hours of deliberation ground on, her future became harder to predict. Hovering lawmen lost their looks of confidence. Reporters' speculations dwindled. The hallways were hushed.

Shortly before 2 P.M. the word came out from the bailiff. The jury had a verdict.

The press rushed into the courtroom, but there was no problem finding space on the wooden benches. There wasn't time for the message to circulate, for the concerned and the curious to arrive.

Paula entered, looking particularly drawn. She wore

brown slacks much too big for her and a white sweater. Court officer Angie Doehlert walked her to the defense table, where Groshong waited. He offered a nod of encouragement.

The bailiff gave his usual warning knock and opened the door to the jury room. The twelve filed in, their faces impassive. Paula's eyes went from juror to juror as they passed. None of them looked at her.

The jury foreman, a middle-aged, bespectacled engineer in the front row, passed the verdict form to the bailiff, who carried it to the bench. Judge Matoesian scanned the form for only a second before reading the first charge, the murder charge, and the jury's verdict: "Guilty."

Paula stared in disbelief at the jurors. A few of them glanced at her. She shook her head slightly, almost imperceptibly, and lowered her gaze to the defense table. Her eyes locked there.

Matoesian read the other three verdicts. "Guilty." "Guilty." "Guilty."

The last word still hung in the air as radio and television representatives dashed from the courtroom. When the noise of the exodus subsided, Groshong, his voice low and tight, requested a jury poll.

Forty-eight times the jurors said "yes."

Yes, they said in answer to Matoesian's questions, we believe Paula Sims murdered her infant daughter, Heather Lee.

Yes, we believe she lied to Officer Eichen when she reported the kidnapping.

Yes, we believe she lied to Detective McCain when she was questioned.

Yes, we believe she concealed Heather's body.

The judge thanked them for their verdict. They would be back to continue the process, he reminded them, to decide if Paula Sims's crimes warranted a death sentence.

As the eight men and four women filed out of the courtroom they passed within inches of Paula. Each was careful not to brush against her, but they looked sidelong at her as they exited.

The attorneys approached the judge's bench, a matter of sequestering the jury a second night. The judge refused to authorize it. Paula, alone at the defense table during their brief discussion, still did not move. She seemed not to breathe. Finally Angie Doehlert put a hand lightly on her back. Groshong leaned over and whispered to her. She rose and walked out silently. Her face was flushed. She looked terrified.

The next morning Peoria's *Journal Star* headlined "Sims Guilty." Coverage included a large picture of Paula taken on the first day of the trial, along with a smaller one of Rob, snapped as he stood in a courthouse hallway minutes after the verdict, cigarette in one hand and Bible in the other. The paper also devoted its "Dial-A-Vote" feature to the case, asking readers, "Should Paula Sims get death penalty?" Those with an opinion were invited to register their sentiments via Touch-Tone phone.

Word reached Peoria that KTVI, the St. Louis ABC affiliate, had offered its viewers a similar poll: "Well, what do you think? Should Paula Sims get the death penalty? Tonight you have a chance to be the jury."

Government officials, news executives, and offended members of the public were quick to decry the "lynch mob" mentality, and the polls' results (eighty-one percent of the TV station's callers voted pro-death) were downplayed or delayed until the trial adjourned.

The day's session was scheduled, as usual, for 9 A.M., but an hour drifted by and nothing happened. Word circulated that Paula's composure had shattered the previous day; in a witness room behind the courtroom she had wept after hearing the verdict. Rumor grew that she was seeking some kind of deal with the prosecution. A guard whispered that she and Groshong had been talking to Weber. Everyone waited.

"It was Don [Groshong]'s idea," Paula said. "I didn't want to. I got paranoid. But he said it would be off the record. He had paperwork ready for Weber to sign, promising it was off the record and it would never be revealed.

"So I told him [Weber]. I told him what happened with Heather. He didn't believe me. He said he was a Christian, too, and had compassion for me, but I would have to tell him the truth.

"It was Rob he wanted. He wanted me to implicate Rob. He said they were seeking the death penalty, and if I would implicate Rob he would call his boss and see if they could get the death penalty withdrawn.

"I said, 'I already told you the truth.'

"He didn't believe me. He said, 'Why are you protecting him?'

"And I said, 'I'm not.'

"And he asked me how I could love a man that much, to face the death penalty or else go to prison for the rest of my life.

"I guess he figured he would get me at my weakest point, which he did. I was drained from the long trial and then from the impact of the verdict. I was really drained. But there wasn't anything else I could say. I told him the truth, and he wouldn't believe it."

Rob did not believe her either. He walked into the witness room shortly after Weber left. "When he came in he said, 'Is it true that you murdered our daughters?'

Paula said yes.

"He said he didn't believe it. He kept askin' me why. I said I didn't know why. He said I couldn't have done it alone; someone must have helped me. He wanted to know who it was.

"I told him there was nobody, just this strange voice in my head that told me to do it.

"He said, 'Who was that?'

"I said, 'I guess it was the devil.'

"And he stood up and he walked over to me and he put his hand on my shoulder. And I must have pulled back, away from him. He said, 'Did you think I was gonna hit you? I'd never do that. I love you, no matter what.'"

Finally, at 11 A.M., the session began. Paula entered shakily, her face gray, her eyelids red and puffy within dark circles. Her lips trembled as she came through the door, but she sat as usual, thin legs crossed, bony hands folded in her lap.

The judge explained the day's business. It was phase two, time to determine if the defendant was eligible for the death sentence. This would be more a judgment of the crime than the criminal: Does this *crime* deserve the death penalty? There might be yet another phase in which the jury would be asked if Paula Marie Sims, personally, deserved to die. The verdict in this phase would have to be unanimous, the judge explained. The prosecution had to prove that the "statutory aggravating factors exist," that "death resulted from exceptionally brutal or heinous behavior indicative of wanton cruelty." In simpler terms, was Heather's death premeditated, prolonged, or torturous?

Weber faced the jurors, beginning with the issue of premeditation. "The burial cloth of Heather Sims was a half-cent trash bag purchased at a blue-light special," he said, a bag purchased the day of the murder or shortly before expressly to contain her body. He cited the "careful planning" of her death, arranged to coincide with a weekend when the Blews were away. "Heather probably lived a little extra time because the Blews were not out of town until the twenty-ninth."

He turned to "heinous behavior." Paula transferred the baby's body from her parents' refrigerator to her own, he theorized, and had sex with Rob upstairs while Heather's body lay below in the kitchen.

The drama was saved for the issue of "prolonged and torturous." Dr. Case had said it would take two minutes for Heather to lose consciousness, Weber reminded the jury, two minutes of struggling for breath. Clutching the sides of the lectern, he painted an awful picture of Heather's last moments. During that time of oxygen deprivation her chest would have been burning, he said quietly. She would have kicked her little legs, trying to push away the suffocating hand of her "mother-protector."

Weber offered the jurors two minutes to reflect on the picture, two minutes to think about Heather, pushing at a hand that denied her breath. A few seconds were consumed by Groshong's objection to the "courtroom stunt" and by Judge Matoesian's overruling of the objection. Then the room sat quietly to experience the time that remained.

Weber stared at the lectern, his hands still gripping its edges. Groshong rocked slightly in his chair at the defense table. Paula's eyes remained focused on the now-familiar spot on the judge's bench. The court reporter put down her pad. Soon even the pens and pencils of the press stopped, and the silence was absolute. Spectators glanced self-consciously at one another and eventually lowered their eyes. No one moved.

Groshong's task was difficult. For weeks he had tried to persuade the jurors of his client's innocence, and they had disbelieved him. Now, without insulting their decision and without offending their sensibilities, he had to convince them that the crime they had judged did not warrant the death penalty. "Exceptionally" was the key, he said, *"exceptionally* brutal and heinous behavior." In the ranking of murder methodology, death by smothering might not be the cruelest.

He turned to premeditation. There had been no evidence to suggest the trash bags were bought to contain Heather's body, he pointed out. If the crime had been carefully planned, Paula would have created a more impressive wound on her own neck. She would have arranged some indications of a struggle. It was possible that the child was killed without any planning at all. Spontaneously. His presentation was calm, quiet, deliberate.

The jury returned in less than two hours. The crime, they decided, warranted death.

The next day it was phase three, time to weigh the "aggravating" and "mitigating" factors, time to decide if anything in Paula Sims's life should prevent imposition of the death sentence. It was February 1, her son Randy's second birthday.

For Paula the agenda held an unexpected indignity. Since

the trial's second day she had been delivered each morning to the shelter of the newly completed sally port, where the overhead door slid down before she emerged from the jail van. As a result, there had been no new photos of her for more than three weeks. On the trial's last day—the day she would learn whether she was to live or die—Peoria County officials acceded to press requests and altered the delivery route. Paula was deposited on the sidewalk, close to a waiting photographer and a TV cameraman who would share their results with the rest of the media: "pool coverage." Their cameras went to work as she was paraded into the courthouse.

In the courtroom, the defense offered only two witnesses, her parents. Paula looked up momentarily as her mother took the stand. Tall and slender, her dark hair combed carefully, Nylene Blew was tense. It was hard for her to find the words. She explained that her son Dennis had been diagnosed as epileptic after suffering a bout of measles just before his third birthday, that her son Randy had died in an auto accident when he was nineteen. "For three years I didn't know if I was gonna make it or not." The jurors watched her intently.

Groshong asked if she loved her daughter. Nylene looked at Paula. "Yes, I do, very much."

"No questions," said Weber.

Paula's father was next. Was his daughter's marriage happy, Groshong asked.

It was happy at the beginning, Orville speculated, but then things changed. Paula did not often visit her parents, although she lived, at most, fifteen miles away. Rob came only on special occasions. "She was under a lot of pressure. She was kinda caught in between. She tried to satisfy her husband, and she tried to satisfy us. I guess we put a lot of pressure on her. We had different life-styles entirely. We needed people, where it seemed like it was the other way around with them. Rob told her that they had each other and they had the baby, and they didn't need anybody else."

Some jurors looked at Paula. She was angled toward her father, but her face had turned to stone.

Paula had always been "real thoughtful," Orville went on, sending birthday cards to all the family members. His voice thickened as he explained that on his own birthday just days earlier she had called "from the place she's at" (he wouldn't say *jail*) and had sung "Happy Birthday" over the phone.

One of the woman jurors shook her head sadly. "No questions," said Weber.

There was no rush to enter when the bailiff opened the courtroom doors to signal that the jury was ready. The press took places in front. Courthouse workers quietly slipped into seats at the back. A dozen observers were scattered in the rows between.

"You can open the door," crackled someone's walkie-talkie, indicating that Paula had been brought from a holding cell below; but Paula did not appear. Instead the surprised bailiff told Judge Matoesian, "She doesn't want to be here."

Attorney Groshong entered to say it more formally: "She waives her privilege to be present."

The judge raised his eyebrows and considered the situation. Paula must come in, he decided, so he could ask her personally if she did indeed waive her right to hear her fate pronounced. She entered slowly, silent on the crepe-soled shoes she had worn throughout the trial. "Mrs. Sims, do you not wish to be present?" Matoesian asked.

She shook her head. He reminded her to speak aloud. "No," she replied.

"You're sure of that?"

"Yes." She turned and made a soundless exit.

The first statement on the jury's verdict form was negatively worded, and the press required a moment to understand: "We, the jury, do not unanimously find that there are no mitigating factors . . ."

As the meaning of the words dawned, those who reported via the airwaves rushed from the courtroom, dashing to microphones or telephones to inform the public that Paula had escaped lethal injection. Judge Matoesian marveled at the exit. "Anyone else want to leave?" he said with a chuckle.

The jurors retreated to the jury room to collect their possessions, and the judge requested that the defendant appear for sentencing. Paula was brought in just as the jurors returned, some of them heading for a press conference in the lobby, some heading for a back-door exit, some wanting to stay and chat with the attorneys. Paula froze partway to the defense table. Jurors halted en route to their destinations. The half-filled room was suddenly too small, too close, too silent.

The judge quietly suggested that those jurors who wished to remain take seats among the spectators. Paula found her way to a chair.

William Haine, the Madison County state's attorney, stood at the prosecution table to recommend sentence. The state, he said, requested "natural life." Donald Groshong asked for a finite sentence, one that might allow Paula someday to leave prison, one that offered "hope at the end of the tunnel."

Matoesian paused for interminable seconds. ". . . For the rest of your natural life," he pronounced at last. The words "no possibility of parole" floated in the air, as did "the right to appeal" and "the Illinois State Department of Corrections."

The judge, who never used a gavel, rose from his bench. It was over. Jurors crowded in to shake the hand of the prosecutor. One shook the hand of the defense attorney. Reporters tried to steer everyone to the waiting press conference.

Paula remained motionless amid the activity, the still center in the whorl. Groshong leaned over to whisper to her, as he had so many times before. She rose slowly and walked silently from the courtroom.

VI

Continuations, Confessions, Conclusions

=== 29 ===

THE JURY FOREMAN TOLD THE POST-TRIAL PRESS CONFERENCE
that jurors had required only one ballot to reach a decision in each of the trial's three phases. "On each vote we
always totally agreed." But they seemed at a loss to explain *why* Heather was killed: "We don't know," answered
one.

Paula was returned temporarily to the Madison County
jail. Officials placed her on a suicide watch.

Newspapers ran stories about the questions unanswered,
the issues unresolved. Rob's possible complicity was at the
top of most lists. "We thought after this trial was over,
everybody thought, that we would have answers," complained Rhonda Scott. While Paula was awaiting trial
Rhonda had given unqualified support. She had welcomed
Paula's phone calls from the jail; she had offered consolation
and encouragement. "I've been waiting all these months,"
she said, fighting sorrow and frustration. "Where are the
answers? Where are they?"

Paula was transferred to the Dwight Correctional Institute in northeastern Illinois. Officials weighed her regularly,

to be sure she wasn't starving herself. Because her wedding ring contained a diamond she was not allowed to keep it. Rob offered to purchase a replacement. "We can't afford it," she reminded him. Instead he made her a new one, fashioned from the metal of a bolt.

"I know the way to the appellate court," Groshong told reporters. He began a process that he estimated might require as long as five years. His first step was to request that Judge Matoesian grant a new trial or set aside the jury conviction. He filed papers specifying more than a hundred reasons the judge should do so: extensive publicity that followed the case to Peoria; failure to sequester the jury; the accountability instruction; admission of the Loralei evidence (a "trial within a trial," Groshong argued); an Illinois trial venue for a crime whose victim was found in Missouri; the showing of the reenactment videotape; the surprise neurology testimony of Dr. Case ("trial by ambush"). Arguing the motion before Matoesian in late March, nearly two months after the verdict, Groshong cited "not just one error [but] the cumulative effect of them all." Matoesian denied the motion, clearing the way for the case to go to the Fifth District Appellate Court.

On the same occasion Paula appeared before the judge to be sentenced on the obstruction and concealment charges, a matter that had not been handled in Peoria. She entered wearing a bright yellow jail-issue rain slicker. Her eyes were focused on the floor, but the dark circles were gone. Her face had fleshed out a bit. Her step was less shaky than it had been at the trial. She looked thirty again. Matoesian issued two three-year sentences and one five-year sentence, to run concurrently. The added punishments were, in Groshong's words, "almost superfluous," since Paula was already serving life.

Rob watched from the front row. Days earlier State's Attorney Haine had announced plans to ask a grand jury to indict him on charges of murder, solicitation to commit murder, obstruction of justice, concealment of a homicide, conspiracy, and perjury. A copyrighted story in the March

25 issue of Alton's *Telegraph* announced Rob had failed another polygraph, this one taken a month earlier at the Illinois State Police crime lab in Springfield. Groshong complained about the continuing publicity.

When the grand jury met, reporters hovered in the courthouse hallway, ready to write the story of Rob's indictment; but instead of hearing evidence grand jury members were sent home. Haine issued a written statement saying consideration of charges against Rob had been postponed in an effort "to avoid any adverse effect on the grand jury that recent publicity may have generated."

Speculation was rampant among the press that prosecutors had nothing more on Rob than they had had before—a failed but inadmissable polygraph and the hope that Paula might turn against him. That theory was supported by a family court hearing at the end of April, a hearing to determine whether Rob's temporary custody of Randy should be made permanent. Haine told Judge Ellar Duff that Rob was "living a lie." His "evidence" was Paula's conviction; by finding Paula guilty, Haine reasoned, the jury had rejected Rob's story. "That evidence can be *construed,*" Haine told the court.

A lawyer appointed to protect Randy's interests labeled Haine's arguments "extraordinary leaps of logic."

The judge declared the state had failed to convince her Rob Sims was implicated in the crime. She gave him permanent custody of Randy and said the boy could be taken to visit Paula as long as a prison official was present during their time together. Rob called the ruling "wonderful." He said he was tired of listening to the prosecution's allegations.

"The truth is Paula's to tell," Haine said unhappily, "and she is not telling."

At a press conference the following day Haine admitted there was no new evidence against Rob. Predictions of an indictment had been based upon a presumption that "she [Paula] would tell the truth." He refused to forecast future grand jury action.

In May the charges still pending against Paula in Jersey

County were resolved with a plea agreement. The county agreed not to file a murder charge, and Paula agreed to a no-contest plea on two charges of obstructing justice in Loralei's death. In the arrangement, known as an Alford plea, she did not admit guilt but acknowledged that the prosecution had enough evidence to convict her. She was given two five-year sentences to run concurrent with all her other sentences. Defense attorney Groshong explained her reasons for accepting the deal: "It won't cost her a day in jail. She's already serving that time." And besides, he said, "Where could she get a fair trial? Brazil?"

Weber and Haine used renewed press interest as an opportunity to say they believed Rob was guilty, at a minimum, of perjury. Their statements added paragraphs to the news stories but didn't bring about an indictment. By midsummer the Sims case was old news.

Rhonda Scott waited for Rob to visit, as he had before Paula's conviction. When he didn't come in the days after the verdict she assumed he was grieving, adjusting, coping. When winter became spring and still he didn't come, she wondered. People told her he had ceased attending the Baptist church up the street and no longer carried the Bible that had been his ever-present prop before the trial.

Rhonda saw his silver Jeep pass her house, but he never stopped. He drove by one day when she was in the yard. She waved. He looked the other way. "I think he's acting very strange," Rhonda declared.

Shortly after Paula Sims had sobbed at the sight of Heather's little white casket, another woman named Paula had visited the grave. She was Paula Elizabeth Welch, and she was not the first in her family to respond to the tragedy. Her sister had once paraded before the Blews' house with a sign proclaiming she loved her little girls, "all five of them."

At times, Paula Welch's interest in the Sims case had neared obsession. She was lured not only by the unremitting publicity but by peculiar coincidences in her own history and that of Paula Marie Sims. They shared a name. They shared a birth month, May. They had both lost brothers to sudden death. They had both given birth in 1986 and again in 1989. They had chosen the same middle names, Marie and Lee, for their daughters.

They were to share even more. On June 7, 1990, Paula Welch answered an ad for a baby-sitter and met Rob Sims.

Welch needed to supplement her income in some quiet, informal way, something that wouldn't interfere with the state aid she received. Regulations limited her employment opportunities. So did her lack of education and experience. She had been a pregnant bride at fifteen, just as she was about to enter her sophomore year in high school. She had her first child, *Diana, when she was sixteen, and her second, *Erick, when she was eighteen. Her husband let her know he didn't believe the second baby was his; she let him know she couldn't tolerate his drinking. The marriage didn't last. Her third child, Michael, was born when she was twenty-two. She intended to marry his father, but the relationship fell apart before the ceremony took place. Her fourth pregnancy came two years later. There was a wedding this time, but the marriage crashed before the baby, Tiffany, was born. After that Paula had her tubes tied. No more kids, she said.

None of her pregnancies had been planned, but thankfully, she enjoyed babies. And when she needed extra money baby-sitting was an area in which she could claim real experience.

Paula Welch recognized Rob Sims, of course (there were few people in southern Illinois who would have failed to recognize him), but Rob's demeanor was a surprise. "He seemed like a polite, gentle man. His kindness seemed so pure, like he wouldn't hurt a fly. Somewhat like a preacher, so soft-voiced." Randy clung to Rob's leg. The boy had had several sitters who had proven unreliable, Rob said. He stressed his need for someone he could count on.

Paula didn't hesitate. She needed the money, and she was too curious to decline. "I said, 'I'll be more than a baby-sitter to him. I'll be like a mom. I'll treat him like he's my own son.'

"He said, 'No, nobody could substitute for my son's mom.'"

Paula Welch found Randy was not a difficult child to tend, despite the fluctuating hours he spent in her care. Rob continued to work rotating shifts at Jefferson Smurfit. To keep Randy's schedule regular he sometimes delivered the boy early or let him stay through the night. The flexibility was fine with Paula. "I would tell him, 'Don't worry about Randy. Just go home and get some sleep, and when you feel good enough come on over and get him, or come over and visit. You don't necessarily have to pick him up.' And I guess that's when our relationship started."

Within days Rob began bringing Randy an hour or two before his shift began and staying to talk, or coming to get Randy in the afternoon and staying for dinner. He seemed comfortable in the little bungalow Paula rented, but he also seemed careful. He smoked no pot. He had to be persuaded even to have a beer. He paused before he answered questions. "He would listen to hisself before he would say somethin'" was Paula's conclusion.

No topics were off-limits to her. "I asked him how long it's been since he had a woman, and he told me it's been since his wife went to jail, and I felt so heartbroke for him. I thought this poor man hasn't had a woman in his life, and he's hurtin' so bad for his children, and I just felt for him." First it was a hug good-bye, then a kiss. "One thing led to another." Soon Rob, as well as Randy, was spending the night.

Summer weather meant the two older children in the Welch household were often outside playing with friends. Seven-year-old Erick accepted the presence of Rob and Randy; nine-year-old Diana didn't. She seldom liked the men who passed through her mother's life. She particularly disliked Rob Sims.

Little Tiffany appeared to be Rob's favorite. "Tiffany was callin' him Daddy. He'd pick Tiffany up and give her a big hug and kiss on the cheek. He treated Tiffany like he loved her."

Rob never complained about the disarray produced by

five children and their playthings, but he bought chip clips when he noticed Paula just crunched up the tops of potato chip packages, and he supplied a bottle brush when he saw she used a dishcloth to clean bottles and nipples. A window in the children's bedroom at the back of the house bothered him. It had a curtain but no shade. "People can see *in* here," he said.

"So what?" Paula shrugged. "They ain't gonna see much." He installed mini-blinds.

Because his son Randy rode in her car, Rob bought Paula new tires. She was impressed. "He was kind to me. He didn't treat me like crap. He treated me good. I guess I started lettin' things go to my head."

When their relationship turned personal, so did the gifts: a Garfield nightshirt and a teddy. "Not a teddy bear," Paula emphasized. "A teddy." There was also a bottle of Ciara perfume (his favorite, he said). On the enclosed card he wrote, "The longer we're together, the more connected we'll be."

For her the gifts, and the words, hinted at commitment. "He used to tell me, about a month after we first met, 'I love you, Paula. I'd like to be with you for good.'

"He's not one of these 'Lay down, let's—'. He treated me with kindness, caressing. Lovemaking. And I've never been treated like that. It wasn't all sexual. It may have been all sexual for *him*. But a lot of feelings went in for me."

Paula began to hope that somehow they would all blend into a family. "I just want one man. That's all I've ever wanted. I told that to Rob." For a while she thought it might happen. When she described a beautiful dress that she had seen, he told her to buy it. It was long and pink with a matching headpiece, the kind of dress a bridesmaid might wear. Or a bride, if the wedding was her third.

There were obstacles, however, in the way of Paula Welch's desire to mold a family. The first was Diana. "Diana didn't want anything to do with family activities when Rob was here. She said, 'I ain't goin' nowhere with him.'"

When Paula and Rob went to look at houses that might be available, Diana's resistance reached a new peak. "She would blare out 'Your wife's a baby-killer' and stuff like that. She knew all about it. She seen it on the news. So when we started doin' things together and Rob was stayin' here, Diana couldn't handle it. She said, 'You give *all* your love and time to him.' And maybe I did. Maybe I didn't realize what I was doin'."

Another impediment to the relationship turned out to be Paula Welch's interest in Loralei and Heather. Rob was upset that she talked so much about his dead daughters. "He said, 'You love my children so much that I would hear about them for the rest of my life.'"

It angered him when she compared Randy to his sisters. "It pissed Rob off. I'd stand there and look at Randy and I'd say, 'Look at him. He looks just like Loralei and Heather. It's just like havin' them right here.'

"And he would just go nuts. He would say, 'No, he doesn't! They're all different people!'"

The ultimate obstacle in the way of Paula Welch's wish for a total commitment was the woman whose name she shared. Paula Sims was miles away, in prison for the rest of her life, but Rob was still married to her.

In mid-August, slightly more than two months after they met, Rob Sims and Paula Welch and their children (all but Diana) undertook a whirlwind week of activities. They went to see the stalactites at Meramec Caverns; they went to the St. Louis Zoo. "It was a *family,*" Paula Welch insisted, "goin' to have fun."

Then they made one more trip, one that she thought might really let them be a family. They drove to the Dwight Correctional Institute so that Rob could tell his wife he wanted a divorce.

Rob's announcement devastated Paula Sims. Rob and Randy were all she had left. "He said how hard it was for him to raise Randy. That's the excuse he gave for why he was divorcin' me, 'cause Randy needed a mother. He said he'd given up hope of me ever gettin' out, and he had to start a new life. I said, 'You found somebody else. That's it, isn't it?'

"And he said, 'No, that ain't it. I still love you. I'll never love nobody else as much as I love you. But I gotta get on with my life.'

"He promised he would bring Randy to see me. He promised. He said he'd never keep Randy from me.

"I think he just started hatin' me for what I done, like everybody else. At first I thought he was tryin' to understand. I couldn't give him much help, 'cause I didn't understand it either. We didn't talk about it very often.

"But with everybody out there hatin' me so much—I think he believed when he divorced me the public would stop thinkin' bad things about him. They'd say, 'Oh, he got rid of her. He must be okay.'

"Maybe that was it. Maybe it was this other woman. Maybe it was because he couldn't forgive me. Maybe it was just everything."

Paula Welch believed the trip to Dwight signaled the real beginning of her union with Rob Sims. Instead it proved to be the beginning of the end. In the days that followed he began to behave in ways that surprised her. "He called me up one day from work, and he asked me if my son Erick was black. 'What makes you ask me that?' I wanted to know.

"And he goes, I heard this from Paula [Sims].'

" 'Well, how the hell would she know?' I asked him. 'She don't know me.' He said he'd had a grandfather who was in the Ku Klux Klan. I said, 'What makes you think my kid is black?' "

Rob's next objections were leveled at Diana. The anger and rudeness he had put up with for weeks were no longer acceptable, he told Paula. "My daughter would say to me, 'I hate you, Mama. I wish you would die.' And Randy was sayin' to his dad, 'Wish you die, wish you die,' because he heard Diana sayin' it to me."

Within days of their most intense "togetherness" Rob told Paula Welch that she couldn't care for Randy any longer. "It's for the best," he announced.

While Paula Welch wondered how to put things back together, the Sims divorce petition made the news, and members of the press found their way to her door. A television reporter came first, asking if she was the cause of the breakup. She went on camera to say she and Rob were "just friends." Reporters from the *Telegraph* followed. Again she said, "Just friends," but the banner headline on the September 13 issue let readers come to their own conclusions. "Woman Denies Romance With Robert Sims" was splashed across page one.

Whatever was left of the relationship crumbled under the publicity. Rob was angry about the stories. So was the agency in charge of social security payments. When authorities learned Welch had been supplementing her income through baby-sitting they cut off her assistance.

At the end of September Rob asked Paula Welch to meet him at a park, where he told her that he wouldn't be seeing her anymore; his divorce attorney had advised him not to see *any* women. Besides, he said, it was obvious that things wouldn't work out between them. He wanted another child, and she had had a tubal ligation after her last pregnancy. "He told me, 'You can't have any more children. I want another child. I want a little girl. You can't provide one.' "

Tubal ligations could be undone, she explained. That wouldn't make any difference, he said. The relationship was over. "Then he said he wanted a woman with great big tits. A small body and great big tits. And red hair would be a plus. Can you believe it? Red hair."

It was easy for Paula Welch to blame her daughter Diana. If Diana hadn't hated Rob, if she hadn't refused to take part in family activities, if she hadn't been such a loudmouth, smart-aleck kid. Paula let the girl know how she felt.

On October 7 Diana turned ten. Three days later tensions in the Welch household reached a new peak. Diana didn't want to go to school. She didn't want to wear the clothes her mother told her to wear. She didn't want to do anything her mother told her to do. She got into a scratching, kicking, fist-flying fight with her seven-year-old brother Erick. "I took her, laid her over my lap, and I beat her ten-year-old ass," said Paula. "I beat her butt with my hand."

Diana went to school. After school she went to neighbors and said she didn't want to go home because her mother had beaten her. The neighbors took her in. When Paula came to their door and asked for Diana they refused to send the girl out. Paula called the police to demand her daughter's return.

Officers took Diana to the station, where she told them that her mother had beaten her with a belt, kicked her, and stepped on her head. The police took photos of her red ear and her bruised thigh and released her to the custody of her paternal grandparents. The following day Paula Welch was arrested for felony child abuse. The press was waiting when she surrendered at the station.

The situation was rife with implications. Parallels were almost too obvious. Two women named Paula. Both with strong connections to Rob Sims. Both accused of a crime against their children, their *female* children. Reporters created their own sardonic shorthand. Paula Elizabeth Welch was dubbed "Paula II."

By the next morning, when she was arraigned at the Wood River Courthouse, the crowd of reporters and photographers had swollen to proportions reminiscent of the legal events surrounding Paula I. The charges against her were reduced to battery, a misdemeanor, and she pled guilty even though she didn't feel she was. Diana was left in the temporary custody of her paternal grandparents. Both mother and daughter were ordered to receive therapy. Paula Welch agreed not to see Rob Sims.

It was a commitment she found difficult to keep. Rob called in February, after he had visited a striptease bar with some men from the plant. She told herself she had too much pride to go to his apartment, but she went anyway.

In April she phoned to wish him a happy birthday. He said he was by himself, alone, lonely. She went to see him once again. He had put an ad in a tabloid, he told her, and was amazed at the number of replies he had received. "An ad for what?" she asked. He read it to her: Man, thirty-eight, with small child, looking for steady relationship, possible marriage.

"He showed me pictures of girls and letters. He had like seventy replies. He said, 'I got so many I don't know who to choose from.'" He'd already traveled to Florida to meet one of the best prospects, he explained, a woman who had promised to visit him in Illinois for his birthday. Apparently she had changed her mind; she didn't show up.

He suggested that Paula try putting an ad in the paper. "You can kiss my ass," she retorted. "I ain't that desperate."

"Well, I'm not desperate," he protested. "I'm doing it for—"

She didn't let him finish. "So you can meet somebody that don't know you is why you're doing it. You don't wanna meet anybody around here 'cause they all know you. They all know your face, they know your name, they know where you been, they know what you been through. Shit, what's not to know about you?"

Family court sealed the file on the Sims divorce to protect Randy, but bits of information leaked out each time Rob and Paula met at the courthouse. Paula wanted Randy to visit her at the prison, as Judge Duff had ruled he could. But now Rob didn't want to take the boy to the prison; he didn't even want the child to know his mother existed; he wanted Paula's name chiseled off the family tombstone that marked the graves of Loralei and Heather.

Public and press speculation mounted as the acrimony became known. Might Paula break her silence now? Or did Rob's divorce petition signal that she was no threat to him, that he was really not involved in the crime?

Lawyers hammered out an agreement. Rob told reporters to leave him alone. Paula said nothing.

By mid-1991 the Madison County state's attorney's office no longer spoke publicly of prosecuting Rob. Weber and Haine claimed their victory and announced their satisfaction, but others recognized the lack of closure. The jury had said Paula was guilty, but there was something unsatisfying about the verdict. It had been Paula Sims vs. the officialdom of two counties and the sentiment of the entire region, a period of sound and fury that had achieved relatively little. The babies were dead, and nothing had been learned about the impulse that killed them.

Jim Bivens, the DCI officer who headed the 1986 search, shook his head. "I'd rather see Rob Sims punished than Paula. . . . To me, Rob Sims set this in motion, even if he didn't touch that child, as far as physically causing her death. That's my feeling. . . . He may not have pulled the trigger, so to speak, physically, but he did mentally. I blame him more than I blame her."

Retirement from the Department of Criminal Investigation offered Bivens a chance to close the book on the case, but he couldn't let it go. "I don't suppose I'll ever know what really, really happened," he said with a sigh as he contemplated the four years of investigative pressures applied to Paula. "She's been through some pretty tight situations with police officers, and they haven't been able to faze her."

Sheriff Frank Yocom, who led the investigation with Bivens, did not agree. "Oh, she's gonna talk at some point in time," he predicted. "I've been sayin' that forever, and I still say it. It amazed me in the trial that she held herself together like she did. I can't believe she did that. But there'll be a point when she's gonna have to say something to somebody."

=== 30 ===

NEARLY TWO YEARS PASSED BEFORE SHERIFF YOCOM'S PREDIC-
tion proved true. When Paula finally phoned me in January
of 1992 she seemed ready to talk. She corroborated what I
already knew about the sorry state of her marriage and
admitted the pain she felt about the collapse of her relationship with little Randy.

Four days later she called again; our discussions began to
range further. Paula described her life with Rob, her feelings
during the trial, her fears about her son's future; but any
mention of her daughters brought an emotional retreat. "I
gotta go now," she said time after time when the topic
veered toward Loralei and Heather.

Gradually she began to speak of them, seeking safety
in specifics—their smiles, their actions, the gifts they received —but she would not talk of their murders. "It won't
do no good to talk about it," she said, weeping. "They're
gone."

Nevertheless, they crept repeatedly into her conversation.
She recounted their births and their short lives, chronicling
the moments that meant most to her. Soon she had told me

everything about the little girls, everything but the details of their deaths; that was a topic too heavy to be shared over long distance. "I was wondering," she said at last, "if you'd like to visit me."

The Dwight Correctional Institute sits on the flat, fertile Illinois prairie, a mile off the interstate highway that links Chicago with the southern regions of the state. The stately administration building is made of brick, as is a wall that hides the units that house eight hundred inmates. The wall is interrupted by turrets, too small and low to be guard towers, eccentric enough to momentarily distract a visitor from the function of the facility. The oddly poetic cylinders, their cone-shaped roofs topped with multicolored shingles, suggest a medieval castle; but as the brick wall reaches a corner it converts to chain link, and two high parallel fences, each topped by shining rolls of razor wire, stretch into the distance.

Inmates meet their visitors in a cafeterialike setting, a room furnished with round tables and plastic chairs. At one end is a snack bar; at the other a play space for children. Near the room's center, at a desk on a raised platform, sits a correctional officer. Other guards come and go; some keep watch behind a one-way mirror.

Words come haltingly to Paula. She stares at her hands, or at the tabletop. "There are times in life when you try to do the right thing, but it doesn't end up the right thing. There are times you think you could never do something like— something. But then you do—something, something that you would never, never dream in a million years. It don't make no sense. I don't know. I know I never planned nothing, like they say I did. But something happened."

Paula has had little help in understanding what happened. Her first weeks at the prison were spent in the mental health unit; the official diagnosis was "major depression." She met with a psychiatrist, a man, but whatever empathy might have allowed her to speak was lacking.

She attended a meeting for battered women but felt out of

place. "That's physical abuse. They have scars. I don't have scars, at least not on the outside."

Another inmate, also convicted of murdering her children, offered a pamphlet on postpartum depression. Paula glanced at it and handed it back. "I was pretending I wasn't interested even though I really was."

Among the several women at Dwight who have been convicted of infanticide there is little communication. In the hierarchy of homicide they are at the bottom of the pecking order, reviled even by other murderers, for they have killed children, their own children, babies who had done no wrong and who could not fight back. Feelings against them run strong enough that they find it easier, even safer, to avoid one another's company, to lose themselves in the crowd.

"I got some of it figured out, I think. Maybe. But other things I don't understand at all. There was something goin' on in my head, and I don't know where it come from. I didn't know what to do about it, so I had to pretend it wasn't there."

There are no breathy sobs like those that once bothered investigators, but tears stream soundlessly down her cheeks. Certain words she cannot bring herself to utter: die, kill, murder. Even the names of her daughters are hard for her to say. She couches the awful truth in safe phrases.

"The first time it happened, in eighty-six, Rob wanted a boy. Okay, he didn't get a boy, but he got a healthy, beautiful girl, and he assured me that he was thrilled with her. But still I knew that I had disappointed him because he wanted a boy. He wanted a boy first, and then I could have my girl. His and mine. He never understood they were *ours*.

"I had been cryin' ever since I come home from the hospital, whether it was somethin' small or somethin' big that upset me. I cried almost every day. Things weren't how I thought they were gonna be or how they should be, how I expected motherhood to be, and a family to be.

"I wanted to take her to the mailbox with me to pick up the mail, but Rob said no. I said, 'Sunshine's good for the baby.'

"He said, 'No, keep her down in the basement where it's cool.'

"I thought, what a place. The basement.

"And then all the problems about people comin' over, friends, my family. Anytime someone came I got jumped on. I got instructions before they arrived, and I got jumped on after they left. I didn't do it right. It was my fault. I always got the blame.

"And I was feelin' so bad, so strange. I didn't know what was wrong with me."

She fought bad feelings as she always had, with pills and pot, and a beer now and then. The pattern was not new, but she had abstained during her pregnancy, and after nine drug-free months she felt the effect of the marijuana and the tranquilizers almost as much as she had when she first began her experimentation with narcotics more than a decade earlier. Still, the anxiety that hung over her was more powerful than anything she could swallow or inhale.

She cried about anything, about everything: a memory of her dead brother, an article on crib death, an argument with Rob, the possibility that an accident might befall Loralei. She watched the infant sleeping peacefully, so peacefully that sometimes she laid a hand on the tiny chest to feel for a heartbeat. She wept with relief when she felt the dainty pulse tapping.

Most of the time she didn't know why she was crying. She wanted some reassurance, some promise that no bad thing would ever happen, that life would be the way she had dreamed it would be when she was young and innocent enough to have dreams. But even if some fairy godmother had offered a pledge of happy-ever-after, she wouldn't have believed it, for there was something dark and heavy in the air she breathed, pushing at her in ways she couldn't explain.

"I didn't know it was gonna happen. It was not long after Rob left. I was gonna give her a bath. I had been givin' her sponge baths, like the book said I was supposed to do until that little piece of her umbilical cord fell off. And then it came off, so I thought it would be good to put her in the tub and give her a nice warm bath. I thought it would help her to sleep."

Paula's preparations were careful and loving. A few inches of water in the tub, just the right temperature. Gentle shampoo for the bright red hair. Special soap for the alabaster skin. A soft little washcloth. A plastic duck.

"I put her in the bathtub. And then I walked out. I didn't *decide* to walk out. I didn't decide anything. I just walked out."

She prowled the house from one corner to another. Down the hallway to the nursery, half expecting to see the baby there. Back the other way, past the closed bathroom door. "I was cryin'. I was always cryin'. I said to myself, am I really doing this? And first I said, no, I'm not. And then I said, well, maybe I am."

Out to the kitchen for no reason except that she had to keep moving. Back to the nursery, past the bathroom door once more. "It was like someone was tellin' me go back in there. And then someone was tellin' me no, don't. It was a fight that was goin' on inside of me. I would start to go toward the bathroom, and then somethin' would say no, don't, don't. And then I wouldn't. I would go light me a joint. And I would pace or light me a cigarette. Pop me a pill. Whatever. And my mind was goin' a hundred miles an hour. And my heart was racin'. I was real, real nervous. I had been nervous since she was born. And I had hardly ate, and I had hardly slept."

To the dining room, around the table. To the kitchen, looking for something, unable to remember what it was. Back to the nursery, circling, hurrying. "I felt like I was rushing, but I also felt like I was moving real slow." And when all the bungalow's corners had been explored, when there was nowhere else to wander, when her expectation overcame her dread, she paused before the closed door of the bathroom and turned the knob. The door swung open slowly, silently.

Loralei lay mute and motionless. The once-warm water spread like a sheet of glass over her, and her pale skin had turned faintly blue. Paula knew there would be no dainty, reassuring beat in the tiny chest.

She couldn't make herself touch the little body, not flesh-to-flesh contact. She drained the tub and reached for a bathroom towel. Fears churned in her head, ironic, erratic: "I thought, Rob is gonna be mad at me. My folks are gonna be mad at me. Everybody is gonna be mad."

Scooping up the tiny bundle, she fled down the steps that led to the basement family room, past the bassinet where Loralei should have been sleeping soundly. "I just went right on down the stairs. Right out the patio doors."

The hill dropped down at the edge of the yard, only feet away. "It was a rough, rough hill. It had little trees and leaves and things that had been there forever. There was almost a full moon out that night. There was enough light that I could see. There was moonlight and branches, black branches, sharp branches. I just went down the hill a little bit. I had a towel. I never touched her. I couldn't. I held her in a towel. I carried her out there very carefully, and I unwrapped her and laid her down very carefully. And I told her I was sorry. I told her I loved her and I was real, real sorry, and then I turned around and walked back up the hill and went in the patio doors.

"When I got back inside I paced some more. I thought, what am I going to do? I had the TV on. The news was on, the ten o'clock news. I thought, I'll sit down and watch the news. Nothing's happened. Nothing's happened. And I kept on looking over to the bassinet, and she wasn't in the bassinet. I thought, did that really happen? I started thinking about a shovel or something. I thought, I've got to do this proper-like. A coffin. But then I thought if I had a coffin, we'd be having a funeral, and she'd be gone, and she's not gone. She's upstairs. So I went upstairs, but she wasn't there. So I thought, oh, it did happen! I thought, gosh, are you just gonna leave her there without doing something proper? But I thought, I can't go back out there. I can't. It's like I wasn't me, like I had lost my mind, and I had lost control. Lost control of everything. And I finally thought, what will I say? I gotta come up with somethin'.

"I remember I had these sticktights all over me, like cockleburs when you go through the woods. I had on blue jogging pants, and they were covered. All over me. All over my socks. I had to pick all those things off me. I changed my clothes. I don't know what I changed into. I had to get them things off. Little sticktights."

The towel that had shrouded the small corpse went into the clothes hamper, crammed into a corner, never to be used again. The knife that cut a jagged slash in the screen door came from the kitchen and was returned to its place. "It was just a steak knife. I put it back in the drawer, in my silverware drawer. And then I went down the lane to the Hyatts.

"That's what happened. You know the rest."

Knowing what happened, admitting it, saying it aloud for the first time brings her no visible relief. She focuses on things around her, rotating her can of Pepsi, running her finger over a nick in the Formica tabletop, pushing away the dreadful pictures in her mind. "I think about it. I try not to, but sometimes—"

Clear definition of her own motives eludes her, but she sees hazily the complications, the interactions, the overlaying web of circumstance and character that influenced her actions. It was more than the depression that settled over her after the births of her babies, for she might have handled that if she had spoken to someone, her mother, her husband, a friend, a psychiatrist. It was more than the stifling and unhappy marriage that trapped her, for if she had been someone else, even if she had been her former self, the "hell-raiser" from the past, she would have broken out of any trap that ensnared her. It was more than the drugs that kept her becalmed and dependent. It was more than any one thing. It was everything together, tangling, twisting, complicating, confusing.

She plays her life over in her mind. If she had listened to her parents when they told her not to marry Rob. If she had told the truth after Loralei's death. If she had stayed off drugs, as she and Rob told each other they would. If she had accepted her aunt's offer of refuge. "There's always that *if, if, if.* If I had done this. If I had done that. But the *if*s don't matter anymore. There's that bottom line.

"There was no reason to do what I did, no matter what. I feel guilty. I feel ashamed. I feel I should have stopped myself somehow. I did once. I did stop myself with Randy.

"And after that, don't you see, after I managed to get through it with Randy, I thought I'd be able to control it, to control myself. I thought it could never happen again. But it did.

"I was glad to be pregnant that last time. I was real happy about it. Not too many people will believe that. But I was. In eighty-nine. Very happy. She was precious. She sure was. And they all looked so different, all my babies.

"Before something happened she was smiling all the time. You know how they smile when they're little and they got their eyes closed. She would smile, and I thought, oh, she's havin' little baby dreams. She was a good baby. Randy loved her. I'd say her name and say, 'Where is she?' and he'd point to her. He really loved her, too.

"She smiled all the time. I sure do miss her. I miss 'em both."

Paula pushes the tears from her cheeks and stares, unfocused and unseeing, at some distant point where memories gather.

"I kept on flashing back to eighty-six, to what had happened. I said this is not gonna happen again. I'm stronger than this. I can handle it. I promised I would handle it. I promised myself. I promised Heather. I promised God.

"I said, I've got a beautiful, healthy baby girl here. This will pass, I kept on telling myself. It will get better. And then maybe I'd drink another beer or smoke another joint or something.

"And I'd look at her, and she was so beautiful, and she was just what I wanted. And I thought about Randy, about how they would be so close, and play with one another, and grow up together. I thought, I've got my dream here. I can handle it.

"And then I would make myself think of something good, like me and her doing mother-daughter things together, and how close we were gonna be, like I had always wanted and had always thought a mother and daughter should be. And how beautiful she was. And how beautiful she was gonna be. And me fixin' her hair and dressin' her up and goin' out and showin' her off and sayin', 'That's my little girl.' I had so many plans. I thought I could overcome it. I really did.

"And I'd look at Randy and remember I overcome it with him. I thought I could do it.

"But I guess I knew it was gonna happen. It was in my head. I had been feelin' bad for so long. Hot. Queasy. Thoughts. Bad thoughts. Remembering.

"It's really hard to put into words or explain. It was just something that was inside of me. It was like, I gotta do this. I gotta do it. I cannot handle things. I'm a failure.

"And it come to me, am I gonna raise my children in this kind of atmosphere? In this kind of turmoil? They're gonna be like me, like two different people, living one way when their father is home and one way when he's gone. That's not the kind of life they should have. I can't give 'em what they should have. I had pretty much given up on their father, on him getting any better. It just seemed like a dead end. I thought this was a way out, to end it.

"I thought, I need to do myself in, too, 'cause I can't stand this. I can't stand it no more. Something's got to be done 'cause I can't take it. I can't take all this pressure. I just felt a tremendous pressure, pressure in my head. I thought about killing myself. But then I thought about Randy. I can't do him in. And who will take care of him? And then I thought, no, no, no! I tried to get the thoughts out of my head.

"And I saw it was such a beautiful day. I wanted to go to the park. Take 'em to a park, I thought. After I give her a bath, and after Randy wakes up from his nap, I'll take 'em to a park. And I thought, no, I can't do that. Rob will be callin' in about an hour. But then I thought maybe I could take 'em afterwards, I could sneak out after his call. But then I thought, no, this isn't working. This isn't working. This isn't what I wanted our lives to be. I don't want this. It's just not working.

"And I thought about killing him, killing Rob. I thought about it. I thought, this would solve it. I thought, no, I can't do that. What am I thinkin' here? I'm not the kind of person to go around takin' people's lives.

"And then it come to my mind, you already did it once. You can do it again.

"And I said, no, I can't!"

With these thoughts racing through her head, Paula paced. She smoked. She poured some whiskey into her Pepsi. She took a Valium, or a Xanax, whatever fell into her hand. "A couple here, a couple there."

She looked at Randy, asleep in the playpen in the living room. She looked at Heather, lying contentedly in the bassinet in the dining room. "It's just like I was fightin' with somethin'. I thought, what am I going to do? Here I go again. And I cried out for God to help me. I was in tears, and I cried out, and I said, 'God, help me! I don't want to do this.' I cried out to Him."

Even as she picked up Heather and mounted the spiral staircase she denied her intention. "I said, I'm just going to give her a bath. I was still fighting with myself. I was fighting it."

Holding the infant in one arm, she paused in the bathroom to turn on the faucet. She held her hand under the cascading water, testing its temperature. She put the stopper in the tub and folded the little towel that she always placed under Heather's head, a pillow to keep her chin above the water.

The reality of the tub and the water was too much to retract. She knew what was coming. She carried the smiling baby to the bedroom and undressed her. "I told her how sorry I was. I told her I loved her. There was somethin' goin', 'Do it. Do it. Do it and get it over with.'"

Cradling Heather in her arms, she sobbed as she walked,

transfixed and determined, across the hallway to the bathroom. She lowered the baby into the inviting water, the water that was just the right temperature.

"Some voice was sayin', 'No one is gonna believe you. They didn't believe you in eighty-six.'

"And somethin' else said, 'Yeah, they gotta prove it. Do it.' And I did."

In a motion as quick and impersonal as she could make it she turned the baby over onto her stomach, her face against the little towel that should have cushioned her head. She rose quickly and walked away, closing the bathroom door behind her. If there was to be any noise, she didn't want to hear it.

She descended the circular stairway, one hand grasping the rail, the other suppressing the sounds of her own mouth, sounds that were neither moans nor sobs but some combination of relief and regret. She paced. She lit a cigarette, barely able to get the shaky flame to its end. She stared out the window but saw nothing. She circled through the kitchen, the living room, the dining room. "I kept on wantin' to go upstairs, but I didn't."

She looked at the playpen where Randy slept and at the bassinet, achingly empty. She returned to the kitchen and waited there, staring at objects that were thoroughly familiar, memorizing their form, listening to the awful tick of the clock.

When enough seconds had turned to minutes and enough minutes had made the outcome inevitable, she found a black plastic bag and clutched it in her hand as she climbed the stairs. She stared straight ahead as she opened the bathroom door. "I didn't look at the tub. I tried not to. I glanced when I walked in, I guess. I let the water out, pulled the plug. I had the bag already layin' on the floor when I thought about the gloves. They were in my bedroom, in my closet, in my coat pocket. I thought, I need to get them."

She shoved her fingers into the beige and brown gloves, an old pair that she'd had for years, but when she returned to the bathroom, she realized the precaution was too late; she had already touched the bag. Her fingerprints were there, marking her, condemning her. She used her gloved hands to wipe them from the plastic.

"There was a towel hangin' up there, and I put that over her so I didn't have to look at her or touch her. That's how I picked her up. I was real careful with her. I wasn't rough. I wanted to be gentle, 'cause I was sorry for what I'd done. I didn't want her sufferin' any more."

The plastic slid through the gloves as she struggled to turn the top of the bag into a knot. Her hands wouldn't work. "I tied it. I carried it downstairs and set it on the kitchen floor. I went to check on Randy, and he was still asleep, so I put it out by the front seat of the car, on the passenger side floorboard." The black plastic bag rested atop a brown paper sack left over from a forgotten errand.

"And then after that I went back in the house. I paced and paced. I went upstairs. I don't know exactly what steps I took. I wrung the towel out. Cleaned the bathtub 'cause there was some blood on it, a little bit. And there was, like, I don't know, something else. Something else that was in the water. It was like, maybe, formula from her stomach. I don't know. It wasn't clear water. And then I took the towel down to the basement. I don't know if I washed a load of clothes then or after I got back, but I know I washed a load of clothes.

"And then Randy woke up shortly after that. I grabbed him. I had a bottle ready for him, and some crackers that he ate in the car seat. I didn't know where I was goin' when I left. I just knew I had to go somewhere."

She thought of going to the house she and Rob had first bought, the one with the damp basement. No, that made no sense. Maybe a park, somewhere serene and secluded. Maybe the Mississippi River, just blocks away. She headed toward the wide expanse of flowing water that bordered the town. A road paralleled the river on the Illinois side; it would lead her somewhere.

"And then all of a sudden I turned to go across the bridge. It was like I was in a daze. I went across the bridge, and I thought of goin' down the railroad tracks, parkin' on the side, walkin' down there, and just layin' it out real carefully somewhere. And then I thought, no, something could happen like it did in eighty-six. Something could get ahold of her, some animal. And I thought, I can't stand that. I can't stand the thought of that."

So she crossed the railroad tracks, and the station wagon entered the parking lot of the lock and dam. A solid row of cars filled every space near the grass, but she could go no further, not with the plastic bag just inches from her hand. She double parked. "I got out. I locked my car door. Randy's door was already locked. And of course the other door in the back was locked; it was always locked. I went around and I opened the passenger side, up front, and I got out what I had to get out, and I locked that door. I had gloves on. One, just one. I had the other one in the front seat."

In a parked car nearby sat a man staring idly at the fishermen on the curving wall. He must be waiting for someone, she decided. Leaving Randy in the locked station wagon, she walked to the nearest trash barrel and studied its dark depth. "I thought, well, an animal's not gonna get in this can here." She deposited her baby in the silver drum. "I didn't just drop her in. I reached down and set her on the bottom. Careful."

She turned to leave, anxious to be away, but the man in the parked car worried her. Was he watching? She saw the lavatories at the top of the hill and walked up the path. Her double parking would seem more sensible if the man thought she was in a hurry to reach the bathroom.

She entered the bright green building. It was empty. "There was a mirror. I stood there and looked at myself in the mirror. I took off the glove. I don't know what I was thinking about. I just looked at myself in the mirror."

With the beige and brown glove clutched in her fist she hurried down the path and unlocked the car. "As I drove off, right before I got to the railroad track, I threw out the paper sack that was on the floorboard. Then I crossed the railroad tracks, and I looked at the gloves, and I thought, I gotta get rid of them. I threw them out the window, too. And then I looked in the rearview mirror, and I seen 'em layin' out in the middle of the road, and I thought, oh, they're right out there in the middle of the road. Someone's gonna find 'em. So I started to stop and back up, and then here come a car from the highway into the park, and I thought, well, no, I just might as well keep on goin'. But when I crossed the highway and pulled into a gas station there it was still in my mind to go get those gloves. But then I looked at that road, and there was a couple more cars pulling in there. And I thought, no, I'm not going back. I'm just going home.

"In my dining room there was this picture of Jesus on the cross, a picture that my grandma gave me, my mother's mom, a real beautiful picture. And I looked at it, at Jesus, and I said, 'Forgive me. Forgive me for what I have done, the way you forgave people for what they did to you.'"

The queasiness that had bothered her for weeks was gone, but terror had replaced it. What would she say? What should she do?

Rob called, as she knew he would. "Are you feeling any better?" he asked. "You looked pretty sick when I left."

"Yeah," she replied. "I feel a little better."

"How's Randy doin'? How's my buddy?"

"He's fine," Paula replied. She had no idea what she might say if he asked about Heather. "It sure is nice out today," she offered, heading off his question. Then she remembered that she wasn't supposed to go outside, not with the children. "We was lookin' out the window," she added quickly.

"Yeah," Rob said, "it's a beautiful day. Well, I'll see you about eleven."

Paula spent the hours pacing, smoking, worrying, trying to make herself think. She fed Randy. She drank a beer. She took more pills, at least two, maybe three. She dumped the remainder in the toilet, pushed the handle, and watched them swirl away. She wondered how she would manage without them.

Just before eleven she opened the back door and stepped into the coolness of the night. She set a bag of dirty diapers on the back porch step. At the sound of Rob's Jeep she lay down on the kitchen floor. It never occurred to her to mess up the house or inflict an injury on herself, as an intruder might have.

"Rob come in, and he shook me, and he looked around, and he said, 'Where's Heather?'

"I said, 'She's in her bassinet.'

"And he said, 'No, she isn't.'

"And so I told him about the masked man. It was all I could think of to say. I told him the story, and he looked at me. He just looked at me. He might have, maybe, kind of thought something, but he never said nothin'. He believed me.

"He went downstairs to his workshop, and he flushed his pot down the toilet. And he asked me, 'Is there anything you got hid? They're gonna go through this house.'

"And I told him, 'No, I already thought about that.'

"And then he called the police."

The words are quiet, whispery, as though controlling the volume could mute the horror. Her fingers tremble as she speaks. She dries her cheek with the back of her hand, but she does not sob.

There are questions she cannot answer, details she cannot supply, issues that she herself raises.

What caused the tiny cuts inside Heather's lip? Was it the pressure of her face against the folded towel, the towel that should have been used to hold her head above the water?

How did the black plastic bag remain from Saturday to Wednesday, four days, in the dark interior of a trash can that was, theoretically, emptied on Monday?

How could Heather's body have resisted decomposition so successfully that the medical examiner believed it might have been frozen? Did nighttime temperatures in the forties preserve her? Was the night chill enough to counteract daytime highs in the sixties?

Why was there no water in Heather's lungs? A medical expert could tell Paula that the epiglottis, the flaplike covering of the windpipe, clamps shut when anything but air threatens to enter, a spasmodic reaction most people have experienced when something "goes down the wrong way." As long as the epiglottis remains closed, keeping out food or liquid, it also keeps out air. If any water did get into Heather's lungs, it would have been quickly absorbed by her system.

"I don't know." Paula shakes her head. "I don't know nothin' about things like that. I only know what I did."

Her story will not be believed, she predicts, at least not by prosecutors. They want a confession that substantiates their version of the crime. They want her hand over Heather's mouth. They want a tale of freezers and refrigerators, of sex on the water bed and a frozen baby in the kitchen. "It just wasn't like that," she sighs. "There was never nothin' like that."

The prosecutors also want a story that implicates Rob. Although William Haine, the Madison County state's attorney, has said "the door is still open" for Paula to tell the truth and perhaps mitigate her sentence, he has made clear that it would have to be a truth he finds satisfactory.

"I can't say Rob did it. I can't lie about him. No matter how I feel about him, I can't lie. It got to the point, at the end, where I despised that man 'cause he controlled my life so much. But I allowed him to. I allowed it. I'm not blaming him for all of it. I know it takes two. And I *allowed* it. I don't know why I allowed someone to treat me like that, but I did."

Although Paula has just begun to sort through the jumble of emotions that plagued her after the births of her children, the possibility of postpartum psychosis occurred almost immediately to a number of St. Louis psychologists. Among them was Dr. Diane Sanford, who, along with psychiatrist Christa Hines, was at the time of Heather's murder in the second year of a four-year study titled "A Clinical Profile of Women with Postpartum Disorders."

Paula's blank stare in TV and newspaper photos caught Sanford's attention, and she wondered if she was seeing a "flat affect," a sign of the emotional detachment that sometimes accompanies postpartum problems. When she learned that Paula's children had been closely spaced—an indicator of potential risk—she considered contacting authorities to ask if they had given the possibility any consideration.

Dr. Hines, too, thought that some heed should be paid to the psychological condition of a woman who would murder two infants and tell the same unbelievable story about the disappearance of both. So strongly did she feel that before Paula's trial, she prepared a packet of postpartum material and sent it to the defense attorney. She received no reply.

Since 1986, when the topic first appeared on popular national talk shows, postpartum conditions have received enough attention that even ordinary people questioned whether this might have been Paula's "motive." Other women who killed their babies had told complex stories of kidnappings; a Pennsylvania woman believed her own story so completely that she passed two polygraph tests before hypnosis drew the truth from her. Some U.S. courts have dealt sympathetically with such defendants; some have not. Other countries have been quicker to recognize and respond to the problem; under Britain's Infanticide Act of 1938, a mother who kills her child in its first year of life is routinely charged with manslaughter, not murder.

Dr. Sanford and Dr. Hines feel certain that postpartum psychosis should at least have been considered in Paula's case. Their statistics corroborate the patterns that others have recognized. Many new mothers, perhaps even a majority of them, experience an emotional letdown (the "baby blues"). They are, for a few weeks, moody, overly sensitive, and quick to cry. Some of them—probably eight to twelve percent—suffer a reaction that goes deeper and lasts longer; they fall victim to a clinical depression or a major anxiety disorder. Fantasies of killing their babies may creep into their thoughts. A few—one or two in a thousand—become psychotic, sometimes acting on their impulses, turning fantasy to fact. Dr. Sanford and Dr. Hines suspect that Paula might have been one of those.

At the time of Paula's trial Sanford and Hines knew

nothing of her beyond the stories that had been reported; even so, there were several things that concerned them. Paula's "flat affect," suggesting a disassociation from reality, was apparent each time her face appeared on the TV news, and the close spacing of her children increased her risk of suffering a postpartum reaction of one degree or another. The duplication of the crime was also relevant, they felt, in light of the fifty-fifty chance that a woman who has suffered a postpartum disorder with one pregnancy will experience it again.

Once they knew her history Dr. Hines and Dr. Sanford discovered that Paula's background contained several other elements that coincided with their own list of risk factors: She had experienced an unplanned and difficult pregnancy; she was involved in a strained marital relationship; she endured a daily existence that was restricted and isolated; she had been sexually abused in her childhood; she had been unable to resolve her grief and guilt over the death of a loved one.

Another important concern was heredity, for her mother Nylene had experienced repeated spells of melancholy severe enough to require medication and occasionally send her into seclusion. (In the postpartum research of Sanford and Hines, thirty-seven percent of the women studied had a first-degree relative who had experienced some form of depression.) A related factor was the hesitation Nylene felt about her ability to cope with motherhood, a hesitation that Paula would have mirrored naturally, although unconsciously, as she struggled to deal with her own responsibilities. "That's how we learn to relate to other people," Dr. Sanford explains, "from what we observe of our parents and how they interact with us."

In like fashion Paula's strong positive bonds with her father and her brother Randy would have predisposed her to expect a similar connection with a husband. Since the men in her early life were authoritative, caring, supportive, and dominating, those are the qualities she would have anticipated in a mate. If that mate turned out to be dominant without being supportive, authoritative without being caring, she would have found herself in a situation that demanded increasing submission.

"It's clear that over time, the more the balance of power in a relationship becomes unequal, the more the woman allows the husband to dominate and stops questioning and begins sacrificing herself, not visiting friends or restricting her activities, the more she puts herself in a position to be controlled, rather than asserting herself and getting out," says Dr. Sanford. "It sounds as though, with Paula, it was just a downward spiral."

Paula's failure to leave her unhappy marriage was not an uncommon response. "There is a level of denial that goes along with it," Sanford explains, "a belief that things will be different, that they will get better. A lot of women believe that their husbands will change, that they will be able to *make* them change. While there is a direct or implied threat, there can also be periods of very intense attachment."

Rob's "thank you for a beautiful daughter" note was evidence of such attachment, Dr. Sanford speculates, just as the loving references to Heather on the calendar were testament to affection that Paula actually felt. In contrast to the warm phrases ("Heather loves to smile," "Heather Lee Sims is beautiful"), the stark Saturday notations of Heather's age strike Dr. Sanford as ominous. The weekly words served no purpose but to establish the obvious—the fact that Heather, for the moment, continued to exist. "That's one of the peculiarities that make me question Paula's mental state," Dr. Sanford says. "That's a very odd thing to do."

Had Dr. Sanford and Dr. Hines, or any other psychologist or psychiatrist, examined Paula, their conclusions might have influenced the course of the trial. But Paula was never interviewed by any mental health professional, nor did she take any psychological tests.

Sanford is amazed that neither the prosecution nor the defense considered the accumulation of factors significant enough to warrant an exploration of Paula's mental state. "This is an issue that women should regard very seriously, that it has been dealt with in this manner. Some people are working very hard to advocate looking into whether, or to what degree, postpartum difficulties have played a role in these scenarios. It's an injustice, really, not just to Paula but to *women* that it's been dealt with as 'This woman murdered her baby, so she should get what's coming to her.' We should be thinking about the broader issues. Because of the attitudes toward women in our society we have a wall up, and I think this case just reinforced that wall instead of starting to take down some of the bricks."

During the years she has been at Dwight Paula has completed photography and business courses. She works as secretary to the prison chaplain, an assignment that offers her some contact with other people, visitors as well as inmates.

At the suggestion of women outside the legal and correctional systems she has taken four psychological tests, two versions of the Minnesota Multiphasic Personality Inventory and two versions of the Millon Clinical Multiaxial Inventory. The tests indicate that at the time of Heather's murder Paula was experiencing extremely high levels of depression, anxiety, paranoia, and disordered thinking. The test scores, along with Paula's description of the crime, were evaluated by Diane Sanford. "I would say that Paula experienced a postpartum psychosis," Dr. Sanford judged, "or at least a very, *very* severe postpartum depression which interfered with her ability to make rational decisions."

Dr. Sanford also noted that Paula's responses indicate she was dependent and self-defeating, attitudes that helped to keep her locked in her unhappy relationship with Rob. "In many ways her profile is that of an abused wife."

The divorce decree orders Rob to bring Randy to the prison once each month for a two and one-half hour visit. It is a long trip—three hours—and by the time they arrive, Paula believes, Rob has programmed Randy to be "hateful."

"I don't love you," the child announced recently as he met Paula in the waiting room. "We only come because we have to." He has also said, "You're scum" and "You're gonna rot here," unlikely conclusions for a four-year-old to reach without some prompting.

"I begged Rob. I said, 'Please, please, don't do this to Randy.' But Rob said that I'm the one that's doin' it. He said, 'You're the one that insisted on seein' him. This is what you get.'

"One time Randy said, 'Why did you take away my sisters? Why?' I didn't answer him. He's too young. And I don't know why, not really. I just said, 'I'm sorry, Randy.' And he said, 'Sorry ain't good enough. Sorry ain't good enough.' That's Rob talkin'. Those are Rob's words.

"And one other time Randy handed me a toy, something from the play cabinet, and he said, 'Here, bad lady.'

"I told him, 'Randy, that's not nice. I'm your mother.'

"He said, 'No, my mommy lives inside of Daddy.'"

On one particularly violent day the little boy hit her, kicked her, slapped her face, and pulled her hair.

"It's breakin' my heart," Paula said. "I thought my heart couldn't be broke no more."

The Blews visit monthly, always bringing Dennis and usually staying for two days. "My dad, he's a really good guy, and he always tries to look on the positive side of things. He believes I'm comin' home someday. He's all ready for me. He'll tell me, 'I'm savin' Girl Scout cookies for you' and 'I'll take you out for a steak dinner.' But my mom—she said one time, 'I didn't raise you, Paula, for you to be in prison.'

"And I said, 'I know you didn't, Mom. You did your best.'

"And she said, 'No, I didn't, or you wouldn't be here. It has to be my fault.'

"I told her she wasn't responsible for it. Not for any of it.

"She said, 'I keep thinking about the time you called on the phone the night before we left, and you were crying, and I just brushed it off. I didn't really think that you needed me because you were always a strong person. I was all excited about going to Kansas City, so I just kind of brushed you aside. I'm sorry.'

"She's said that many times. She keeps on thinkin' about it. She can't get it out of her mind.

"And one time—well, more than one time—she said, 'Promise me, before I die, that you'll tell me what really happened. Don't you think I deserve that?'

"I agreed. She deserves it."

But when Paula makes an effort to approach the truth she finds that her parents cannot allow themselves to hear it. "I got something to tell you," she says. Then her father changes the subject and takes Dennis to the snack bar, or her mother sighs and lays her head on the visiting room table. So instead of offering the truth she is waiting to tell Paula delivers a shorter message: "I want you to know that I'm sorry about everything."

"It wasn't supposed to be like this," her mother sobs.

"I know," Paula says, stroking her head.

They sit, silent, in the prison visiting room, contemplating the blunted, tangled course of lives that should have run straight and true. Each of them has, in one way or another, lost all three of her children.

If one path had veered in another direction, if one player had passed a moment sooner or later, if a chosen word had been softer or kinder, things might have been different. Simple dreams might have flourished. Children might have grown up and produced more children.

But as mother and daughter both know, no ifs can deliver them from reality. The dreams die here.

"It wasn't supposed to be like this," Paula echoes, staring into the empty distance.